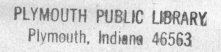

Encyclopedia of
Film Stars

Encyclopedia of
Film Stars

DOUGLAS JARVIS

GALLERY BOOKS
An Imprint of W. H. Smith Publishers Inc.
112 Madison Avenue
New York City 10016

4

The Contents

Endpapers: *Jack Nicholson and Jessica Lange display star status.*

Half-title page: *An invitation from the "It" Girl, Clara Bow.*

Title page: *Orson Welles — "it's like meeting God without dying".*

These pages: *Dustin Hoffman and Faye Dunaway in* **Little Big Man** *(1970).*

This book was devised and produced by Multimedia Publications (UK) Ltd

Editor: Richard Rosenfeld
Assistant editors: Sydney Francis, Anthony Hall
Editorial assistant: Harriet Kinloch
Production: Arnon Orbach
Design: Michael Hodson Designs
Picture Research: Jane Puttick

First published in the United States of America 1985 by Gallery Books, an imprint of W. H. Smith Publishers Inc., 112 Madison Avenue, New York, NY 10016

ISBN 0 8317 2795 0

Typeset by Letterspace Limited
Origination by **Scan Studios Ltd**
Printed in Italy by Sagdos

Note: Where two or more films were released in the same year, the release date is given after the first film only.

The Silent Era

R ight from the earliest days of the movies, the stars were the great attraction. They were created by the public, not the moviemakers. However, the moviemakers certainly played their part by choosing the same lead roles for a series of films to speed up the production process; the audiences quickly selected their own favorites and the star system took off.

The earliest stars

The first identifiable movie "name" was Onésime, a Frenchman whose comic adventures delighted spectators in the early 1900s. Among his successors was the brilliant Max Linder, whose skillfully developed movie persona included a silk hat and elegant clothes; Linder raised laughs as the "upper-class twit" blundering his way through an obstacle course of embarrassing moments. By 1910 he was a guaranteed box-office draw, so laying claim to being the first real film star.

Another early star was a Danish actress, Asta Nielsen, who appeared in **The Abyss** (1910), a story of a girl's seduction. The film's sensational success led to her making many similar movies in Denmark and Germany — and she was still a star when the Talkies (sound era) arrived some 20 years later.

Pawn players

By 1910 the rivalry between the film studios had so intensified that Biograph billed one of its actresses as "The Biograph Girl" to attract larger audiences. They refused to reveal her identity in case she demanded more money, though this was quickly offered by a competitive studio which

◀ *Going through chaos to get the girl, Buster Keaton plays a street photographer turned cameraman in* **The Cameraman** *(1928).*

rigged up a publicity stunt to make her vanish and later reappear in St Louis, under the name Florence Lawrence. The affair soon died down but, as a direct result, within two years all the major players were being individually billed.

The film studios recruited many stars from the stage. Sarah Bernhardt, for instance, was persuaded in 1912 to join the French film studios and in America leading theater players were tempted by lucrative contracts. The transition didn't always enhance their careers; opera singers Mary Garden and Geraldine Farrar were not the successes the studios hoped they would be though both still acquired small fortunes.

Comic capers

The studios not only had to bow to the public demand for stars, but also cater for new tastes in subject-matter and length. Audiences preferred fiction to "joke" films and what were later termed documentaries — and they demanded longer films. Accordingly the Americans, following the lead of European film makers, began producing features extending over several reels, instead of the customary one- and two-reelers. But until well into the Talkies these feature films were supported by shorts, newsreels and cartoons.

By far the most popular shorts were the comic capers produced by Mack Sennett and Hal Roach. Sennett's "Keystone Cops" were stars of a sort, as were the great silent screen clowns Buster Keaton, Harold Lloyd and Charlie Chaplin. All spent years of valuable training making these shorts and all achieved huge box-office success long before they had made any features.

Hollywood idols

The industry was so keen to exploit the craving for stars that it created fan magazines. The articles fulfilled a completely different kind of function to those appearing in today's magazines; the stars were presented as incandescent, faultless, idealized versions of their real selves. The image was everything. The public lapped up this carefully prepared diet, with just about every home in America taking at least one fan magazine.

The studios began to gather together a stable of talent, with likely youngsters being "groomed for stardom". In return for this investment, studios demanded exclusive services, usually for seven years.

The studios had options in these contracts, but the players did not. Once dropped, a "name" player might find work at another studio if very lucky – but when a star became free he or she would be snapped up, providing they weren't considered trouble. As long as the studio system prevailed, an unofficial blacklist operated among the Hollywood moguls; temperamental or argumentative stars were left with two choices – working in the minor studios or not working at all.

Stardom in the twenties was precious and highly prized. Movie players knew they had made it when their name was billed above the film's title: that was the "official" elevation to stardom. The rule of one star/one film

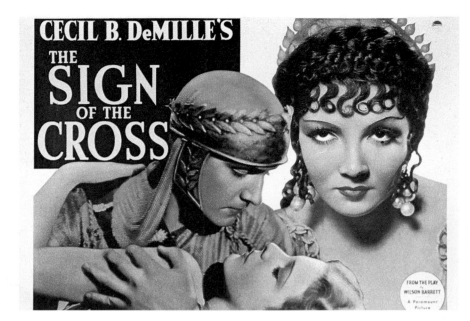

made it difficult to match players of equal status until some teams became so popular with audiences that studios became eager to cater to the demand, creating Greta Garbo and John Gilbert, Ronald Colman and Vilma Banky, Janet Gaynor and Charles Farrell and other romantic partnerships.

The Hollywood machine
Few other national film industries were as successful as Hollywood in providing the public with movie idols – but when they did Hollywood soon snapped them up. By the end of the First World War the studios had become so rich and powerful that they could purchase any player who made a sensation in Europe.

The chief raiding ground was

▲ *Claudette Colbert's first major part was in* **The Sign of the Cross** *(1923). The teaming with Fredric March was repeated in* **Tonight Is Ours** *(1933).*

Germany, especially after audiences had been spellbound by Pola Negri in **Love and Passion** (1914), the American version of Lubitsch's **Madame Dubarry** (1919). Paramount soon took Negri on, and studio publicists played up the supposed rivalry between her and their reigning queen, Gloria Swanson.

The public eye was fixed upon the stars alone – such as Rudolph Valentino and Greta Garbo – whom they flocked to see and longed to know about, but the big Hollywood studios had perfected a system by which stars were merely cogs in a vast machine. And this machine promised to deliver entertaining products in its efficient way forever, until one small maverick company, Warner Brothers, decided to test the public with sound movies.

Talkies hit the screen
Up to now, movies had been given live orchestral accompaniment in cities and piano accompaniment in smaller towns. In **Don Juan** (1926), Warners had already experimented successfully with a system using recorded music and sounds synchronized to the action on screen. At its New York premiere, **Don Juan** was shown along with some shorts in which celebrated musical stars appeared to sing or play from the screen. The success of these films

▼ *MGM spent an unprecedented $2 million on making* **Conquest** *(1938), giving the lead role to top box-office star Greta Garbo, and co-starring Charles Boyer.*

▲ *A sure way to tropical paradise ...
Clara Bow in a feature from the same
year as the birth of the "It" girl, 1927.*

▶ *Charlie Chaplin in* **The Pilgrim**
*(1923) just before he formed United
Artists with Douglas Fairbanks, Mary
Pickford and D.W. Griffith.*

made the producers go further; it was
decided that Al Jolson would sing in
parts of **The Jazz Singer** (1927), the
dialogue being conveyed by intertitles
and synchronized music. But between
one pair of songs Jolson said, ad-
libbing, "Ma, you ain't seen nothin'
yet!" − and the public loved it.

Only very few people in films
believed that Talkies would last; they
were just a passing fad. Movies didn't
need to talk; that was for theater − or
radio, which was beginning to com-
pete for moviegoers' leisure time.
But Warners decided that Jolson
would sing and *talk* through portions
of **The Singing Fool** (1928) and
when this proved an even bigger
financial success the rush to make
Talkies was on. Studios and cinemas
were wired for sound − and soon
those expensive European stars of
the silent screen were glumly returning home on transatlantic liners.

◄ *Theda Bara was the first star "made" by publicity. She was said to be of mysterious Oriental parentage, though in reality born of a Jewish family in Ohio. Her first name was an anagram of "death", her second "arab" spelled backwards.*

small independent company; she burlesqued her image in a Hal Roach short, **Madame Mystery** (1926), but didn't film again — though casting directories listed her as "at liberty" till her death from cancer in 1955.

♥ Married: Charles Brabin in 1921, who had directed her two penultimate Fox films, and who outlived her by two years.

❝ She was the *femme fatale*, the she-demon. She was deadlier than the male. She was lustful, lascivious, carnal. She had no heart; she had no soul." — *Douglas Heyes.*
"She is pretty, but her acting is as incredible as her behavior, moving from petulance to gloating triumph in a glance." — *David Shipman.*
"Which person impressed me most during the silent era? Theda Bara. She was one of the best informed women I have ever known. She knew who she was. She was Theodosia Goodman." — *Adele Whitely Fletcher.*

Theda Bara

🎥◄ The screen's first "vamp" was born in Cincinnati, Ohio, in 1890 and made a mild impact on the New York stage as a *femme fatale*, before being discovered by director Frank Powell for **A Fool There Was** (1915), a lurid melodrama about a vile beauty who lures a man from his wife and drives him to ruin. The publicity — she was said to have been born in the shadow of the Sphinx — made her, and she in turn made the film's producer, William Fox, so rich he founded the studio that later became 20th Century-Fox. Born Theodosia Goodman, she changed her name to Theda Bara for films.

Only the first of the 39 films she made for him over the next four years survives: the titles include **The Two Orphans** (1915), **Sin, Carmen, East Lynne** (1916) **Romeo and Juliet, Camille** (1917), **Cleopatra, Madame Dubarry** (1918), **When a Woman Sins, Salome** and **The She-Devil** (1919).

Her popularity plummeted when she insisted on playing a colleen in **Kathleen Mavourneen** (1919) and she went on to make only two more films for Fox.

She returned to the stage but attempted a comeback in **The Unchastened Woman** (1925) for a

▼ *Theda Bara and Wyndham Standing in* **The Unchastened Woman** (1925). *This, her intended triumphant return, was given the thumbs down by her one-time fans.*

Clara Bow

The novelist Elinor Glyn coined the word "It" to denote sex appeal and audiences in general agreed with Miss Glyn that no one had more "It" than Clara Bow, who was otherwise the quintessential "jazz baby" of the Silent screen.

She was born in Brooklyn in 1905

▼ *If publicity made Theda Bara, it was the public who made Clara Bow, a vivacious brunette. She was, said Scott Fitzgerald, the quintessence of the term "flapper". However, the image didn't last long and was replaced by a tawdrier one involving an excess of drink and drugs.*

and entered movies via a beauty contest in 1922. She was averaging a dozen films a year for the optimistically entitled Preferred Company, run by B. P. Schulberg, but her huge popularity didn't begin till he took her with him when he returned to Paramount in 1926. Her best movies for that company were: **Dancing Mothers** (1926), **Mantrap, It** (1927), **Children of Divorce, Wings** (directed by William A. Wellman, who said in 1977 that she was "magnificent" — the reason the film still stands up), **Hula, Red Hair** (1928) and **The Wild Party** (1929), her first Talkie.

Scandal erupted in 1930 when she sued a former secretary for embezzlement and in the court case that followed there were revelations of

booze, lovers and drugs. The public turned against her, and she was dropped by Paramount. Two comeback pictures at Fox, **Call Her Savage** (1932) and **Hoopla** (1933), didn't help, nor did her burgeoning figure. She didn't film again and died in 1965.

♥ Married: cowboy star Rex Bell in 1931, but they were separated some years before her death. Lovers include Gary Cooper, Victor Fleming, Richard Arlen, Eddie Cantor, Bela Lugosi, Gilbert Roland, "Slapsie" Maxie Rosenbloom and Fredric March.

❝ The embodiment of the independent-minded flapper

with bobbed hair and cupid bow lips." — *Ken Wlaschin.*

"Clara Bow, with her tousled mane of red hair and intense black eyes, who generated sex appeal and excitement with breath-taking ease." — *Maurice Chevalier.*

"A little ball of fire named Clara Bow attracted attention. Here was another new type, and cute as a *boutonnière*. In fact, she could have found her way home on any masculine lapel." — *Frances Marion.*

Lon Chaney

"The Man of a Thousand Faces" was born in Colorado Springs in 1883 to deaf and dumb parents. He started humbly in the theater at 17 to gain all-round experience, began in movies as an extra and received his first credit in 1913.

In hundreds of supporting roles over the next six years he specialized as a villain and became increasingly absorbed in makeup to change his appearance. His most popular role at that time was **The Miracle Man** (1919), in which he played a phony cripple. Thereafter he was chiefly cast as someone maimed, ugly, scarred, mad or simply unfortunate. In 1919 he also made **The Wicked Darling,** his first film with Tod Browning, who directed nearly all of his most famous films, but not **The Hunchback of Notre Dame** (1923), the title role of which made Chaney a box-office attraction.

Universal, which produced that film, had not — to its chagrin — got Chaney under contract, but he returned to that studio to be **The Phantom of the Opera** (1925). Meanwhile he had become one of MGM's most precious assets, in such films as Sjöström's **He Who Gets Slapped** (1924), George W. Hill's **Tell It to the Marines** (1927) and Brenon's **Laugh, Clown, Laugh** (1928). In these he looked like himself; his intense dark eyes made him a

▼ *A portrait of Lon Chaney clearly showing that he was just as capable of being frightened as were his audiences. You may not immediately recognize him here, but this is the way he looked when not disfigured by disguise and make-up on the film set.*

notable Silent actor. He played grotesques for Browning in **The Unholy Three** (1925), **The Blackbird** (1926), **The Unknown** (1927), **London After Midnight, West of Zanzibar** (1929) and **Where East Is East,** among others. He made one Talkie, a remake of **The Unholy Three,** before dying of throat cancer in 1930.

♥ Married: Cleva Creighton (1905-14), the mother of Lon Chaney Jr, character actor of the thirties and forties; secondly and happily Hazel Hastings (1914).

❝ Chaney not only was a great actor; he was a magnificent dancer. The most famous ballet stars, like Nijinsky, could express every emotion and every shade of meaning in the movements of their bodies. Chaney had that gift. When he realized that he had lost the girl, his body expressed it — it was as though a bolt of lightning had shattered his physical self. Extraordinary, really!" — *Charles Laughton.*

"But that he was a cathartic figure there is no doubt. His creatures were vulnerable and sympathetic, immensely powerful and real; though considering the extent to which they were maimed and mutilated — armless, legless, one-eyed, hunchbacked — we might well wonder about his audience." — *David Shipman.*

Charlie Chaplin

Charlie Chaplin was, for most of his life, considered the supreme comic genius of the screen: contemporary critics put him ahead of his rivals because of his gift for pathos, but that is not a quality admired today and the sixties' re-evaluations of Harold Lloyd and Buster Keaton showed that Chaplin was only one of a triumvirate of Silent clowns.

He was born in Lambeth, South London, in 1889, and was a boy actor before joining a music-hall company. That brought him to the US, where he joined Mack Sennett at Keystone making one-reel comic cut-ups. Chaplin's début was in **Making a Living** (1914) and he appeared for the first time in his tramp costume in his second film, **Kid Auto Races in**

Charlie Chaplin in **MODERN TIMES**

Venice (1914). By the time he moved on to Essanay a year later he had achieved world popularity; he continued to develop his comic skill during his year with Essanay, before moving on to Mutual for a series of two-reelers which wonderfully exploit the Tramp's personality — his vulgarity and nimbleness, his impishness and his rejection of authority, his gallantry to women and, above all, his timing and invention. **The Pawnshop** (1916), **Behind the Screen, The Rink, Easy Street** (1917), and **The Immigrant** also have a marvelous foil for Chaplin, the huge and fearsome Eric Campbell.

After another huge salary increase Chaplin moved to First National, where his films include **A Dog's Life** (1918), **Shoulder Arms** and his first feature, **The Kid** (1921), which was second only to **The Birth of a Nation** as the most financially successful movie yet made. With the director of that film, D. W. Griffith, plus Pickford and Fairbanks, Chaplin formed United Artists. A perfectionist writer and director, as well as performer, Chaplin presented his remaining films only at intervals: **The Gold Rush** (1925), **The Circus**

(1928), **City Lights** (1931) and **Modern Times** (1936). These last two, made after the Talkie revolution, qualify as Silents, and Chaplin was much admired for holding out against Sound. He played a dual role, the

▲ *Chaplin as seen by the poster artist.*
▼ *And this is how the film ended. Chaplin walks off towards the sunset and marriage with Paulette Goddard.*

Tramp and a comic Hitler, in **The Great Dictator** (1940), finally abandoning the Tramp's costume when he played a dandyish mass murderer in **Monsieur Verdoux** (1947).

The film's stance, together with Chaplin's left-wing views and a paternity case (though he was acquitted) made him an unpopular figure in the US, and the State Department indicated that it was unlikely to grant a re-entry permit (he had remained a

British citizen) if he went to Europe for the premières there of **Limelight** (1952). From his home in Vevey, Switzerland, he journeyed to Britain to make two films of little merit, **A King in New York** (1957) and **A Countess from Hong Kong** (1966), appearing in the latter in a cameo role only. He was awarded an honorary Oscar and knighted in 1975; he died in 1977, aged 88.

▲ *Chaplin the director, here seen in 1915. There was usually a strong element of autobiography in his work hinged around a rags-to-riches theme.*

♥ Married: Mildred Harris (1917-20); Lita Grey (1924-7), after several public revelations about their private life; Paulette Goddard (1936-42) — at least studio biographies said so, but the couple are not believed to have gone through any ceremony; and Oona O'Neill (1943), daughter of the playwright Eugene O'Neill. Oona's eight children, added to two sons by Miss Grey, made Chaplin a father ten times over. Lovers include, among others, actresses Edna Purviance, Marion Davies and Pola Negri.

❝ In a company in which he feels himself at ease he will play the fool with delightful abandon. His invention is fertile, his vivacity unfailing, and he has a pleasant gift for mimicry . . . the unbelievable charm that graces all his actions." — *W. Somerset Maugham.*
"Pathos has nearly ruined Chaplin, who is an artist of genius." — *Graham Greene.*
"That obstinate, suspicious, egocentric, maddening and lovable genius of a problem child." — *Mary Pickford.*
"But the best comics are also good actors. Chaplin is a wonderful actor." — *Zero Mostel.*

▲ *"Doug", as the world loved him, in* **Around the World in 80 Minutes** *(1931). This shot was taken towards the end of his career when his popularity was fading and he was unsure about the sort of films he should be appearing in.*

Douglas Fairbanks

🎥◁ The screen's first great swashbuckling hero was born in Denver, Colorado, in 1883, to well-off parents. He started acting in 1902 and two years later made his début on Broadway, where he established a reputation as a juvenile lead before deserting the stage for movies. Beginning with **The Lamb** (1915), he made a series of comedies and action adventures for Triangle and then Paramount, increasingly becoming involved in their production and sometimes supplying the plotlines — which were often similar, about a madcap young man whose enthusiasms and energy carry him into and out of trouble.

His eternal optimism was shared by audiences, who recognized that he was a regular guy, no matter what mayhem he caused. As one of the founding members of United Artists, he produced and starred in three more such pictures before taking up a sword to vanquish his foes in **The Mark of Zorro** (1920). He made another comedy, **The Nut** (1921), in case the public would not accept him in his new role, but the other film was so popular that he achieved a long-held ambition by playing D'Artagnan in **The Three Musketeers.**

Thereafter he appeared only in films — each one more accomplished than the last — in which his derring-do and athletic prowess endeared him even more to moviegoers: **Robin Hood** (1922), **The Thief of Bagdad** (1924), **Don Q Son of Zorro** (1925), **The Black Pirate** (1926), **The Gaucho** (1927) and **The Iron Mask**

(1929). With the coming of Talkies he and his wife gave in to the urging of their fans by appearing together, but their version of **The Taming of the Shrew** was unappreciated by critics and public alike. Thinking himself too old for swashbuckling, Fairbanks returned to comedy in **Reaching for the Moon** (1931), but the audiences of the Depression found him passé. He made only three more films: a travelogue, **Around the World in 80 Minutes; Mr Robinson Crusoe** (1932); and **The Private Life of Don Juan** (1934), a British picture made with, and out of admiration for, producer Alexander Korda. He died from a heart attack in 1939.

♥ Married: Beth Sully (1907-18), mother of Douglas Fairbanks Jr, whose likable personality and swordsman's skills never quite equaled his father's; Mary Pickford (1920-35), a match which made them

▲ *Douglas Fairbanks about to fall in love with Mary Pickford on a tour during World War I, accompanied by Charlie Chaplin (l. to r.).*

the king and queen of Hollywood, entertaining regally at their mansion, "Pickfair", and being mobbed on their foreign tours; and Sylvia, Lady Ashley (1936), who outlived him and later married Clark Gable.

❝ Fairbanks' glory, the mystery of his visual imagination, is that he could throw away all the textbook tricks on the make-shift apparatus of ordinary life. To Fairbanks a narrow lane with high walls is a risky, but workable, set of parallel bars; a spear is a pole to vault with . . . ." — *Alistair Cooke.*
"Douglas Fairbanks was make-

believe at its best, a game we youngsters never tired of playing, a game — we are convinced — our fathers secretly shared. He was complete fantasy, not like Disney's, which has an overlayer of whimsy and sophistication, but unashamed and joyous. Balustrades were made to be vaulted, draperies to be a giant slide, chandeliers to swing from, citadels to be scaled." — *Frank S. Nugent.*
"A little boy who never grew up." — *Mary Pickford.*
"He had extraordinary magnetism and charm and a genuine boyish enthusiasm which he conveyed to the public." — *Charlie Chaplin.*

Lillian Gish

🎥 Lillian Gish was born in Springfield, Ohio, in 1896, and made her stage début at the age of five to earn money, since her father had left home and her mother could not get herself a job as an actress. Lillian and her sister Dorothy knew Mary Pickford, who persuaded D. W. Griffith to give them contracts. They both made their movie débuts in **An Unseen Enemy** (1912), and after leading roles in Griffith's two epics, **The Birth of a Nation** (1915) and **Intolerance** (1916), Lillian starred in some of his popular melodramas, often as a waif: **Hearts of the World** (1918), **Broken Blossoms** (1919), **True Heart Susie, Way Down East** (1920) and, with Dorothy again, **Orphans of the Storm** (1921).

She had an unhappy spell with Inspiration but made two good films. She was hardly happier at MGM, but the successes continued with King Vidor's excellent **La Bohème** (with John Gilbert) (1926), and her two best films, **The Scarlet Letter** and **The Wind** (1927), both directed by Victor Sjöström — ironically a friend of Garbo, whose presence at the studio was one reason executives had lost interest in Miss Gish. A contract with United Artists resulted in only one film, **One Romantic Night** (1930), also her Talkie début; she left Hollywood after just one more movie, **His Double Life** (1933), to concentrate on the stage.

She returned to movies in a supporting role in **The Commandos Strike at Dawn** (1942) and she made over a dozen such appearances in the intervening years, most notably in **The Cobweb** (1955), **The Night of the Hunter, The Unforgiven** (1960) and Altman's **The Wedding** (1978). Her most recent film is **Hambone and Hillie** (1984). In 1971 she received an honorary Oscar.

♥ Has never married, but her name was romantically linked in the thirties with the critic George Jean Nathan.

▼ *Lilian Gish under the lustful eye of Montagu Love in* **The Wind** *(1927).*

▲ *Lillian Gish not long after she first began starring in movies. The director D.W. Griffith helped guide her early career, when she developed into one of the "greats" of the silent screen.*

❝ I do not say that this little girl is as great an actress as Sarah Bernhardt. For all I know she may not be able to speak the President's American. What I do know is that in this one picture [**Broken Blossoms**] she ranks with the world's great artists . . . . It is curious that this plain little American girl should give the world an exact image of the great actress in far-off youth." – *James Agate.*

"Miss Gish had a place in the world of movies comparable to that in the theater of a Sarah Bernhardt or an Eleanora Duse." – *Bosley Crowther.*

"Her career is proof of the fact that the entire history of the feature film is contained within a lifetime." – *Kevin Brownlow.*

William S. Hart

The first star of Westerns was a Jewish man from Arkansas, "Bronco Billy", who couldn't even ride a horse. The second was born in Newburgh, New York, in 1870, and was a middle-aged Shakespearian actor. William S. Hart, however, grew up in the West and was a cowboy before taking up acting. An old friendship with Thomas H. Ince, perhaps the most celebrated producer/director of the time, took him into films, and after one two-reeler he wrote **The Bargain** (1914) with his own star part. Ince gave him

a free hand in the movies that followed (sometimes he produced and directed), all of them now considered authentic representations of what the Old West was really like – tough and treacherous.

Hart perfected his character of "The Good Bad Man", a rotten critter – and usually a loner – who reforms for the love of a good woman, often a widow with a wee tot. As he reforms or is redeemed, the camera lingers on the great stone face, gradually registering remorse. Although he sometimes appeared in city duds – as in **Between Men** (1915) – audiences preferred him in leather chaps, especially in **The Return of Draw Egan** (1916), **Hell's Hinges, The Narrow Trail** (1917), **The Toll Gate** (1920) and, in the same year, **The Testing Block.**

The last three films were all made for Paramount despite his quarrel with Ince over the use of his famous

▲ *William S. Hart introducing Maurice Chevalier to the rough and tumble world of the Western.*

pinto pony, Fritz. Eventually he left the studio when it started demanding greater artistic control since box office returns were falling – probably because plots were so similar. United Artists signed him up, giving him the capital he wanted to make **Tumbleweeds** (1925), but its failure sent him into retirement – apart from a personal introduction from the screen when it was reissued in 1939 (because of the success of **Stagecoach**). He died in 1946.

♥ Was briefly married to Winifred Westover.

❝ Bill Hart was dynamic. He was deeply emotional, having the uncanny ability to project his feelings to audiences. His impact on women, whether teenager or dowager, was powerful, even though his profile was something less than Greek and his expression about as warm as chiseled granite." — *Walter Seltzer.*

"That strange face, blinkered and hard, was surely like that of Marley's which Scrooge found on the knocker, haunted and hunted, and not needing intertitles like 'Realizing that the road of the outlaw closes all others'." — *David Shipman.*

Buster Keaton

The man now generally acknowledged as the funniest — or at least the most modern — of the Silent clowns was born in 1895 in Piqua, Kansas, to a touring vaudeville team of acrobats, whom he joined on stage at the age of three. A chance meeting brought him into movies: watching Fatty Arbuckle at work on **The Butcher Boy** (1917) he joined in and thereafter played support to Arbuckle in 14 shorts. At the same time as he made his first feature, **The Saphead** (1920), for Metro, Arbuckle defected and producer Joseph M. Schenck selected Keaton to replace him as the star of his two-reel comedies.

Keaton's athletic skill in his shorts is matched only by their considerable inventiveness, for which he was chiefly responsible. Of the score he made,

▲ *"The Great Stone Face", Buster Keaton in a predicament in* **The Navigator** *(1924), usually regarded as one of his masterpieces.*

many are among the movies' richest treasures: **Neighbors, The Goat** (1921), **The Playhouse, The Boat, The Paleface, Cops** (1922), **The Frozen North, The Electric House, Daydreams, The Balloonatic** (1923) and **The Love Nest.** More masterpieces followed when

Schenck put Buster into features: **The Three Ages** (1923), **Our Hospitality, Sherlock Junior** (1924), **The Navigator, Seven Chances** (1925), **Battling Butler** (1926), **The General** (1927), **College** and **Steamboat Bill** (1928).

When Schenck contracted Keaton to MGM, without autonomy, there

▼ *An ironic shot of Keaton who, towards the end of his career, had little control over his films.*

▲ *Harold Lloyd in* **Safety Last**
*(1923). His antics on high buildings
are among the cinema's abiding
treasures.*

Harold Lloyd

Although Harold Lloyd experimented with comic costumes (as was usual), he found real fame as a go-get-'em all-American boy. He was born in Burchard, Nebraska, in 1893 and was so movie-mad that he was an extra before he was 20. Hal Roach was another, and they worked together from the moment Roach set up his own company in 1915, but without success on the part of Lloyd, whose character Willie Work didn't catch on. Lonesome Luke did better, but it was the college boy he first played in **Over the Fence** (1917) which established him.

He made 90 shorts, and as his popularity grew so did his propensity for daring gags — despite losing some fingers in handling a prop bomb which exploded. **High and Dizzy** (1920) was his first essay into what would be his speciality, being stranded on the top (or side) of skyscrapers; and it was soon after that that he moved to three- and then four-reelers: **A Sailor-Made Man** (1921).

Although others helped him to develop his routines, he had complete creative control and halfway through the decade broke with Roach to sign for Paramount. With such films as **Grandma's Boy** (1922), **Dr Jack, Safety Last** (1923), **Why Worry?, Girl Shy** (1924), **Hot Water, The Freshman** (1925), **For Heaven's Sake** (1926), **The Kid Brother** (1927) and **Speedy** (1928), he established himself as the public's favorite Silent clown. Despite more antics on a tall building in **Feet First** (1930) his other early Talkies are chiefly notable for his attempts at novelty through plot or gag: **Welcome Danger** (1929), **Movie Crazy** (1932) and **The Cat's Paw** (1934).

When the box office returns of **The Milky Way** (1936) and **Professor Beware** (1938) showed that Lloyd's public was finally losing interest, he retired, unwisely emerging for a doomed collaboration with Preston Sturges in **The Sin of Harold Diddlebock** (1947). In the early

was a falling-off, noticeable in **The Cameraman** and even more so in **Spite Marriage** (1929), Keaton's first Talkie. For a while Keaton's popularity surged, but the films themselves were only shadows of his Silents and the public drifted away. When MGM fired him, there were no Hollywood offers, partly because of his drinking; his divorce had crippled him financially and two cheapies he did for money in Europe (France and Britain) did not help his career at all. He survived in Hollywood making two-reel comedies of no great merit and returned to features in a supporting role, as a Silent clown, with **Hollywood Cavalcade** (1939).

He continued in occasional features and television until 1963 when a 10-minute ovation at the Venice Film Festival confirmed his star status as *the* master clown, an actor close to genius. He worked until his death in 1966, unsmiling to the end. His penultimate film, and one of his most enjoyable, was **A Funny Thing Happened on the Way to the Forum** (1966).

♥ Married: Natalie Talmadge (1921-32), whose sister, Norma, was married to producer Joseph M. Schenck; Mae Scribbens (1933-5) and Eleanor Norris (1940), who outlived him.

❝ **Sunset Boulevard:** there he was again, superbly glum in the entourage of Gloria Swanson as the forgotten star. The trouble was that with Keaton on the screen other faces, other gestures, were apt to fade; even the greatest performances were diminished. In the famous duet in **Limelight** it was Keaton, struggling with the vagabond sheets of music, whom one watched, not Chaplin." — *Dilys Powell.*
"He taught me most of what I know about timing, how to fall and how to handle props and animals." — *Lucille Ball.*

sixties, two compilations of his old movies had audiences laughing all over again. He was awarded a special Oscar in 1952 and died in 1971.

 Married: his leading lady, Mildred Davis, in 1923.

" Lloyd depended more on story and situation than any of the other major comedians (he kept the best stable of gagmen in Hollywood, at one time hiring six); but unlike most 'story' comedians he was also a very funny man from inside. He had, as he has written, 'an unusually large comic vocabulary'. More particularly he had an expertly expressive body and even more expressive teeth, and out of this thesaurus of smiles he could at a moment's notice blend prissiness, breeziness and asininity, and still remain tremendously likable." – *James Agee.*

"He gave us an eager young man whose fortitude and initiative more than made up for any lack of special talent or ability. He simply took off the makeup and put himself on screen. And it worked." – *Richard Koszarski.*

▲ *An ad for one of Lloyd's occasional Talkies (later remade as* **The Kid From Brooklyn** *(1946) with Danny Kaye).*

▼ *Lloyd as a wealthy do-gooder whose efforts clearly are not appreciated by everyone. The film is* **For Heaven's Sake** *(1926).*

19

Legs (1919) and she had another huge hit with **Pollyanna** (1920), the first for United Artists, of which she was one of the founding members. She played a dual role in **Little Lord Fauntleroy** (1921), the title role and his mother.

Pickford longed to play the successful part of a grown-up but when the adult Mary failed in **Rosita** (1923) and **Dorothy Vernon of Haddon Hall** (1924) she soon returned to playing adolescents in films like **Little Annie Rooney** (1925) and **Sparrows** (1926). Defiantly grown up again she made her best film, **My Best Girl** (1927). She abandoned her old image completely in her first three Talkies: **Coquette** (1929), for which she won an Oscar, **The Taming of the Shrew** and **Kiki** (1931), but the last two fared poorly. She was a desperately old-fashioned creature to Depression-hit America, and after a third failure, **Secrets** (1933), she retired. She died in 1979.

♥ Married: actor Owen Moore (1911-20); Douglas Fairbanks (1920-35); and Charles "Buddy" Rogers (1937), who outlived her.

Mary Pickford

"America's Sweetheart" (elsewhere, "The World's Sweetheart") was born in 1893 in Toronto, Canada, and made her stage début in that city at the age of five, keeping the wolf from the family door. In 1907 she was on Broadway, but when there were no further stage offers she applied to Biograph. Movie players were not then identified but when, in her 27th film − **The Little Teacher** (1910) − the intertitles called her "Little Mary", Biograph was inundated with requests for more of Little Mary's films. She was also known as "The Girl with the Curls" and so began a popularity which was to make her the most famous woman in the world, and one of the richest. In 1913, on Broadway, she proved that movie actors could not only act on the stage but also draw vast crowds to the theater. Money, however, was not to be found in theater.

Adolph Zukor of Paramount met her constantly escalating terms while

she made such films as **Tess of the Storm Country** (1914), **The Poor Little Rich Girl** (1917), **Rebecca of Sunnybrook Farm, The Little Princess** and **Stella Maris** (1918), but he was then outbid by First National, who offered autonomy and huge fees to her business manager − Mother. Pickford's three films for First National included **Daddy Long**

▶ Few 32 year old actresses would contemplate playing a 12 year old, but Pickford succeeded in **Little Annie Rooney** (1925).

"It was always Mary herself that shone through. Her personality was the thing that made her movies memorable and the pictures that showed her personality were the best." – *Lillian Gish.*

"It was easy for me to act the part of a child because I adored children. I forgot I was grown up. That was the way I did **The Poor Little Rich Girl.** While I was playing that part I *was* a poor little rich girl, suffering all her unsatisfied yearnings for the things that money couldn't buy." – *Mary Pickford.*

"Mary Pickford is the only member of her sex who ever became the focal point of an entire industry. Her position is unique: probably no man or woman will ever again win so extensive a following." – *Benjamin B. Hampton.*

Gloria Swanson

Gloria Swanson's film career really finished with the Silents, but so strong were both her impact on her contemporaries and her one comeback film that she remained someone to reckon with till her death.

She was born in 1898 in Chicago. Her first role was in **The End of a Perfect Day** (1914) for Essanay Studios where she stayed, eventually playing leading lady to such comics as Wallace Beery and Bobby Vernon. Later she moved to Triangle but began her ascent to fame at Paramount in such Cecil B. De Mille films as **Don't Change Your Husband** (1919) and **Why Change Your Wife?** (1920), marital comedies thought sophisticated at the time.

Her last film for De Mille was **The Affairs of Anatol** (1921), after which Paramount showcased her in movies in which the plots were secondary to her extravagant wardrobe. When public interest began to fade, she changed her image, playing working girls, most remarkably in **Manhandled** (1924) and **Stage Struck** (1925). Her popularity by now exceeded even Pickford's and she took the opportunity to become her own producer at United Artists: her second film there, **Sadie Thompson** (1928), proved her mastery of the Silent screen, but there were difficulties with the next, **Queen Kelly,** which was not shown in the US because of the Talkies.

At first it seemed that Swanson would have a glorious career in Sound films after **The Trespasser** (1929), but she had faded by the time she did **Perfect Understanding** (1933) with Laurence Olivier. The British production was a financial disaster, and although several studios expressed an interest in Swanson she was off the screen until **Father Takes a Wife** (1941) and then again until Billy Wilder's **Sunset Boulevard** (1950), when her magnificent portrayal of a fading Silent movie queen set the world buzzing. But the offers that resulted were not exciting, and she made only two minor films (one American, one Italian) and played herself in **Airport 1975** (1974). She died in 1983, aged 85.

Married: Wallace Beery (1916-19); Herbert Somborn (1919-23); Henri de la Falaise (1925-30), a match that set Hollywood talking since he was a French marquis; Michael Farmer (1931-4); William Davey (1945-6); and William

▲ *Gloria Swanson, who came to prominence via Cecil B. De Mille's bedroom farces, here seen on the lookout by the seaside.*

Dufty (1976), a fellow health fanatic who, in the event, wasn't around very long. Lovers include (according to her memoir) film director Jack Conway (1916); Craney Gartz, a "Pasadena millionaire" (1919); film director Marshall Neilan (1921); co-star Rod La Rocque (1924); Joseph P. Kennedy (1927-30), father of the future president; and actor Herbert Marshall (1934).

She is courageous in a business where courage is as necessary as beauty and artistry. She has had to fight every inch of her way to her present high place in pictures. But there always seemed to be something pathetic about courageous little 5½-foot Gloria." – *James R. Quirk.*

"Is there anyone who can flaunt a superb wardrobe with more dash than

Gloria Swanson? To the smallest detail of ornament such as a buckle on a headdress or a wrist trinket, this young woman has a knack of lending to her apparel a certain significance of modernity that makes you unconsciously think that whatever she happens to put on is, of course, the very latest thing." – *Marshall Neilan.*

"Miss Swanson does more whole-souled and convincing acting than ever we have seen her do in all the years we have admired her [in **The Love of Sunya**]. Furthermore, we never had any idea that she was so beautiful . . . we decided the only way to describe her is to say that she is at least three Greta Garbos, and let it go at that." – *Harriette Underhill.*

Rudolph Valentino

The name "Valentino" has passed into legend like that of the other great lovers, Don Juan and Casanova. Yet in the few of his films that are revived he is unimpressive, and not notably virile, doing little more in his love scenes than snarl at his leading ladies: offscreen he was sexually ambiguous.

He was born in Castellaneta, Italy, in 1895 and emigrated to the US in 1913; he was poor, and seems to have made a living by dubious means, including blackmail and sleeping around. His skill as a dancer led to a

fleeting appearance in **Alimony** (1918), and although he had parts great and small he was generally unknown when June Mathis chose him to play the lead in **The Four Horsemen of the Apocalypse** (1921). He was a sensational success as the playboy who becomes a war hero, and the studio which benefited was Paramount, to which Mathis

▼ *Rudolph Valentino kidnapping an apprehensive Vilma Banky in* **The Son of the Sheik** *(1926), before riding away with her into the desert.*

▲ *Valentino's funeral in 1926 was an unprecedented event in Hollywood history, with thousands of female fans verging on mass hysteria.*

moved him after a salary dispute. **The Sheik, Blood and Sand** (1922) and **Monsieur Beaucaire** (1924) kept the female fans palpitating, but Valentino's second wife so interfered that he was allowed to go to United Artists, where he made **The Eagle** (1925) and **The Son of the Sheik** (1926). His early death from peritonitis in 1926 added to his mystique.

♥ Married: Jean Acker (1920), but it lasted only one night; Winifred Shaughnessy, known professionally as Natacha Rambova.

❝ That Valentino was certainly a very splendid fellow. And his unique glamor was not entirely due to the fact that he was unhampered by banal dialogue. Modern dialogue is not always banal, and the screen hero who could match Valentino's posturing technique with an equally polished vocal technique has a perfectly fair chance of becoming his romantic peer. It was his magnetism and dignity that assured him a peak of magnificent isolation." – *James Mason.*

"A curiously naïve and boyish young fellow, certainly not much beyond 30 and with a disarming air of inexperience. To my eyes, at least, not handsome, but nevertheless rather

attractive. There was an obvious finesse in him; even his clothes were not precisely those of his horrible trade." – *H.L. Mencken.*

Erich von Stroheim

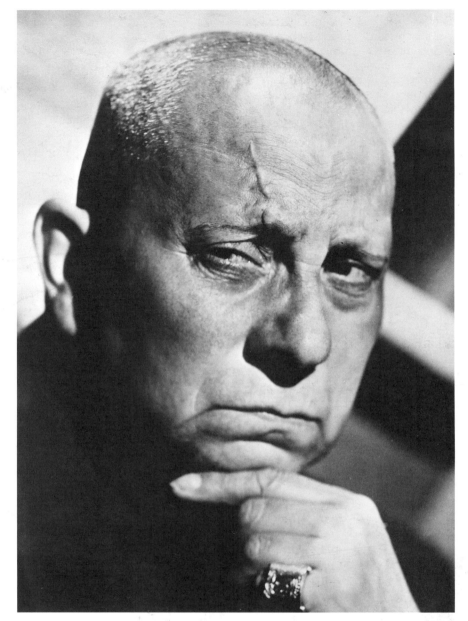

"The Man You Love to Hate" was born in Vienna in 1885 and emigrated to the US in 1906. He invented an aristocratic Austrian background before entering the film industry, where he most frequently advised on uniforms and wore them in Hollywood's war movies, in which his bullet-headed, monocled, fierce appearance made him a sinister Hun. His first credit was as **Captain McLean** (1914) and he worked regularly until the demand for Huns dried up. He then sold himself to Universal as writer, director and star of **Blind Husbands** (1919), as a lecherous – and uniformed – European count, and he played the role again in **Foolish Wives** (1922) and **The Wedding March** (1928), both of which were made in the midst of dissension and charges of extravagance, as were the other movies he directed between these two.

His high esteem among critics could not save him when his film with Gloria Swanson – **Queen Kelly** – became a débâcle – and the industry was just interested in him as an actor, though his only worthwhile roles were in **The Great Gabbo** (1929), **The Lost Squadron** (1932) as an autocratic movie director, and **As You Desire Me** with Garbo. He was invited to France to play a German officer in **Marthe Richard au Service de la France** (1937) and he stayed on to appear in Renoir's **La Grande Illusion** and other films, including **Les Disparus de St Agil** (1938) and **Menaces** (1940), two of his rare sympathetic appearances.

In Hollywood during the Second World War his few important roles included Rommel in Billy Wilder's **Five Graves to Cairo** (1943), but when work didn't improve he returned to France to star in **La Foire aux Chimères** (1946), the best of his postwar French movies. One last American movie was noteworthy: Wilder's **Sunset Boulevard** (1950), in which he was Swanson's butler. He died in 1957.

Married: Margaret Knox (1914-18); May Jones (1918-19); Valerie Germonprez. In 1939 he met Denise Vernac, his companion until his death.

▲ *In his early films Eric von Stroheim invariably played a lecherous, uniformed aristocrat. This portrait was taken later in his career, when his roles required pathos.*

❝ He was fascinating, *le grand seigneur* at all times. There was something very noble about him, although he wasn't a 'von' at all, his accent belonged to one of the rougher suburbs of Vienna. Of course he influenced me as a director: I always think of my style as a curious cross between Lubitsch and von Stroheim. When I first saw him at the wardrobe tests for his role as Rommel, I clicked my heels and said: 'Isn't this ridiculous, little me directing you? You were always ten years ahead of your time'. And he replied 'Twenty'." – *Billy Wilder.*

"A figure at once superb and pathetic: an artist with integrity, a supreme contempt for conventions and a disastrous inability to be practical; a man with courage, arrogance and, from the beginnings of his career, with grievances so overwhelming that recriminations became second nature to him." – *Catherine de la Roche.*

"The experience of working with him was unlike any I had had in more than 50 pictures. He was so painstaking and slow that I would lose all sense of time, hypnotized by the man's relentless perfectionism." – *Gloria Swanson.*

The Golden Years of Hollywood

Once the Talkies had arrived, stars not only had to speak but to sing, too — Joan Crawford, Gloria Swanson, even Gary Cooper, sang. Film techniques took a back seat in favor of the all-powerful microphone so that many of the "All Singing! All Dancing! All Talking!" movies now look primitive beside some of the expertly tailored late films of the silent screen.

By 1933, though, the problems of sound had been mastered and the Talkies really took off. Musicals were once again popular after their understandable eclipse in the silent era and every studio was equipped to turn out a program of romances, thrillers, comedies, musicals and action spectaculars. Westerns were the exception, for in the thirties they still had the status of B movies, supporting the main feature.

The Hollywood moguls
By general consent the leader of the industry was Metro-Goldwyn-Mayer, which not only boasted "more stars than there are in heaven", but spent more on its individual productions than the other studios. The other studios in the "Big Five" were Paramount, Warner Brothers, RKO and Fox, which became 20th Century-Fox when it was absorbed by Darryl F. Zanuck's dynamic new company, 20th Century Pictures.

Universal, Columbia and United Artists made up the "Little Three", so regarded because they owned

◀ *Lending new meaning to the phrase "a strong supporting cast",* **Night at the Opera** *(1935) was the first Marx Brothers film to be given adequate resources for big production numbers.*

none of the cinema circuits that automatically booked their products. During the early thirties, Columbia emerged from its "poverty row" status, helped by the films directed by Frank Capra and, more generally, by the swell in audiences seeking to escape their Depression blues.

In spite of some changes at Fox, Universal and most of all at RKO (which seldom made any profit), the companies were run by their founders and continued to be so until the fifties. RKO was the first to go out of business, ruined by the whims of its new boss, the millionaire Howard Hughes, whose interest in movies and female movie stars proved disastrous for the studio.

Each studio turned out three to four major pictures every month and as many minor ones, as well as several films of indeterminate status known as "programmers". These were designed chiefly to keep the audiences coming in.

The "Big Five" turned out an average of 10 prestigious movies each year. The old one film/one star concept had long been in decline, but was finally abandoned with MGM's **Grand Hotel** (1932) into which — in a typically grandiose way — this giant studio poured *five* stars, an event regarded with unparalleled excitement.

Two or three stars per film remained the average and they were supported by a wonderful brigade of character players, many of whom were familiar enough to receive fond murmurs of recognition from audiences. Some of these supporting actors were also under contract — Warner Brothers had a particularly enviable stock company — while others went from studio to studio, chalking up to a dozen credits a year.

New breed of stars

In the early thirties some stars made as many as eight movies a year, and worked hard for their money. The notorious Hollywood parties of the silent period became much rarer once it was necessary for the artists to arrive on set having learned their lines the previous night!

The influx of stage-trained actors into films was essential as much for reasons of discipline as for acting and vocal skill. Stars were expected not only to act in front of the cameras but to endure make-up tests, costume fittings, stills photography and personal appearances on tour. But over and above this, the Depression caused moviegoers to reject their former idols of the frivolous twenties.

During the Depression, films had to be made cheaply and quickly. By the end of the thirties and throughout the forties this was no longer the case and studios began the habit of rationing their box-office stars so that audiences would not tire of them. Minor names made only two or three films a year, while the really big stars made just one, which would be all the more eagerly anticipated.

Studio monopoly

Less than a handful of popular — and brave — stars freelanced; others kept deals going with two or perhaps three studios at a time. The close ties between studio and star were of mutual benefit. Those stars under

▲ *The love between a research chemist and a cafe owner forms the basis of this 1932 Marlene Dietrich star vehicle: one of her six Hollywood films directed by Josef von Sternberg, the man responsible for* **The Blue Angel** *(1930).*

▼ *Searching for the nearest exit, Humphrey Bogart, Ann Sheridan and George Raft in* **They Drive by Night** *(1940).*

▲ *An early publicity still of Ingrid Bergman, shortly after her arrival in Hollywood to star in Selznick's version of* **Intermezzo** *(1936).*

exclusive contract may have complained about having no say whatsoever in the material they were handed, but the studios protected them closely (so that no off-screen affairs or personal weaknesses made the papers) and ensured that they remained in the public eye. Several big names found themselves shelved entirely once they had left the studio which helped to promote them.

Grooming new stars

In spite of their power, studios could not guarantee success for a new "star". Samuel Goldwyn once signed up an actress, Anna Sten, who had been stunning in her Russian and German films. He spent over $3 million in remolding her for the Hollywood publicity machine, but when the public shunned her third film, in which she played opposite the immensely popular Gary Cooper, she was hastily dropped.

Once the artist showed star potential, however, he or she would be billed opposite established stars in order to get the widest possible audiences. If the reviewers were negative and the fan mail sparse, the artist returned to supporting roles, or was not offered a renewed option.

Silent survivors

Actors such as Ronald Colman and Gary Cooper, along with Greta Garbo, Norma Shearer and Joan Crawford, were survivors of the silent screen; they had been active in that frank, free period of the early

thirties when Hollywood could still make honest dramas. When a Production Code was enforced in 1930 by the official guardians of morality, sex could not be portrayed on the screen. But despite this censorship, the industry was buoyant enough to continue producing racy entertainments – even if these lacked the bite of earlier movies. The flair and confidence with which the studios entertained audiences during the thirties and forties made these Hollywood's "golden years".

The war years

Surprisingly, the Second World War had little adverse effect on the health of the film industry, and actually helped to increase cinema attendance. It did, however, create a demand for even more escapist movies – and for younger stars.

War audiences could hardly identify easily with the stars of the thirties. These had been authoritative figures, leaders of men, like Clark Gable, Ronald Colman and James Cagney; or dapper men-about-town like William Powell, George Brent and Franchot Tone. The female stars – from Greta Garbo to Kay Francis – had been glamorous, beautifully dressed and remote. There were a few "friendly" stars like Joan Blondell and Ann Sothern, but the only boy-next-door type was Mickey Rooney.

It was to this more approachable type that the young filmgoers were drawn, and Mickey Rooney and Judy Garland were closer to their aspirations than Robert Taylor or Marlene Dietrich. Couples separated by the war sought idols more like the sweethearts they were missing, and so made stars out of Van Johnson, June Allyson, Dorothy McGuire, Maureen O'Hara, Jane Wyman and Robert Walker. Though these artists were not exactly ordinary, they were certainly more accessible than the near-mythical Valentino or Garbo.

Perhaps that is why these stars seem less interesting now (none of them is included here). But among the female actresses, some at least replaced the leading ladies of the past. A few male stars, such as Clark Gable and Spencer Tracy, looked set to go on forever, but Tyrone Power increasingly found that parts once earmarked for him were now going to the handsome newcomer, Gregory Peck.

In 1946 audience attendance hit an all-time peak, after which the long, sad decline began. By the end of the decade the film industry's golden years were over.

▼ *An immortal scene of screen romance that needs no description: Clark Gable and Vivien Leigh in* **Gone With the Wind** *(1939).*

Jean Arthur

The delicious comedienne with the corncrake voice was born in 1905, the daughter of a photographer who frequently used her as a model. A photograph of her led to a Fox contract and a small role in **Cameo Kirby** (1923). Small roles at various studios and a Paramount contract followed, but she made little or no impression until **The Whole Town's Talking** (1935). She became queen of Columbia in three of Capra's comedies, **Mr Deeds Goes to Town** (1936), **You Can't Take It With You** (1938) and **Mr Smith Goes to Washington** (1939), in the meantime bringing her distinctive, warm personality to some equally fine

▼Jean Arthur, before she became a much admired comedienne, taking a rest while posing for a glamor still.

films: **History Is Made at Night** (1937), **Only Angels Have Wings** (1939) and **The Devil and Miss Jones** (1941).

Further comedies included two directed by George Stevens, **The Talk of the Town** (1942) and **The More the Merrier** (1943), after which she retired when her contract expired. Paramount brought her back in Billy Wilder's **A Foreign Affair** (1948) and George Stevens's **Shane** (1953). As the favorite actress of so many film-makers she might be filming to this day, but her timidity and lack of self-confidence won the day.

♥ Married: Julian Anker (1928) and producer Frank Ross (1932-49).

" Jean Arthur is my favorite actress. Probably because she was unique . . . . Those weren't butterflies in her stomach. They were wasps. But push that neurotic girl forcibly, but gently, in front of the camera and turn on the lights — and that whining mop would magically blossom into a warm, lovely, poised and confident actress." — *Frank Capra.*

"One of the greatest comediennes the screen has ever seen. When she works she gives everything that's in her, and she studies her roles more than most of the actresses I've ever known." — *George Stevens.*

Fred Astaire

The screen's greatest dancer was born in 1899 in Omaha, Nebraska, and within a few years he and his sister were showing their skills in local halls and theaters. In the twenties they both starred in major musical shows on both sides of the Atlantic and, when she retired, he

signed a contract with RKO. Uncertain of what to do with this lean, unromantic actor they loaned him out for **Dancing Lady** (1933) and gave him hardly a bigger role in **Flying Down to Rio** but his dance with another supporting player, Ginger Rogers, caused the studio to co-star the pair in **The Gay Divorcee** (1934) and then **Roberta** (1935). Rogers' sassiness and his modesty blended well, and their dances were invigorating. They sang and danced to excellent songs by Berlin, Kern and Gershwin – in **Top Hat, Follow the Fleet** (1936), **Swing Time** (the best of the series), **Shall We Dance?** (1937) and **Carefree** (1938). The team split with **The Story of Vernon and Irene Castle** (1939).

As a freelance, he danced with Eleanor Powell in **Broadway Melody of 1940** and Rita Hayworth in **You'll Never Get Rich** (1941) and **You Were Never Lovelier** (1942); and he had two big hits with Bing Crosby, **Holiday Inn** and, later, **Blue Skies** (1946). **Ziegfeld Follies** introduced him to a more balletic dancing style. He retired but was coaxed back to partner Judy Garland in **Easter Parade** (1948) and then in **The Barkleys of Broadway** (1949), but she had to be replaced – by Ginger Rogers. He continued to make major contributions to the glorious MGM musicals: **Three Little Words** (1950), **The Belle of New York** (1952), **The Band Wagon** (1953) and **Silk Stockings** (1957), the first two with Vera-Ellen and the others with Cyd Charisse; and at Paramount he danced with Audrey Hepburn in **Funny Face** (1957). He did dance some

▶ *Fred Astaire with one of his best partners, Cyd Charisse, in the balletic dance which climaxed Vincente Minnelli's bright musical* **The Band Wagon** *(1953).*

STAGE

THE MAGAZINE OF

After Dark

35¢

Fred Astaire and Ginger Rogers
as Vernon and Irene Castle
in the R K O — Radio picture,
The Castles

FEBRUARY
1939

steps in **Finian's Rainbow** (1968) and in the introduction to an MGM compilation film, but his other late movies were "straight" ones, in which he had supporting roles.

 Married: Phyllis Potter (1933 until her death in 1954); Robyn Smith (1980).

" He's the greatest dancer who ever lived — greater than Nijinsky." — *Noël Coward.*
"Except for the times Fred worked with real professional dancers like Cyd Charisse, it was a 25-year war." — *Hermes Pan.*
"He's a supreme artist, but he is constantly filled with doubts about his work — and that's what makes him so good. He is a perfectionist who is never sure he is attaining perfection." — *Rouben Mamoulian.*

Lauren Bacall

It isn't such a great profession, she once observed, being a widow, and one sympathized with the strong and stylish Lauren Bacall. But her teamings with husband Humphrey Bogart are among the enduring pleasures of the cinema; when they sparred, his world-weary

◄ *Fred Astaire and Ginger Rogers in the last of the famous musicals they made for RKO,* **The Story of Vernon and Irene Castle** *(1939).*

cynicism was an admirable foil to her little-girl looks, husky voice and overt sex appeal.

Bacall was born in New York in 1924, had an early stage career, but was discovered as a model by director Howard Hawks, who cast her opposite Bogey in **To Have and Have Not** (1945). After **Confidential Agent** (1945) with Charles Boyer, she was teamed with Bogart in **The Big Sleep** (1946), **Dark Passage** (1947) and **Key Largo** (1948).

▲ *Bogart and Bacall, sea captain and cabaret singer in* **To Have and Have Not** *(1945), her first film directed by Howard Hawks. In life, as in the film, they fell in love.*

Quarrels with Warners, to whom she was under contract, resulted in only two further movies, **Young Man with a Horn** (1950) and **Bright Leaf** — and she has filmed infrequently since. Apart from three comedies, **How to Marry a Millionaire** (1953), **Woman's World** (1954) and **Designing Woman** (1957), her most memorable non-Bogart movies were **The Cobweb** (1955), **Harper** (1966) and **Murder on the Orient Express** (1974). During this period she had several Broadway successes.

♥ Married: Humphrey Bogart (1945, widowed 1957); Jason Robards Jr (1961-9). Between the two marriages she was expected to marry Frank Sinatra.

◄ *The second Bogart-Bacall teaming is also classic: he's Raymond Chandler's private eye, Phillip Marlowe and she? Well, she's very mysterious.*

We discovered Bacall was a little girl who, when she became insolent, became rather attractive. That was the only way you noticed her, because she could do it with a grin. So I said to Bogey, 'We are going to try an interesting thing. You are about the most insolent man on the screen and I'm going to make this girl a little more insolent than you are' . . . . It was sex antagonism, that's what it was, and it made the scenes easy." – *Howard Hawks.*

"She has a javelin-like vitality, a born dancer's eloquence in movement, a fierce female shrewdness and a special sweet sourness. With these faculties, plus a stone-crushing self-confidence and a trombone voice, she manages to get across the toughest girl a piously regenerate Hollywood has dreamed of in a long, long while." – *James Agee.*

Ingrid Bergman

Ingrid Bergman was the forties idea of a great actress, partly because she was one of the few shining stars to follow Bette Davis' lead in playing both nice and evil women. In fact, she was seldom convincing in her unsympathetic roles, but she had a freshness and a radiance surpassing the qualities in other Hollywood ladies.

She was born in Stockholm in 1915 and brought up by relatives when her parents died; she studied acting and made her film début in **Munkbrogreven** (1934). She starred in half a dozen Swedish movies, one of which was seen by David O. Selznick, who decided to remake it with her: **Intermezzo: A Love Story** (1939). Her beauty and natural qualities impressed Selznick and everyone else; but he loaned her out for most of her years under contract.

She was impressive in **Adam Had Four Sons** (1941), **Rage in Heaven** and **Dr Jekyll and Mr Hyde,** but **Casablanca** (1943) made her a box-office star, partly because of the unlikely chemistry of her teaming with Humphrey Bogart. After that film, she commanded the biggest directors and co-stars in Hollywood: Sam Wood's films **For Whom the Bell Tolls** and **Saratoga Trunk** (1945), both with Gary Cooper; Cukor's **Gaslight** (1944), for which she won an Oscar, with Charles

Boyer; Hitchcock's **Spellbound** (1945) with Gregory Peck; Leo McCarey's **The Bells of St Mary's** with Bing Crosby; and Alfred Hitchcock's **Notorious** (1946). The great success of these was not equalled by **Arch of Triumph** (1948), **Joan of Arc** or Hitchcock's **Under Capricorn** (1949) – and even less so by Roberto Rossellini's **Stromboli,** despite the publicity engendered when she left her husband for Rossellini and bore his child out of wedlock. The other films she made for him in Italy were financially disastrous, and their marriage was in ruins by the time Jean Renoir invited her to France to make **Paris Does Strange Things** (1956).

Hollywood asked her back for **Anastasia** and awarded her a second Oscar; **Indiscreet** (1958) and **The Inn of the Sixth Happiness** further helped to restore her popularity but, now living in Europe, she didn't pursue her film career with any determination and chose new parts badly. She made rare TV appearances and acted in the US and in Britain. She had only two successes among her last half-dozen films, **Cactus Flower** (1969) and **Murder on the Orient**

▼ *Ingrid Bergman soon after her arrival in Hollywood in the late 1930s; her natural look heralded a new kind of star.*

Express (1974), for which she won her third Oscar (as Best Supporting Actress this time), but, for her famous compatriot Ingmar Bergman, **Autumn Sonata** (1978) contains her greatest performance. One of her rare TV appearances was as Golda Meir, which was shown just after her death from cancer in 1982.

♥ Married: Dr Peter Lindstrom (1937-50); Roberto Rossellini (1950-8); Swedish impresario Lars Schmidt (1958), but it didn't last.

❝ There has never been anything like her." – *Cary Grant.*
"She's so great that when she walks on screen and says 'Hello' people ask 'Who wrote that wonderful line of dialogue?'" – *Leo McCarey.*
"Miss Bergman was everything that the publicity sheets would have one believe of the majority of film stars (though only the minority qualify): she was unaffected, intelligent, unconceited." – *Rodney Ackland.*
"Her great quality is that the moment she understands a part, her intellect gives way to emotion. When her emotion takes over, it comes out right." – *Anatole Litvak.*

Humphrey Bogart

If ever there was a case of the public making a star, it happened to Humphrey Bogart. The critics and his own talent helped, factors against which Warner Brothers fought since they could only see him as a supporting actor. As a

▲ *When cast opposite Spencer Tracy in* **Dr Jekyll and Mr Hyde** *(1941), Bergman asked to change roles with Lana Turner, and ended up playing a cockney barmaid.*

villain he never played for sympathy and was a loner, contemptuous of phonies and "authority", with a pessimism compounded by his own stubborn integrity.

Bogart was born into comfortable circumstances in New York in 1899 and drifted into acting because of his friendship with the actress Alice Brady. As a reasonably successful Broadway child actor he was put under contract by Fox and made his feature début in **A Devil with Women** (1930). No one was particularly impressed with the half-dozen movies he made, so he returned to New York to play a gangster in **The Petrified Forest** with Leslie Howard, who insisted that Bogart play the same role in the movie, made in 1936. Warners signed him only reluctantly, but soon found that they had a fine foil for their other tough guys – Edward G. Robinson in **Bullets or Ballots** (1936), **Marked Woman** (1937) and **Kid Galahad,** James Cagney in **Angels with Dirty Faces** (1938) and **The Roaring Twenties** (1939), and George Raft in **Invisible Stripes** and **They Drive by Night** (1940).

Despite Bogart's outstanding performances in **Dead End** (1937) and **Stand-In,** he was only offered the lead part in **High Sierra** (1941) after just about every other star male had turned it down. Ironically George Raft

▼ *In* **The Big Sleep** *(1946), real-life husband and wife Bogart and Bacall proved to be one of the great screen teams.*

also turned down **The Maltese Falcon** and **Casablanca** (1943), the two now-classic movies which made Bogart the biggest male star of his contemporaries. John Huston's **Across the Pacific** (1942), and **The Treasure of Sierra Madre** (1948) and **Key Largo** are other milestones in Bogart's career, as are Hawks' **To Have and Have Not** (1945) and **The Big Sleep** (1946); the other late Warner movies are poor, except the last of all, **The Enforcer** (1951).

As his own producer, Bogart made only one outstanding film, **Knock on Any Door** (1949), but he is at his best and most typical in such others as **In a Lonely Place** (1950) and **Sirocco** (1951). Reverting to character roles, he was the cheery skipper in **The African Queen** (1952) and the neurotic one in **The Caine Mutiny** (1954), earning new laurels – and an Oscar for the former. The best of the rest are John Huston's **Beat the Devil**, Billy Wilder's **Sabrina**, Joseph L. Mankiewicz's **The Barefoot Contessa** and

William Wyler's **The Desperate Hours** (1955). His last film was **The Harder They Fall** (1956). He died of cancer in 1957.

♥ Married: Helen Mencken (1926-8); Mary Phillips (1928-38); actress Mayo Methot (1938-45) and Lauren Bacall (1945), who outlived him. He was reputedly the lover of Alice Brady.

❝ Bogart's a helluva nice guy till 11.30 p.m. After that he thinks he's Bogart." – *Dave Chasen.*
"Was he tough? In a word, no. Bogey was truly a gentle soul." – *Lauren Bacall.*
"He was a real man – nothing feminine about him. He knew he was a natural aristocrat – better than anybody." – *Katharine Hepburn.*

▼ *Bogart in 1939; this was during his most prolific period – 28 films between 1936–40.*

Charles Boyer

No other screen lover was quite so effective as Charles Boyer, with his soulful eyes and deep, French-accented voice. He wanted to be taken seriously as an actor, but was too intelligent not to know when he was on to a good thing.

Boyer was born in 1899 in Figeac, France, and was studying acting at the Conservatoire when Marcel l'Herbier chose him for a role in **L'Homme du Large** (1920). He was a great star of stage and screen when both Germany and Hollywood engaged him to play in the French versions of their early Talkies; he also played supporting roles in the US and was eventually starred in **Caravan** (1934), but it was **Private Worlds** (1935) which established him with American audiences.

The French **Mayerling** (1936) was one of the great hits on the art-house circuit and started his run of popular movies: **History Is Made at**

▲ *Boyer and Bergman in* **Gaslight** *(1944). Don't worry about him: for most of the film he drove her towards suicide.*

Night (1937), **Conquest, Tovarich, Algiers** (1938), **Love Affair** (1939), **All This and Heaven Too** (1940), **Back Street** (1941) and **Hold Back the Dawn.** A spot of villainy in **Gaslight** (1944) didn't hurt his image, but few of his postwar films worked out as planned, especially the expensive **Arch of Triumph** (1948) with Ingrid Bergman. After a short time in the theater he returned with beard and smaller billing in **The Thirteenth Letter** (1951), as if to announce that he had made the transition to character actor.

▲ *Suave and sophisticated Charles Boyer, the ideal screen lover.*

At the height of his career he had returned to France at intervals to film, and continued to do so over the next two decades, playing supporting roles in both French and English movies. His last fine chance was in **The Earrings of Madame De . . .** (1953) and he played it with all his old mastery.

 Married: British actress Pat Paterson (1934), who died in 1978. Boyer committed suicide two days later.

❝ Just as [Leslie] Howard was the perfect Englishman, Charles Boyer was the perfect movie Frenchman, ideal symbol of those marginally romantic qualities with which Anglo-Saxons have always invested the Gallic male. His deep and vibrant voice spoke a promise of new adventures in love, his deep, sad eyes bespoke a worldly knowledge untarnished by cynicism." – *Richard Schickel.*

James Cagney

Stocky, pugnacious, dynamic, self-assured, cocky, charming: Cagney was all of these things in his gangster roles. Although equally convincing as killer or cop, the persona hardly varied — with Cagney's *range* it didn't matter, it was simply enlivening to be in his presence.

He was born in 1899 in New York and had a number of jobs before trying vaudeville. He was a minor star on Broadway when Warner Brothers decided to film the play he was in, asking him to repeat his role: thus he made his movie début in **Sinners' Holiday** (1930). Four supporting roles followed, including one in **The Public Enemy** (1931), but after three days was upped to the star role of gangster.

The rest is now history. Here was a new type of leading man, and the public lapped him up in such films as **Taxi** (1932) and **Hard to Handle** (1933). **Footlight Parade,** a musical, revealed his buoyancy as a dancer, but, as he showed in **Frisco Kid** (1935), **G-Men, Ceiling Zero** (1936), **Angels with Dirty Faces** (1938),

▲ *James Cagney as psychotic gangster Cody Jarrett in* **White Heat** *(1949). Off-stage he was a quiet, charming, peaceful guy.*

Each Dawn I Die (1939), **The Roaring Twenties, Torrid Zone** (1940) and **City for Conquest,** he was too valuable as a shoot-'em-up (or down) tough guy to do much of that. He also played Bottom in **A Midsummer Night's Dream** (1935) and his constant quarrels with Warners (over salary and overwork) resulted in two movies for a minor

▲ *Cagney won a Best Actor Oscar for his ebullient performance as showman George M. Cohan in* **Yankee Doodle Dandy** *(1942). He began life as a talented dancer.*

company (because no major studio would risk Warners' wrath by employing him).

The patching up of the quarrel and some of the excellent films listed above did not change Cagney's determination to leave Warners — nor did the greatest triumph of his career, **Yankee Doodle Dandy** (1942), for which his portrayal of song-and-dance-man George M. Cohan won him an Oscar. None of his four films as a freelance made much of a mark, but a return to Warners to play an aging gangster in **White Heat** (1949) was lucky for him (and them). Slightly less engaging as he aged, he nevertheless was a fascinating villain in both **Mister Roberts** (1955) and **Love Me or Leave Me;** and he showed he had lost none of his old comic panache in a (fairly) sympathetic role in Billy Wilder's **One Two Three** (1961). With that, he retired, but came back (on doctor's orders) to appear in **Ragtime** (1981).

♥ Married: Frances Vernon (1920).

❝ James Cagney rolled through the film like a very belligerent barrel." — *Noël Coward.*
"Cagney was and is spruce, dapper and grinning: when he hits a friend over the ear with a revolver-butt, he does it as casually as he will presently press the elevator button on his way out. By retaining his brisk little smile throughout he makes one react warmly, with a grin, not coldly and aghast . . . . He was never a romantic figure himself — at his height you can't be — nor was he sentimental — Cheshire cats never are — but he possessed, possibly in greater abundance than any other name star of the time, irresistible charm." — *Kenneth Tynan.*

Maurice Chevalier

🎥 Like the other major stars of the early musicals — Al Jolson and Fred Astaire — Maurice Chevalier was not in his first youth when he delighted audiences. He was

born in poverty in 1888 in Paris and began entertaining in cafés. He was an extra in **Trop Crédule** (1908) and made intermittent movie appearances over the next 20 years while forging a name for himself in revue and cabaret. In 1929 he was screen-tested by MGM but signed by Paramount, who starred him in **Innocents of Paris.**

▼ *The Hollywood image of Maurice Chevalier: in straw hat and surrounded by eye-popping female admirers in* **Folies Bergere** *(1935).*

His debonair, roguish personality and thickly accented charm were sparklingly used by Ernst Lubitsch in **The Love Parade,** the first of several musicals where he was teamed with Jeanette MacDonald to deliciously *risqué* effect: **One Hour with You** (1932) and **Love Me Tonight** and, at MGM, **The Merry Widow** (1934). MGM now held Chevalier's contract, but there was a dispute about billing and he returned to France after a loan-out, for **Folies Bergère** (1935). In Britain, he made **The Beloved Vagabond** (1936) and René Clair's **Break the News** (1938); the best of his French movies are **Personal Column** (1939) and Clair's **Man About Town** (1947).

Hollywood beckoned again, with **Love in the Afternoon** (1957), and then the ever popular **Gigi** (1958): the movie took a number of Oscars and he was awarded an honorary one. His twinkle brightened many (mainly poor) American movies till 1967. He died in 1972.

♥ Married: dancer Yvonne Vallée (1927-35). Reputed lovers include music-hall co-star Mistinguett, movie stars Marlene Dietrich and Kay Francis, dancer Nita Raya, former actress Mrs Odette Melier and Jeanette Macdonald.

❝ He is unique, and, being so, he is indestructible. As a performer, he was totally integrated and the whole of him was much bigger than the sum of his various talents. His stylized silhouette, the saucy angle of his straw hat, his smile, the way he moved, sang and talked was not only artistically perfect, but spiritually up-

▲ *Chevalier and Jeanette Macdonald in the musical* **Love Me Tonight** *(1932). She suffered from what is now called frigidity – he was a tailor employed to do some defrosting.*

lifting to young and old. He radiated optimism, good will and above all the *joie de vivre* that every human being longs for." – *Rouben Mamoulian.*
"M. Chevalier is as enjoyable as ever. There is his smile and also his stare – a stare of discomfort when he is dumbfounded. But whether he is solemn or laughing, he is always engaging." – *Mordaunt Hall.*
"You're the greatest thing to come from France since Lafayette." – *Al Jolson.*

Claudette Colbert

📽◁ Although she could be bubbly and over-bright, Claudette Colbert was never anything but elegant — in manner as well as looks. She was a great comedienne in an era of light comediennes. She was born in Paris in 1905 but was brought up in New York, where at the age of 20 a playwright recommended her for a role in a play. During several years on Broadway she made one movie, **For the Love of Mike** (1927), but her stage training made her an asset with the advent of Talkies and Paramount signed her up: the high spots include **The Smiling Lieutenant** (1931), **The Sign of the Cross** (1932), **Three-Cornered Moon** (1933), **It Happened One Night** (1934) – on loan and winning her an Oscar – **Cleopatra, She Married Her Boss** (1935) and **Tovarich** (1937), the last two on loan, **Bluebeard's Eighth Wife** (1938) and **Midnight** (1939).

As one of the highest-paid and most popular players in Hollywood she freelanced successfully in **It's a Wonderful World, Drums Along the Mohawk, Arise My Love** (1940), **The Palm Beach Story**

▼ *Charles Laughton and Claudette Colbert as the Emperor Nero and his mistress Poppaea in De Mille's* **The Sign of the Cross** *(1932).*

(1942) and **Since You Went Away** (1944), her first mother role. After that her vehicles weakened, though **The Egg and I** (1947), one of several teamings with Fred MacMurray, was a big box-office hit. She should have been in **State of the Union** and **All About Eve**, but made inferior movies to them; in 1952/3 she made films in Britain and France, but after **Texas Lady** (1955) and **Parrish** (1961) has confined her work to the stage.

♥ Married: actor/director Norman Foster (1928-35); Joel Pressman (1935, widowed 1968).

❝ A terrific lady and a good actress." – *Lauren Bacall.* "Colbert has supreme command of the comic style [in **Midnight**]." – *Frank S. Nugent.*

Ronald Colman

He managed to be, all at the same time, debonair and courtly, distinguished and dashing, charming and full of integrity. Accordingly, he was one of the screen's great romantic heroes.

He was born in Richmond, Surrey, in 1891 and in his youth acted as an amateur before turning professional; a number of West End appearances and a handful of British films led nowhere, so he went to the US, where after two minor films he was cast opposite Lillian Gish in **The White Sister** (1923).

The starring roles which followed were in such popular films as **Stella Dallas** (1925), **Beau Geste** (1926) and, in **The Winning of Barbara Worth,** he and fellow Goldwyn star Vilma Banky became one of the great love teams of the Silents. She didn't survive the coming of Talkies, but Colman became a bigger star than ever, partly because of his gentle but authoritative voice – in films such as **Bulldog Drummond** (1929), **Arrowsmith** (1931) and **Cynara** (1932).

After breaking away from Goldwyn he freelanced, hitting a peak in **A Tale of Two Cities** (1936), mustacheless, and two magnificent films, **Lost Horizon** (1937) and **The Prisoner of Zenda.** He made some errors after that, both with the scripts

▲ *Ronald Colman and Vilma Banky in the* **Two Lovers** *(1928).*

he accepted and two he rejected **(Intermezzo: A Love Story** and **Rebecca).** He returned to form in **Random Harvest** (1942) and was awarded an Oscar for **A Double Life** (1948), one of his by now rare film appearances. In the fifties he made only two guest appearances, and he died in 1958.

♥ Married: Thelma Raye (1919-34), whom he divorced after a long separation; English-born actress Benita Hume (1938).

❝ Mr Ronald Colman is, I understand, the greatest male exponent of body-urge – the new term for the old-fashioned 'sex-appeal' – possessed by the modern screen. As I am not a flapper I do not know how far Mr Colman makes good the claims made for him; he seems to me to be a good-looking man who probably goes in first wicket down, is scratch at golf, and would be just about as interesting to talk to on any subject as a University Blue." – *James Agate.* "The secret of Ronald Colman's lasting success was that he was a complete original, in personality, good looks, diversity and style." – *Jane Wyatt.*

The young Gary Cooper in an unfamiliar role, as an elegant aesthete. He cut such an attractive figure that Paramount quickly fed his elegant profile into their publicity machine.

Gary Cooper

As cowboy or (light) comedian, Gary Cooper was one of the nonpareils of American cinema, not particularly versatile but able to project a determination and honesty, in addition to the other qualities essential to the heroes he played.

He was born in Helena, Montana, in 1901 to British parents, whose move to Los Angeles enabled him to get work as an extra in movies, chiefly in two-reel Westerns. When one actor failed to show up he was promoted to the role of Ronald Colman's rival (for Vilma Banky) in **The Winning of Barbara Worth** (1926), which brought a Paramount contract. Goldwyn, who produced, had also made an offer, but at a lower salary — which so rankled him that ten years later he made a deal whereby he shared Cooper's services with Paramount.

After two or three supporting roles, notably in **Wings** (1927), he became one of the studio's stalwart leading men, but did not achieve real popularity until his first all-Talkie, a Western, **The Virginian** (1929). Other memorable films of this period include **The Spoilers** (1930), **Morocco** with Marlene Dietrich, Mamoulian's **City Streets** (1931) and Frank Borzage's very fine version of Hemingway's novel, **A Farewell to Arms** (1932).

Starting with Hathaway's **Lives of a Bengal Lancer** (1935), he starred in films which made him one of the world's half-dozen top box-office attractions; among them **Peter Ibbetson,** Borzage's **Desire** (1936) with Marlene Dietrich, Frank Capra's **Mr Deeds Goes to Town, The General Died at Dawn,** De Mille's **The Plainsman** (1937), Lubitsch's **Bluebeard's Eighth Wife** (1938), William Wyler's **The Westerner** (1940), De Mille's **North West Mounted Police,** Capra's **Meet John Doe** (1941) and Hawks' **Sergeant York,** for which he won a Best Actor Oscar.

After two major films with Ingrid Bergman, **For Whom the Bell Tolls** (1943) and **Saratoga Trunk** (1945), he filmed chiefly for Warner Brothers, not always choosing the best material, though he continued to command Hollywood's leading directors — Fritz Lang with **Cloak and Dagger** (1946) and Leo McCarey with **Good Sam** (1948).

▼ *The public however, preferred the more down-to-earth Cooper, liking him best as the Western hero, as seen here in* **High Noon** *(1952).*

Fred Zinnemann's excellent Western **High Noon** (1952) was something of a comeback for him, providing a second Oscar. Aging now, he filmed regularly during the last decade of his life, outstandingly in: **Vera Cruz** (1954), a Western with Burt Lancaster; Wyler's **Friendly Persuasion** (1956), a tale of Quaker folk; and Billy Wilder's **Love in the Afternoon** (1957), as a roué in love with a much younger girl, Audrey Hepburn. He was awarded an honorary Oscar just before he died of cancer in 1961. **The Naked Edge** (1961) was released posthumously.

♥ Married: Veronica Balfe (1933). Lovers include Clara Bow, Lupe Velez, Countess Dorothy di Frasso, Marlene Dietrich and Patricia Neal.

“ I've seen them all come and go, and they all get spoiled. Many begin to believe their image. Gary was never spoiled. He was a natural person with no temper that I ever heard of or saw. It's a little thing, but indicative of the man, that I never received a thank you note from him that wasn't handwritten . . . . Jimmy Stewart is the same way." – *Edie Goetz.*
"He was the most gorgeously attractive man. Bright, too, though some people didn't think so." – *Patricia Neal.*

Joan Crawford

Perhaps the most admirable quality of Joan Crawford's performances was the conviction she brought to her often poor scripts. Her range was minute and she barely knew of subtlety, but she dominated every film she made in her awesomely long career.

She was born in San Antonio, Texas, in 1904. Studio biographies stated that she had been a waitress before a prize in a Charleston contest led her into dancing professionally. MGM executive Harry Rapf was said to have seen her in the chorus of a Broadway show and she was certainly his mistress when given a contract at that studio. She made four minor appearances under her real name (Lucille Le Sueur) and got her new

name and a real role for **Sally, Irene and Mary** (1925). For a while she was just another all-purpose *ingénue,* noted for her intensity, but as a jazz-mad flapper she made her mark in **Our Dancing Daughters** (1928). She sang and danced in her first Talkie, **The Hollywood Revue of 1929,** and essayed a very dramatic role in **Paid** (1930). **Laughing Sinners** (1931) was the first of several teamings with Clark Gable, including, most felicitously, **Possessed, Dancing Lady** (1933), **Chained** (1934) and **Love on the Run** (1936).

The other memorable movies from this period are **Grand Hotel** (1932), **Rain, The Last of Mrs Cheyney** (1937) and **Mannequin** (1938); but with the exception of **The Women** (1939) and **A Woman's Face** (1941) her last MGM films were poor.

Studio bosses agreed with the "box-office poison" label exhibitors gave her, but Crawford, noted for her ambition, refused to be washed up and got herself a contract with Warners at a much reduced salary. In two years she had only one brief role, as herself in the all-star **Hollywood**

▶▶ *A young and exultant Joan Crawford. Apparently she so loved being a star that she kept every fan letter and made sure that her fans knew her every move to ensure a daily mobbing!*

PHOTOPLAY

APRIL

1/6

JOAN CRAWFORD

MR. CHIPS DISCOVERS HOLLYWOOD By James Hilton
Also: The **ASTOUNDING STORY** of **ERROL FLYNN**

▲ *The late Joan Crawford, when her career was revitalized by co-starring with Bette Davis in* **Whatever Happened to Baby Jane** *(1962). Five films followed before she died in 1977.*

Canteen (1944), but then she went after the role of the strong-minded and determined **Mildred Pierce** (1945), winning an Oscar. Some equally choice and absurd melodramas followed: **Humoresque** (1946), **Daisy Kenyon** (1947) and **Flamingo Road** (1949) and, after she left Warners, **Torch Song** (1953) – her triumphant return to MGM – **Female on the Beach** (1955) and **Queen Bee.** Together with the much better **Harriet Craig** (1950), these are the movies in which to savor late, ripe Crawford.

The offers were beginning to get fewer and smaller when at last her career was boosted by **Whatever Happened to Baby Jane?** (1962), in which she co-starred with another veteran, Bette Davis; but this only led to similar Grand Guignol outings, at much lower budgets. Her last film was **Trog** (1970). She died in 1977.

♥ Married: movie star Douglas Fairbanks Jr (1929-33); Franchot Tone (1935-9); supporting player Philip Terry (1942-6); Pepsi-Cola chief Alfred Steele (1956, widowed 1959). Lovers include Harry Rapf, Clark Gable, lawyer Greg Bautzer, gangster/gigolo Johnny Stompanato and others (according to her daughter's memoir).

❝ Nobody suffered on screen quite as she did, the great eyes brimming with manfully-fought-back tears, the wide pillar-box of a mouth quivering occasionally before some frantic contortion brought the impregnable teeth into play to signify an invincible will rising above adversity. As the years passed . . . another new Crawford emerged with **Sudden Fear.** This time the lady was completely dominant, battling her way to success in a man's world and ready to stop at nothing in the process. This was really my favorite Crawford: who, subjected to **Torch Song, Female on the Beach** or **Johnny Guitar** at a tender age, could ever hope for a complete recovery?" – *John Russell Taylor.*

"Joan Crawford won't venture out of her Fifth Avenue apartment to buy an egg unless she is dressed to the teeth." – *Hedda Hopper.*
"I think she is a splendid actress, but I am always a little repulsed by her shining lips, like balloon tires in wet weather." – *John Betjeman.*

Bing Crosby

Bing Crosby's screen presence, like his singing, was relaxed and easy. These factors helped him to his position as the world's favorite entertainer during the Second World War and just after. Later generations, depending on disposition, found him bland or "cool". Few of his movies sparkle but his thousands of records, constantly re-issued, testify that he was one of the best singers of popular songs.

Crosby was born in Tacoma, Washington, in 1904 and became a band singer while still at college. As one of the "Rhythm Boys" with Paul Whiteman's Orchestra he made his feature début (he had already made some shorts) in **King of Jazz** (1930);

▲ *Crosby won an Oscar for playing a priest in* **Going My Way** *(1944): here he's seen in the sequel* **The Bells of St Mary's** *(1945).*

as his popularity grew Paramount signed him to play himself in **The Big Broadcast** (1932) and he remained at that studio for 20 years, ambling through such lightweight musicals as **We're Not Dressing** (1934), **Anything Goes** (1936) and **Doctor Rhythm** (1938).

His teaming with Bob Hope in **Road to Singapore** (1940) set them off on a series of zany adventures, doublecrossing each other for Dorothy Lamour, and though the last two are pretty bad, there is still much fun to be had on the roads to **Zanzibar** (1941), **Morocco** (1942), **Utopia** (1946) and **Rio** (1947). His other hit films included **Birth of the Blues** (1941), **Holiday Inn** (1942) and **Going My Way** (1944), for which his portrayal of a singing priest brought him an Oscar and a sequel, **The Bells of St Mary's** (1945), with Ingrid Bergman. After **Blue Skies** (1946) he was given increasingly poor material except for two films directed by Frank Capra, namely **Riding High** (1950) and **Here Comes the Groom** (1951).

Although he still sang, he handled serious drama with sympathy in **Little Boy Lost** (1953) and **The Country Girl** (1954); and he gave Paramount one last supersized success with the mawkish **White Christmas,** again singing Irving

▼ *Bing singing in his early days in Hollywood, specifically for the publicity department. Curiously, some of the girls seem more interested in that than him.*

Berlin songs. Crosby sang Cole Porter's songs in **High Society** (1956) and his duet with Grace Kelly, "True Love", was the last of his huge-selling records. After a handful of poor films he became a character actor for his two last movies, **Robin and the Seven Hoods** (1964) and **Stagecoach** (1966). His TV shows maintained his popularity, and he made record-breaking personal appearances in London and New York not long before he died in 1977.

♥ Married: movie star Dixie Lee (1930, widowed 1952), and starlet Kathryn Grant (1957), who outlived him. His name was romantically linked with Peggy Bernier, Ghislain de Baysson, Jane Wyman, Mona Freeman and Rhonda Fleming.

❝ Dear Bing had always clutched at conventional heartstrings . . . . Crosby's golfer image is entirely appropriate to a man who never seemed to miss the fairway and whose enduring success has more to do with his faultless swing than with physical commitment." – *Frederic Raphael.*
"He was a tough guy. Make one

wrong move and he'd never speak to you again." – *Phil Harris.*
"A lot of people think that Bing was a loner, but Bing was a very loyal friend." – *Bob Hope.*
"As I look back, I think he was a very shy, insecure man. The world looked upon him as one of the great talents, he just never saw himself in that light." – *Dorothy Lamour.*

Bette Davis

There are few leading roles in today's movies for aging actresses, so Bette Davis, who refuses to take supporting roles, makes only TV films, all of which show that the old fire still burns. But her abiding fame stems from her great years, when sheer acting talent made her one of the biggest box-office stars. When someone complained that her personality got in the way, she scornfully replied: "Show me someone who is not a personality and I'll show you someone who is not a star."

Bette Davis was born in Lowell, Massachusetts, in 1908; she studied acting and was becoming known as an efficient New York *ingénue* when Universal signed her. She made her movie début in **Bad Sister** (1931) but was dropped by Universal a year later; George Arliss asked Warner Brothers for her as co-star in **The Man Who Played God** (1932), and thus she arrived at the studio where she achieved her greatest glory.

There was a vibrancy in all her work, showcased best at this time in **Cabin in the Cotton** and **20,000 Years in Sing Sing** (1933); acclaim did not really come her way until she was loaned out to play the cockney waitress in **Of Human Bondage** (1934), and it continued through **Bordertown** (1935), **Dangerous,** for which she won her first Oscar, and **The Petrified Forest** (1936). Battling for more such roles, she went to Britain to make a film, but Warners filed an injunction. She lost the subsequent case and Warners kept its promise, more or less, to provide better material, starting with **Marked Woman** (1937). She won a second Oscar for her portrayal of a Southern belle in Wyler's **Jezebel** (1938), commencing a run of films which never stop being revived: **The Sisters, Dark Victory** (1939), **Juarez, The Old Maid, The**

She was one of the first big stars not to depend upon sympathy: "no one is as good as Bette when she's bad" went the slogan, but it disguises the variety of her performances. This continued in the postwar period, but the pictures were not as good: she particularly loathed **Beyond the Forest** (1949) and when she decided to leave, Warners didn't demur.

Unbowed, she gave a magnificent performance as a Broadway actress in Mankiewicz's **All About Eve** (1950), after which either she chose badly or she didn't get the right offers until **Whatever Happened to Baby Jane?** (1962), when she enjoyably acted Joan Crawford off the screen. She followed with several other chiller-thrillers, and continues to the present to seek meaty roles in films for cinemas and TV.

♥ Married: Harmon Nelson (1932-8); Arthur Farnsworth (1940, widowed 1943); William Grant Sherry (1945-9); co-star Gary Merrill (1950-60). Lovers include William Wyler.

▲ *Since Bette Davis was not a glamor star, Warners fostered an image of her as a woman of the world.*

▼ *A fine case in point was her role in the Civil War melodrama* Jezebel *(1938), for which she won her second Oscar.*

Private Lives of Elizabeth and Essex (as Elizabeth I), **All This and Heaven Too** (1940), Wyler's **The Letter** (perhaps her greatest performance), **The Great Lie** (1941), Wyler's **The Little Foxes, In This Our Life** (1942), **Now Voyager, Old Acquaintance** (1943) and **Mr Skeffington** (1944).

❝ Whatever Bette had chosen to do in life, she would have had to be the top or she couldn't have endured it." – *Gary Merrill.*
"All she had going for her was her talent." – *David Zinman.*

Olivia de Havilland

One of screen's prettiest, most demure and affecting heroines, Olivia de Havilland was born in 1916 in Tokyo, Japan, to a British family. When her parents separated she went with her mother to California where, later, she was seen by a Warners talent scout in a performance of **A Midsummer Night's Dream.** The studio signed her to play in its film version (1935), but her first film released was **Alibi Ike.** She and Errol Flynn made a storybook romantic team in **Captain Blood** and were seen to even better advantage in **The Charge of the Light Brigade** (1936), **The Adventures of Robin Hood** (1938) and **Dodge City** (1939). Her warm and beautiful Melanie in Selznick's **Gone With the Wind** established her as a serious actress but she was not happy with her roles when she returned to Warners: they included two with Flynn, **Santa Fé Trail** (1940) and **They Died With Their Boots On** (1941), and **Strawberry Blonde** with Cagney.

She made one good film at Paramount, **Hold Back the Dawn,** and she later returned to the same studio after an argument with Warners which kept her off the screen for three years. Her first Oscar followed **To Each His Own** (1946). She won a second with **The Heiress** (1949), though conceivably gave her finest performance in **The Snake Pit** (1948), as the inmate of a mental asylum. Few of her other films

▶ *Olivia de Havilland's villainous role in* **Hush Hush Sweet Charlotte** *(1965), opposite her old friend Bette Davis.*

are memorable — and there were fewer of them after she went to live in Paris with her second husband; the best may be **The Light in the Piazza** (1962). The last to date is **The Fifth Musketeer** (1979).

♥ Married: novelist Marcus Goodrich (1946-52); Pierre Galante (1955), editor of *Paris Match*.

❝ Her face was so beautiful, all I could do was stand and stare." — *Ernie Pyle*.
"If ever there was a born actress it is Olivia de Havilland. Her diction is superb. She can deliver a line with any inflection a director wants, as accurately as if it were played on a piano." — *Mervyn Le Roy*.
"Olivia de Havilland is a lady of rapturous loveliness and well worth fighting for." — *André Sennwald*.

Marlene Dietrich

🎬 If all the stars in this encyclopedia are legendary, then Marlene is more legendary than most. She has, or had, glamor but not great beauty; a screen presence but little real acting talent; no sense of humor and less spontaneity; but early on she made herself the image of a desirable, mysterious woman — admittedly, with help from director

▲ *Marlene Dietrich with James Stewart in* **Destry Rides Again** *(1939), the film which revitalized her career.*

Josef von Sternberg, though he did not discover her, as she claimed.

Dietrich was born in Berlin in 1901 and began in showbusiness by playing the violin. Her first film appearance was in **Der Kleine Napoleon** (1923), in a minute role, but these grew bigger until she starred in **I Kiss Your Hand Madame** (1929). For director von Sternberg she drawled "Falling in Love Again", showed her shapely legs and led Emil

Jannings to his doom in **The Blue Angel** (1930). She accompanied von Sternberg when he returned to Hollywood and he directed her in **Morocco** (1930), **Dishonored** (1931), **Shanghai Express** (1932), **Blonde Venus, The Scarlet Empress** (1934) and **The Devil Is a Woman** (1935). Decreasingly the public went to see her and increasingly the star was like a puppet: Paramount put a professional stop to

▼ *"It took more than one man to change my name to Shanghai Lily": Dietrich in* **Shanghai Express** *(1932).*

the association and entrusted her to Lubitsch, who was the producer for **Desire** (1936) and who later directed her in **Angel** (1937).

Her style suited these artificial comedies but they did not revive her popularity. **Destry Rides Again** (1939) did, however; her bawdy saloon queen a reminder of the flesh-and-blood woman of **The Blue Angel**. At Universal she made some efficient melodramas, including **Seven Sinners** (1940) and **The Spoilers** (1942), both with John Wayne. After **Kismet** (1944) she filmed only irregularly and not, on the whole, impressively. The exceptions are Billy Wilder's **A Foreign Affair** (1948), Alfred Hitchcock's **Stage Fright** (1950), Fritz Lang's **Rancho Notorious** (1952) and Wilder's **Witness for the Prosecution** (1957). After **Judgement at Nuremberg** (1961) she concentrated on personal appearances, but returned to make a brief, sad appearance in **Just a Gigolo** (1978).

♥ Married: Rudolf Seiber (1924), long separated but not divorced. Lovers include Jean Gabin, Michael Wilding, John Gilbert, Gary Cooper and Cary Grant.

❝ What I did was to dramatize her attributes and make them visible for all to see; though, as there were perhaps too many, I concealed some." – *Josef von Sternberg.*
"She has sex, but no particular gender. Her masculinity appeals to women, and her sexuality to men." – *Kenneth Tynan.*

Robert Donat

🎥 Robert Donat did not have a prolific film career, but he left behind half a dozen memorable performances, rich in sensibility and honesty. He was born in Withington, Manchester, in 1905 to a Polish father. While at school he began to give poetry recitals (his grave and expressive voice remained one of his greatest assets) and he went on the stage in 1921. He was a star by 1932, when he turned down an MGM contract and made his film début for Korda in **Men of Tomorrow**; also for Korda he played the juvenile male lead in **The Private Life of Henry**

VIII (1933) before going on to Hollywood to play the title role in **The Count of Monte Cristo** (1934). The British films that followed were **The Thirty-Nine Steps** (1935), **The Ghost Goes West** (1936) and **Knight Without Armor** (1937).

For MGM in Britain he made **The Citadel** (1938) and **Goodbye Mr Chips** (1939), for which he won an Oscar; but just as earlier he had refused to honor agreements with Warner Brothers and RKO, so now he would not go to Hollywood to fulfill his commitment to MGM (roles which he turned down were later played by Robert Taylor, Errol Flynn, Gary Cooper, Spencer Tracy, James Stewart and Laurence Olivier).

During the Second World War, he was in **The Young Mr Pitt** (1942), **The Adventures of Tartu** (1943) and **Perfect Strangers** (1945), but thereafter asthmatic problems limited his work on stage and screen. His last half-dozen films included **The Winslow Boy** (1948); the poor **The Cure for Love** (1949), which he also

▲ *Robert Donat as the advocate in* **The Winslow Boy** *(1948) about to make a speech in the House of Commons and* ▶ *in the title-role of* **The Count of Monte Cristo** *(1934).*

directed; **The Magic Box** (1951), the industry's Festival of Britain film in which he starred; and **The Inn of the Sixth Happiness** (1958).

 Married: Ella Annesley Voysey (1929-46); actress Renee Asherson (1953), but they were separated before his death.

" Robert Donat was one of the greatest actors of his generation and probably the most unlucky. The gods gave him every grace and gift except for one — good health." — *Campbell Dixon.*
"He was as much as anybody responsible for the worldwide success of **The Thirty-Nine Steps.** I am sure that his performance made it so delightful: he was not in any sense a comedian, but he had a beautiful dry quality and that was his great contribution." — *Alfred Hitchcock.*

Irene Dunne

For a while, Irene Dunne specialized in weepies, like her RKO colleague Ann Harding, bringing to them sufficient wit and light-heartedness to make them palatable. When she turned to comedy those same qualities were outstanding; and Cary Grant once told her she had the best timing of the light comediennes with whom he had worked.

She was born in Louisville, Kentucky, in 1898 and trained as a singer. She was a Broadway star when RKO signed her and she made her début in **Leathernecking** (1930); among the big films she made there were **Cimarron** (1931), **Symphony of Six Million** (1932), **Back Street**, **The Silver Cord** (1933), **Ann Vickers** and her first musicals, **Sweet Adeline** (1935) and **Roberta.** Freelancing, she did two of her best-loved vehicles at Universal, **Magnificent Obsession** and **Showboat** (1936); **Theodora Goes Wild** was her first comedy and **The Awful Truth** (1937) her best, if we except **Love Affair** (1939) and **Penny Serenade** (1941), both bittersweet tales. **My Favorite Wife** (1940) was good; **A Guy Named Joe** (1943) and **The White Cliffs of Dover** (1944) were sentimental tales for MGM. **Anna and the King of Siam** (1946), **Life With Father** (1947) (as mother), and **I Remember Mama** (1948) were prestigious items, but when two comedies and **The Mudlark** (1950) — in which she was Queen Victoria — failed, Dunne decided to retire. Her last film was **It Grows on Trees** (1952).

▼ *Irene Dunne in one of the publicity stills issued by RKO to indicate that she was no longer playing suffering heroines, but madcap wives and heiresses in comedies which contemporary audiences still find funny.*

 Married: Francis Griffin (1928, widowed 1965).

" Irene Dunne today is virtually the same woman that millions of moviegoers fell in love with over 30 years ago. She is funny, brilliant and yet somehow wistful . . . . Having just seen all of her 'lost' films I can say with certainty that Irene Dunne's film career was one of the few which fulfilled all of its possibilities, giving American motion pictures an actress of classic beauty, humor and intelligence." — *David Chierichetti.*

Deanna Durbin

Deanna Durbin's fans have stayed remarkably loyal, and every time one of her films turns up on television there is a legion of new fans. What they see is a child (or young woman) of great natural ability as both actress and singer: whether singing arias or (more rarely) jazz, there is never a false note and even when playing "Little Miss Fix-It" her presence is never cloying, but determined, high-spirited and keen.

She was born in Winnipeg, Canada, in 1921 to British-born parents who emigrated to California, where Deanna's soprano voice attracted the attention of neighbors and alerted a talent scout. An MGM contract resulted in only one short, **Every Sunday** (1936) with Judy Garland, who, in error, was kept while Durbin was dropped. Universal put her into one of its programmers, **Three Smart Girls,** and after a few days began to build up her role. The receipts from this movie and **100 Men and a Girl** (1937), in which she found work for some unemployed musicians, saved the studio from bankruptcy. Producer Joe Pasternak continued to showcase her talents in some cunning entertainments: **Mad About Music** (1938), **That Certain Age, Three Smart Girls Grow Up** (1939), **First Love, It's a Date** (1940), **Spring Parade, Nice Girl?** (1941) and **It Started with Eve.** Then Pasternak moved to MGM and the lack of guidance began to show: only **His Butler's Sister** (1943) had the same carefree insouciance.

Durbin made a successful transition to dramatic actress in **Christmas Holiday** (1944), maintaining her huge popularity. But apart from using Technicolor and Jerome Kern songs for **Can't Help Singing,** Universal began to economize, claiming, when they finally dropped her, that her gigantic salary made her movies un-profitable. Her five films of the late forties have almost nothing going for them but her — one of the great injustices in Hollywood history. She retired after **For the Love of Mary** (1948), refusing Pasternak's offer to rebuild her career at MGM.

 Married: Vaughan Paul (1941-3); producer Felix Jackson (1945-8); French producer/director Charles David (1950), with whom she lives happily outside Paris.

 The modern Jenny Lind." — *Lawrence Tibbett.*
"I was always mad about Deanna. I admired her work tremendously and then she disappeared suddenly.

▲ *More publicity stills, this time from Universal, of the girl who was their biggest star, Deanna Durbin.*

▼ *A photograph which amply demonstrates why Deanna's charm won the hearts of fans the world over.*

Whatever became of her? Didn't she settle in France with her family?" — *Gracie Fields*.

"Pure youth rarely gets a chance on the screen . . . . She is asked to behave like what she is — a nice girl of 14. Realizing that she can't sing all the time, and seeking something to fill in the gaps, her picture's producers have hit upon the daring scheme of letting her natural bloom of youth suffice." — *Cecilia Ager*.

Alice Faye

Like Deanna Durbin, Alice Faye retired from movies while she still had much to offer them, and, like her again, she has retained a large army of fans. Her gentle way with a song and a line actually constitute great stylishness.

She was born in New York in 1912 and became a chorus girl and then a singer. In Hollywood she had a minor part in **George White's Scandals** (1934), but Fox upped her to the female lead. She decorated such pleasing musicals as **King of Burlesque** (1936) and **Sing Baby Sing**; and though billed under Madeleine Carroll in **On the Avenue**

▲ *Alice Faye in the days when she had the Rita Harlow look, before Fox gave her a classier image in response to her growing popularity.*

(1937) was soon a much bigger star because of **Wake Up and Live, You Can't Have Everything, You're a Sweetheart, In Old Chicago** (1938) and **Alexander's Ragtime Band,** her best film.

Her other films include: **Rose of Washington Square** (1939), **Hollywood Cavalcade, Tin Pan Alley** (1940), her only teaming with 20th Century-Fox's other blonde musical star, Betty Grable, **That Night in Rio** (1941), **The Great American Broadcast, Weekend in Havana, Hello Frisco Hello** (1943) in which she sang "You'll Never Know", and **The Gang's All Here.** She loathed playing the same role over and over again, and set great store by a non-musical, **Fallen**

▼ *Tyrone Power, Alice and Don Ameche in* **Alexander's Ragtime Band** *(1938), a favorite film for all three.*

Angel (1945), but when she found that Linda Darnell's role had been built up at the expense of her own she left Fox, swearing never to return. Eventually she did, playing the mother in **State Fair** (1962); after her family had grown up she returned to work on Broadway in the seventies and made guest appearances in two undistinguished movies.

 Married: singer Tony Martin (1937-40); comedian Phil Harris (1941).

" You know, Alice Faye at that time, she'd sing a song on the screen and the next morning it sold a million copies. Technically, she wasn't a particularly good singer but she was one of those unusual song salesmen on the screen: she knew how to sing a song to sell it." – *Jule Styne.*
"Alice, dear Alice . . . . Wouldn't it be nice if all the people in the world had as much joy in their lives as I had in making those six pictures with you?" – *Don Ameche.*
"Alice had a quality, a feminine warmth that none of the other girls seemed to have at the time, not Betty [Grable] or any of them; and for that reason I think she was a star." – *Walter Lang.*

W. C. Fields

 Adversity dogged the footsteps of W. C. Fields, as he expected it to: he didn't think much of the world, especially those in authority — like cops and his wives — and it didn't expect much of him. He took refuge in booze and muttered comments. Misogynist and misanthrope, he dreamed up fantastic schemes to revenge himself on the world and often succeeded.

He was born in Philadelphia in 1879 and had a hard childhood; his skills in juggling took him into vaudeville and he made one movie short, **Pool Sharks** (1915). His actual film career started as comic relief in **Janice Meredith** (1924), after which he made a string of films for Paramount, including **It's the Old Army Game** (1926), **So's Your Old Man** and **Running Wild** (1927). Paramount and he called it quits when Talkies came in; he made four shorts for

▲ *Mae West and W.C. Fields: great team, poor film.* ▼ *W.C. chancing his luck in* **Never Give a Sucker an Even Break** *(1941).*

Mack Sennett and did **Her Majesty Love** (1931) at Warners. He returned to Paramount for **Million Dollar Legs** (1932) and stayed to make the classics **Tillie and Gus** (1933) and **Six of a Kind** (1934) (in both teamed up with Alison Skipworth, a match for him in guile) and **You're Telling Me, The Old-Fashioned Way, It's a Gift, Mississippi** (1935) and **The Man on the Flying Trapeze.** He also played Mr Micawber in MGM's **David Copperfield.**

Illnesses caused by his drinking kept him off the screen for a while; but he returned to Universal for a disappointing teaming with Mae West

in **My Little Chickadee** (1939), followed by probably his most brilliant film, **The Bank Dick** (1940). He wrote the script of that and the splendidly anarchic **Never Give a Sucker an Even Break** (1941). His last three appearances were no more than guest spots, culminating in **Sensations of 1945.** He died in 1946.

 Married: Harriet Hughes (1900), but they were long separated. Carlotta Monti, his last mistress, wrote a book about their life together.

" A creative genius. I have only to see his face to laugh." – *John Betjeman.*
"His comedy routines appeared spontaneous and improvised, but he spent much time perfecting them. He knew exactly what he was doing every

moment, and what each prop was supposed to do. That 'my little chickadee' way of talking of his was natural." – *Bing Crosby.*

"The Talkies brought one great comedian, the late, majestically lethargic W. C. Fields, who could not possibly have worked so well in Silents; he was the toughest and most warmly human of all screen comedians, and **It's a Gift** and **The Bank Dick,** fiendishly funny and incisive white-collar comedies, rank with the best comedies (and best movies) ever made." – *James Agee.*

Errol Flynn

"One of the most charming and tragic men I have known," wrote Jack L. Warner of his studio's leading action-adventure hero, whose lithe, lighthearted swashbuckling performances remain one of cinema's enduring pleasures.

Errol Flynn was born in Hobart, Tasmania, in 1909 to an academic family, whose bent he did not follow.

He bummed around in odd jobs, and when a role in a semi-documentary, **In the Wake of the Bounty** (1933), awakened an urge to act he went to England, where he landed a role in **Murder at Monte Carlo** (1934). Its producers, Warner Brothers, sent him to Hollywood, where he had two minor roles before becoming **Captain Blood** (1935) when Robert Donat failed to turn up. He made some fine adventures, often with Olivia de Havilland: **The Charge of the Light Brigade** (1936), **The Adventures of Robin Hood** (1938), **The Dawn Patrol, Dodge City** (1939), **The Private Lives of Elizabeth and Essex, Virginia City** (1940), **The Sea Hawk, Santa Fé Trail** and **They Died With Their Boots On** (1941). He had romanced Kay Francis in **Another Dawn** (1937) and Bette Davis in **The Sisters** (1938) but neither straight drama nor comedy were really his forte. The Second World War provided further chances to be brave and enabled Flynn to be grimmer than his younger self in **Edge of Darkness** (1943) and **Objective Burma** (1945). Also dur-

ing this period he was the prizefighter **Gentleman Jim** (1942).

Apart from **The Adventures of Don Juan** (1949), Warners thought him best cast in Westerns – **San Antonio** (1945), **Silver River** (1948) and **Montana** (1950) – but MGM borrowed him for **That Forsyte Woman** (1949) and **Kim** (1950). After he left Warner Brothers in 1952 it was clear that his career had no direction: in Britain, two co-starring stints with Anna Neagle were mistakes, **Let's Make Up** (1954) and **King's Rhapsody** (1955). His drinking had long affected his work and was now affecting his looks. He played drunks in **The Sun Also Rises** (1957), **Too Much Too Soon** (1958) and **The Roots of Heaven.** These

Errol Flynn in two of his early swashbuckling roles, when he so blithely loved the ladies and overcame his opponents. ◄ In **The Sea Hawk** *(1940) and ▼ with Henry Stephenson and Olivia de Havilland, the loveliest of his partners, in* **Captain Blood** *(1935).*

▲ *The magnificent Flynn in* **The Adventures of Robin Hood** *(1938), one of the first Technicolor films and the role for which he is best remembered.*

were A movies, unlike the last he made, **Cuban Rebel Girls** (1959), which, like many of his efforts of the fifties, was largely unseen. He died of a heart attack in 1959.

♥ Married: actress Lili Damita (1935-43); Nora Eddington (1943-9); starlet Patrice Wymore (1950), from whom he was separated at the time of his death. Lovers include Linda Christian, Betty Hansen, who in 1942 sued him for "statutory rape", and Beverly Aadland, his companion during his last years.

❝❝ He wasn't an admirable character, but he was a magnificent male animal, and his sex appeal was obvious . . . . It seemed not to matter whether he could act. He leapt from the screen into the projection room with the impact of a bullet." – *Hal Wallis.*

"Flynn was a magnificent specimen of the rampant male. Outrageously good looking, he was a great natural athlete who played tennis with Donald Budge and boxed with 'Mushy' Calahan. The extras, among whom I had many friends, disliked him intensely." – *David Niven.*

"Errol Flynn was a joy, a lovely man, and most of the talk about him is nothing but rumor by people who didn't even know him. He loved to talk about how much he could drink and the women he'd made love to, but most of it was just the rationalizations of a disappointed moralist. He was the hardest-working, most down-to-earth actor I ever worked with." – *Henry King.*

Henry Fonda

🎥◁ Without a great range or a glamorous personality, Henry Fonda enjoyed a long career as a leading movie star. The image he projected was of an innately decent, ordinary man, one of thought and feeling, respectful of those around him — an American image, in fact. Frank Capra once explained why he had preferred to use Gary Cooper and James Stewart instead of Fonda, who, "good as he is, is not my cup of tea. I didn't think he *was* America. He represented to me some kind of stylized, eclectic — is that the word I want? — elite intellectual and he was very much of the stage."

Fonda was born in Grand Island, Nebraska, in 1905 and, after acting as an amateur, turned professional. As a Broadway name he signed a movie contract with producer Walter Wanger, though he made his film début for 20th Century-Fox, with which he was most associated. This first film was **The Farmer Takes a Wife** (1935) opposite Janet Gaynor. Though a rather diffident hero, his personality fitted all genres of movie: **The Moon's Our Home** (1936),

▲ *The young Henry Fonda seen here with Sylvia Sidney in* **You Only Live Once** *(1937), one of the few of his early films that he actually liked.*

Wings of the Morning (1937), Fritz Lang's **You Only Live Once, Jezebel** (1938), **The Mad Miss Manton** and **Jesse James** (1939). He was particularly memorable in **The Young Mr Lincoln, Drums Along the Mohawk** and **The Grapes of Wrath** (1940), all directed by John Ford. Lang's **The Return of Frank James,** Preston Sturges' **The Lady Eve** (1941), **The Big Street** (1942) and William Wellman's **The Ox-Bow Incident** (1943) are the best of those he made before joining the navy.

After the Second World War he made John Ford's **My Darling Clementine** (1946) and freelanced; after Ford's **Fort Apache** (1948) he devoted himself to the stage, returning to the screen in **Mister Roberts** (1955), based on one of the plays he had done. After **War and Peace** (1956) and Alfred Hitchcock's **The Wrong Man** (1957), he produced one of his best films, **Twelve Angry Men**; for the same director, Sidney

Lumet, he made **Stage Struck**. Dividing his time between Broadway and Hollywood he eased himself into supporting roles, often cast as an aging Western lawman or a politician. He had disliked most of his early films, but he may have been proud of these films: **Advise and Consent** (1962), **The Best Man** (1964), **Fail-Safe**, **A Big Hand for the Little Lady** (1966), **Madigan** (1968) and **There Was a Crooked Man** (1970). Few of his later films were worthy of him, but he extended his range as fairly fierce patriarchs in **Sometimes a Great Notion** (1971) and **On Golden Pond** (1981). He won an Oscar (having earlier been awarded an honorary one) for the latter not long before he died in 1982.

♥ Married: actress Margaret Sullavan (1931-3); Frances Brokaw (1936, commited suicide 1950), mother of his children Jane and Peter; Susan Blanchard (1950-6); Alfreda Franchetti (1957-62); Shirlee Adams (1965), who outlived him.

❝ If I can be like Henry Fonda, then I look forward to aging, to 60 and beyond — and not just because Hank finally won the Oscar that

▼ *Fonda's quiet but determined personality made him an ideal protagonist in Westerns. He made several in his later years,* **Firecreek** *(1968) being one of the better ones.*

he deserved. He was a good character actor and a good actor in the American tradition of playing variations on oneself." — *Paul Newman.*
"I have never known an actor with such craft, with such professional seriousness; such a pleasant man, full of humor, so reserved and so keenly quick-witted." — *Sergio Leone.*
"He is a better actor than almost anyone you like to name in Hollywood, yet when you come down to it he has not played anything like a wide variety of roles in his 70 or so films. His quality has been demonstrated rather by the intelligence and authority with which he has explored various aspects of one basic attribute: decency." — *John Russell Taylor.*

Joan Fontaine

Joan Fontaine gave three of the greatest screen performances — in **Rebecca** (1940), **Letter From an Unknown Woman** (1948) and **Something to Live For** (1952). In other roles she was variable and sometimes horribly artificial.

She was born in Tokyo in 1917, the sister of Olivia de Havilland, who became an actress before her. She herself made her film début in **No More Ladies** (1935), around the time she was the mistress of Silent star Conrad Nagel. An RKO contract brought some B movies and three roles in important movies directed by George Stevens, **Quality Street** (1937), **A Damsel in Distress** opposite Fred Astaire, and **Gunga Din** (1939), but she was "resting" when David Selznick cast her as the shy second wife in **Rebecca** (1940); the Oscar she won for Hitchcock's **Suspicion** (1941) was thought to be for that earlier performance.

Selznick loaned her out for **This Above All** (1942), **The Constant Nymph** (1943), **Frenchman's Creek** (1944) and **The Affairs of Susan** (1945); freelancing, she started well with **From This Day Forward** (1946), **Ivy** (1947), in which she played her first villainess, **The Emperor Waltz** (1948) and **Letter From an Unknown Woman,** but after **September Affair** (1950) and **Something to Live For** (1952) the offers were either few or uninteresting. Her supporting performance in **Tender Is the Night** (1961) was admired but her only

subsequent film has been **The Witches** (1966). She does occasional stage work.

♥ Married: actor Brian Aherne (1939-45); producer William Dozier (1946-51); producer Collier Young (1952-61), who had been married to Ida Lupino, who co-starred with Fontaine in **The Bigamist** (1953), produced by Young; Alfred Wright (1964-9). Lovers include Conrad Nagel, producer/director/actor John Houseman (c. 1948), and photographer Slim Aarons.

❝ I dreaded working with Joan Fontaine again, but the first day she came up to me during a break and said she was just doing it for the money, she wasn't out to prove anything anymore, and she would act it whatever way I told her. And that's just what she did; she couldn't have been more delightful and fun to work with. We had a ball doing it [**Darling, How Could You!** (1951)]." – *Mitchell Leisen.*
"With her Dresden doll-like delicacy, and her cool, elegant manner, aris-

▲ *Joan Fontaine first appeared in Hollywood as little-Miss-Innocent but she graduated to tougher roles, playing a murderess in Ivy (1947). In real life she combined being a licensed pilot and Cordon Bleu cook with flying balloons and playing golf.*

tocratic Joan Fontaine should have been a ranking international cinema star for much longer than the World War II period." – *James Robert Parish.*

Jean Gabin

🎥 In Gabin's great period he was the quintessential loner, on the run from authority or the army, risking everything for one beautiful woman. It is said that his contracts specified that he always had to die in the last reel.

He was born in Paris in 1904 to a theatrical family and appeared in revue, cabaret and in legitimate drama before making his film début in **Chacun sa Chance** (1930). Although the somber, if not taciturn

image was established while he did standard leading men stints, he did not begin to suffer emotionally on-screen until Julien Duvivier's **Maria Chapdelaine** (1934), the start of a fine run of movies: Duvivier's **La Bandéra** (1935), **La Belle Equipe** (1936) and **Pépé le Moko** (1937); Jean Renoir's **Les Bas-Fonds** (1936), **La Grande Illusion** (1937) and **La Bête Humaine** (1938); Grémillon's **La Gueule d'Amour** (1937) and **Remorques** (1940); Marcel Carné's **Quai des Brumes** (1938) and **Le Jour se Lève** (1939). These films made him France's chief international star, and he was courted by Hollywood. He went there because of the Second World War and made **Moontide** (1942) and **The Impostor** (1944) before joining the Free French army.

Back in France his stock went down when he and Marlene Dietrich left the cast, amid great publicity, of Carné's **Les Portes de la Nuit** (1946); but **Martin Roumagnac**, which they did instead, was no substitute. He regained some of the old esteem with **Au-Delà des Grilles** (1949), in a role similar to his prewar ones, but after that he began to change his image, if not the tenor of his performances. He worked with Max Ophuls in **Le Plaisir** (1951), with Jacques Becker on **Grisbi** (1954), Renoir on **French Can-Can** (1955) and Autant-Lara on **Four Bags Full** (1956), but by and large he no longer commanded the interest of the country's leading directors. Indeed, towards the end he would no longer take direction.

Becker's film, a gangster tale, re-established Gabin as France's most popular star, and so he remained, virtually, to his death, playing men of authority — mobsters, lawyers, *pater familias*, politicians, police commissioners, social workers, aristocrats — in mostly mediocre films. Twice he was Simenon's detective Maigret; he also played the inspector in **Crime and Punishment** (1956) and Valjean in **Les Misérables** (1957). He died after **L'Année Sainte** (1976).

♥ Married: his mistress, dancer Gaby Basset (1928-31); dancer Jeanne Susanne Mauchin (1931-42) and Dominique Fournier (1949) who outlived him and is the mother of his children. His most publicized liaisons were with his co-stars

Jean Gabin at the height of his career ▲ as the tortured railwayman in **La Bête Humaine** *(1938) and as the character actor he became ◄ in* **L'Affaire Dominici** *(1973).*

Mistinguett (c. 1927), Mireille Balin (c. 1937), Michèle Morgan (c. 1938-40) and Marlene Dietrich (c. 1945).

❝ This contemporary mature figure of tragedy and disillusionment in whom the instincts of a poet are choked [in **Le Jour se Lève**] is played with depth by Gabin." – *Richard Winnington.*
"Indeed, masterly performers like Tracy and Donat and Gabin even fox the experts so skilfully as to conceal their art." – *James Mason.*

Clark Gable

"The King" was born in Cadiz, Ohio, in 1901 and joined a stock company while in his teens; he was unsuccessful until a former actress, Josephine Dillon, taught him his

◄ *Just married: Scarlett and Rhett, played by Leigh and Gable, in* **Gone With the Wind** *(1939).*

▲ *Gable relaxing, here seen before the appearance of the ever popular and very famous mustache.*

craft and after some extra work in movies he began making a name for himself on the West Coast stage.

He played villains in **The Painted Desert** (1931) and **Night Nurse** and while making **The Easiest Way** at MGM he was offered a contract. Within a few months he was on his way to becoming the studio's major male star, and not only because he was showcased opposite all the big Metro ladies. He had confidence and toughness, plus a formidable charm, in **A Free Soul, Susan Lenox: Her Fall and Rise, Possessed** and **Red Dust** (1932); he won an Oscar for his comedy performance in **It Happened One Night** (1934) and continued to win new admirers in **Manhattan Melodrama, After Office Hours** (1935), **China Seas, Mutiny on the Bounty, San Francisco** (1936), **Test Pilot** (1938) and **Idiot's Delight** (1939).

He was a popular (indeed, *the* only) choice to play Rhett Butler in **Gone With the Wind,** after which came **Strange Cargo** (1940), the last of several teamings with Joan Crawford, and **Honky Tonk** (1941), the first of several with Lana Turner. After **Somewhere I'll Find You** (1942)

he went to war; he returned in **Adventure** (1945) with Greer Garson, who had become MGM's leading lady star in his absence. They did not make an ideal team. **The Hucksters** (1947) proved that Gable had lost some of his old devil-may-care quality, though none of his authority. MGM was uncertain how to maintain his popularity, and by putting him into indifferent films bungled it.

Mogambo (1953), a remake of **Red Dust,** proved that in the right film he could still draw crowds, but he refused to renew his contract because he had learned that MGM had meant to drop him. He didn't lack offers, but his post-MGM films were not too distinguished until **The Misfits** (1961), in which he played an aging cowboy. He died of a heart attack in 1960.

♥ Married: drama teacher Josephine Dillon (1924-30) and socialite Rhea Langham (1930-9), both ladies considerably older and with whom he didn't stay long; Carole Lombard (1939, widowed 1942), his co-star of some years earlier; Sylvia Hawkes (1949-52), widow of Douglas Fairbanks; and Kay Spreckles (1955), who gave birth to his son after his death. Lovers include Frances Doerfler; actresses Jane Cowl and Pauline Frederick; co-star Joan Crawford (c. 1931); co-star Loretta Young (c. 1937); Jean Harlow and columnist Adela Rogers St Johns.

" It was the joy of your life to know Clark Gable. He was everything good you could think of. He had delicious humor; he had great compassion; he was always a fine old teddy bear . . . . In no way was he conscious of his good looks, as were most of the other men in pictures at that time. Clark was very un-actory." *— Joan Blondell.*
"He was the epitome of the movie star — so romantic, such bearing, such friendliness." *— Elizabeth Taylor.*
"Yeah, Gable was the greatest male ever on the screen. Valentino may have been the greatest women's actor. But men liked Gable and women liked Gable. He had them all." *— Clarence Brown.*

Greta Garbo

Greta Garbo has fascinated every generation of movie audiences that has seen her. She was *the* star with beauty, glamor and charisma.

Garbo was born in Stockholm in 1905 and gained her first film experience in an advertising short for the store for which she worked; that led to a comic short, encouraging her to apply for an acting scholarship. She was taken from drama school for the leading role in **The Atonement of Gosta Berling** (1924), directed by Mauritz Stiller, who became her mentor; they both signed contracts with MGM after she had appeared in Pabst's **Die Freudlose Gasse** (1925). MGM, not knowing what to do with her, cast her as a peasant girl who becomes an opera singer in Ibañez's **The Torrent** (1926). She then played a seductress in **The Temptress,** a role that so pleased MGM that she was virtually typecast in her following films — **Flesh and the Devil** (1927), **Love,** a modernization of *Anna Karenina,* **The Mysterious Lady** (1928), **A Woman of Affairs, Wild Orchids** (1929), **A Single Standard** and **The Kiss.**

The Silent screen was dead by the time the last of these appeared. MGM was fearful that Garbo might go back to Europe, as had so many other European stars left stranded by the Talkies, that they hesitated. Finally **Anna Christie** (1930) appeared with the slogan "Garbo Talks!" and she became an even more potent figure at the box-office. With the exception of **Susan Lenox: Her Fall and Rise** (1931) made with Clark Gable, and the all-star **Grand Hotel** (1932), the succeeding films were unworthy of her, though she magically pulled the material up to her level.

She begged for better roles and MGM acceded to her wish to play **Queen Christina** (1933) — to even greater acclaim than before. She played an adultress yet again in a contemporary story, **The Painted Veil** (1934), which conventionalized a good

▲ *Mauritz Stiller successfully created a new kind of woman, "sophisticated, scornful and superior", with Garbo. The former Greta Louisa Gustafsson became a legend in her own lifetime.*

Somerset Maugham story, but after that MGM starred her in a series of period pieces which were among the big prestige movies of the time: **Anna Karenina** (1935); George Cukor's **Camille** (1936), possibly her greatest performance; Clarence Brown's **Conquest** (1937); and then, as a change of pace, a modern comedy directed by a master of that form, Ernst Lubitsch's **Ninotchka** (1939).

"Garbo Laughs!" said the ads, and so did audiences — which had been diminishing in the US until then. When World War II closed the European markets to Garbo, she made

▲ *"Garbo and Gilbert in* **Love***",
(1927), the advertisements read, but
the couple couldn't hide the fact that
their passionate embraces on screen
were more than just good acting.*
▶ *"Garbo Laughs!" was the slogan for*
Ninotchka *(1939), the first comedy
she appeared in.*

another comedy, **Two-Faced Woman** (1941) and when it failed both
she and MGM decided to call it quits
until the war finished. When it did,
she found that she no longer had the
courage to confront the camera.

 Has never married; and is as
reclusive in retirement as she
was as a star. Reputedly in love with
Mauritz Stiller; had an affair with her
co-star John Gilbert but didn't turn up
for the arranged wedding ceremony.

Others with whom her name was romantically linked include Leopold Stokowski and dietician Gayelord Hauser.

66 What, when drunk, one sees in other women, one sees in Garbo sober." — *Kenneth Tynan.*
"There have been two great personalities in movies in the last 40 years. One was Valentino, the other was Greta Garbo. Today, without having made a film since 1940, she is still the greatest." — *Clarence Brown,* in 1963.
"She was a provocative girl. I found working with her an extraordinary experience. She wasn't a trained actress — and she was aware of that herself — but she had extraordinary intuitions, especially in the realm of erotic experience. Her acting made you feel that here was a woman who knew all there was to know about all aspects of love." — *Melvyn Douglas.*
"She must think that I am trying to imitate her, but there is nobody like Garbo. I am new to the screen, but I think she is the greatest star in the world. She has a magic quality which will survive bad pictures — and even age . . . ." — *Marlene Dietrich.*

Judy Garland

The screen's greatest song-and-dance girl was born in 1922 in Grand Rapids, Minnesota, to a vaudeville family. She made her stage début at the age of three: her verve and attack as a child performer impressed many a showbusiness veteran, one of whom got her an audition at MGM. She starred in a short with Deanna Durbin, **Every Sunday** (1936), and was loaned to

20th Century-Fox for her first feature, **Pigskin Parade.**

MGM didn't know what to do with her until Roger Edens — who later described her as "the biggest thing to happen to the MGM musical" — had her sing "You Made Me Love You" to Clark Gable on his birthday. Both star and song were incorporated into **Broadway Melody of 1938.** When Fox refused to loan Shirley Temple, Garland starred in **The Wizard of Oz** (1939), in which she sang "Over the Rainbow"; audiences loved her and Mickey Rooney as the teenage entertainers in such films as **Babes in Arms, Strike Up the Band** (1940) and **Girl Crazy** (1943).

She played adult roles in **Little Nellie Kelly** (1940) and **For Me and My Gal** (1942), with Gene Kelly; and sang "The Trolley Song" in **Meet Me in St Louis** (1944), which

◄ *Mickey Rooney and Judy Garland were teamed in some high-spirited musicals. This one is* **Strike Up the Band** *(1940).*

▲ *Judy Garland, Ray Bolger, Jack Haley, Frank Morgan and Bert Lahr in the all-time box-office hit,* **The Wizard of Oz** *(1939).*

led to a new era of musicals. She didn't sing at all in **The Clock** (1945), which showed her at her most delicate and vulnerable, but she did in **The Harvey Girls** (1946), **The Pirate** (1948) with Kelly, **Easter Parade** with Astaire and **In the Good Old Summertime** (1949). A combination of nervous illnesses, temperament and overwork led to her suspension from both **Annie Get Your Gun** and **Royal Wedding,** to be replaced by Betty Hutton and Jane Powell respectively. Between the two she completed **Summer Stock** (1950), her last film for MGM. Warners welcomed her back in **A Star Is Born** (1954), but despite warm personal notices Hollywood lost interest until concerts and records proved her one of the great legendary stars, leading to straight roles in **Judgement at Nuremberg** (1961),

A Child Is Waiting (1963) and I Could Go on Singing – in which she sang for the last time on screen. She died in London in 1969 from an accidental overdose.

♥ Married: bandleader David Rose (1941-3); Vincente Minnelli (1945-50), who directed her in Meet Me in St Louis and four other films and is the father of Liza; Sid Luft (1952-65) who produced A Star Is Born – two children; Mark Herron (1965-7); nightclub manager Mickey Deans (1969). Lovers include Tyrone Power (c. 1943) and producer/director Joseph L. Mankiewicz, who left MGM after telling the boss, Louis B. Mayer, and Garland's mother that Garland needed psychiatric help if her life wasn't to become a mess.

❝ When she was good, she was not only very, very good, she was the most sympathetic, the funniest, the sharpest and the most stimulating woman I ever knew." – *James Mason.*
"She is a star; the genius outsize article . . . . She is an actress of power and subtlety; a singer whose way with a song is nothing short of marvelous . . . . She is a great artist. She is Judy. She is the very best there is." – *Philip Oakes.*

Greer Garson

For a while, Greer Garson was a very big star indeed – MGM's "class" lady after the departures of Garbo and Shearer. She dispensed charm, sometimes with a ladylike hauteur, and her performances reflected this duality, for she could come up with gestures and delivery both genuine and artificial in any given scene.

She was born in County Down, Northern Ireland, in 1908 and went from amateur acting to professional in her early twenties; she was discovered by Louis B. Mayer while playing a leading role in the West End, made her movie début in Goodbye Mr Chips (1939) and was seen to advantage in Pride and Prejudice (1940) opposite Laurence Olivier; her first teaming with Walter Pidgeon was Blossoms in the Dust (1941) and her second Mrs Miniver (1942), a wartime drama which brought her an

Oscar. Random Harvest, with Ronald Colman, was another popular success, as were Madame Curie (1943) and Mrs Parkington (1944), both with Pidgeon.

She appeared with Gregory Peck in The Valley of Decision (1945), and Clark Gable in Adventure, but after that her popularity began to wane. MGM tried to restore it by excursions into comedy and other teamings with Pidgeon, including That Forsyte Woman (1949) and The Miniver Story (1950). She and MGM called it quits with Her Twelve Men (1954) and she retreated to the stage and TV after Strange Lady in Town (1955), though she returned to films to play Mrs Roosevelt in Sunrise at Campobello (1960). The last of her three subsequent appearances was in The Happiest Millionaire (1967).

♥ Married: Edwin Snelson (1933-7); actor Richard Ney (1943-7), who played her son in Mrs Miniver; wealthy businessman Elijah "Buddy" Fogelson (1949).

❝ Greer Garson has kinds of vitality and resource which might do very good kinds of work, but ordinarily they are turned to wax. She is waxen in stretches of The Valley of Decision, and embarrassingly actressy in some others; but quite often too, as an Irish servant in a rich Scottish household, she is alive, vivid and charming, and suggests how really good she might be under better

▼ *Greer Garson who, at the height of her career, took over from Greta Garbo as "Queen of the screen".*

circumstances. If she were not suffocated and immobilized by Metro's image of her — and, I'm afraid, half-persuaded of it herself — I could imagine her as a very good Lady Macbeth . . . . But I suppose the best she will ever be allowed is this sort of short trot in pre-conditioned open air. — *James Agee.*

"Garson seems to move in a cloud of sanctity, smiling quizzically to indicate intelligence." — *David Shipman.*

Betty Grable

Betty Grable only just passed muster as dancer, actress and singer; and she was *not* a lady with a great deal of class. She seemed a friendly girl, and she had great legs: perhaps these were the reasons she was the undoubted number one pin-up of the Second World War.

She was born in St Louis, Missouri, in 1916 and became a dancer in her teens. She made her film début in the chorus of **Let's Go Places** (1930) and may be spotted in other early musicals. RKO signed her and made her the *ingénue* in a Wheeler and Woolsey vehicle, **Hold 'Em Jail** (1932), and she did a duet with Edward Everett Horton in **The Gay Divorcée** (1934).

When RKO subsequently dropped her she made **Pigskin Parade** (1936) at 20th Century-Fox and then went to Paramount, who were no more successful in making her a star than RKO had been. Fox, however, had the right idea, if only because Alice Faye was suddenly taken ill, and

▲ *Betty Grable towards the end of her screen career, in the comedy* **How to Marry a Millionaire** *(1953).*

put Grable in a mindless Technicolor musical, **Down Argentine Way** (1940). Within three years she was queen of the American box-office, though her best film is probably a black and white thriller, **I Wake Up Screaming** (1941).

Through **Song of the Islands, Coney Island** (1943), **Sweet Rosie O'Grady** and **The Dolly Sisters** (1945) the audiences kept coming. Fox tried to vary the formula several

▼ *Grable, no doubt overjoyed that her legs were insured with Lloyds of London for the sum of one million dollars!*

times in the postwar period but the only one of these experiments which was successful was **Mother Wore Tights** (1947), the first of several teamings with Dan Dailey.

By 1950 her hold on the box-office was slipping and two years later the studio had a newer blonde, Marilyn Monroe, who was billed above Grable in the comedy **How to Marry a Millionaire** (1953). Neither **Three for the Show** (1955) nor **How to be**

Very, Very Popular indicated that Grable had regained her following and she left Hollywood, though continued to sing and dance on stage until just before she died of cancer in 1973.

 Married: former child star Jackie Coogan (1937-40); Harry James (1943-65).

" She was not only one of the biggest box-office attractions of all time, but her work symbolized that era of gaudy Technicolored escapism for which millions craved in World War II when she became the most celebrated pin-up girl of all time . . . ." – *Tom Vallance.*

"I always called Betty 'princess' 'cause that's how I felt about her. Betty was class. She was a true star. She could light up before the camera. If she had wanted she could have become a great dancer. I'd be suggesting new routines and she'd holler 'Who are you, the director?' She was lazy I guess. Loved that racetrack. But great for the business and wonderful to work with." – *Dan Dailey.*

Cary Grant

▲ *Cary Grant rightly bemused at having to cope with Katharine Hepburn in* **Bringing Up Baby** *(1938) – only "baby" was a leopard.*

He is the quintessential male film star – good-looking, good-natured and someone we've loved for several generations. Like many others, he is not especially talented, inasmuch as he can only play one role – handsome, amiable and long-loved Cary Grant. Although a nimble light comedian, he can misjudge his effects, but he has given more and better light comedy performances than most of his rivals.

He was born in 1904 in Bristol and entered showbusiness as a callboy; he went to the US as part of an acrobatic troupe and became an actor, eventually finding his way to Hollywood, where Paramount gave him a con-tract. After making his début in **This Is the Night** (1932), he played supporting roles, but was showcased opposite Dietrich in **Blonde Venus** and Mae West in **She Done Him Wrong** (1933) and **I'm No Angel**; however it was opposite Katharine Hepburn in **Sylvia Scarlett** (1935) and Jean Harlow in **Suzy** that he really made his mark, leading to concurrent contracts with RKO and Columbia.

Few of his movies have dated: **Topper** (1937), **The Awful Truth**

▼ *"Hollywood's greatest farceur" with co-star Rosalind Russell in* **His Girl Friday** *(1940).*

▲ *Grant in unaccustomedly grim mood, helping Audrey Hepburn fight off the killers in* **Charade** *(1963).*

♥ Married: actress Virginia Cherrill (1933-5); Woolworth heiress Barbara Hutton (1942-5); actress Betsy Drake (1949-59); actress Dyan Cannon (1965-8); secretary Barbara Harris (1981). Among the ladies with whom he has been romantically linked are Marlene Dietrich and Sophia Loren.

66 One learns more from watching Cary Grant drinking a glass of water or opening a door in one of his films than in following months of teaching at the Actor's Studio." – *Tony Curtis.*
"Cary Grant was Hollywood's greatest farceur." – *Frank Capra.*
"These pictures [the comedies of the late thirties] did much to establish the Cary Grant we know and love 45 years later: the comic actor in high polish, plowing through all manner of screwball commotion with unassailable suavity, emerging from many an ordeal-by-slapstick with dignity tattered but intact. He had only to repeat this formula for the remainder of his career, but, as easy as it looked, he never coasted: he is the most finely tuned farceur in the business, with a comedy timing as elegant and impeccable as his attire." – *Harry Haun.*

with Irene Dunne, **Bringing Up Baby** (1938) and **Holiday,** both with Hepburn, **Gunga Din** (1939), **Only Angels Have Wings** with Jean Arthur, **His Girl Friday** (1940) with Rosalind Russell, **The Philadelphia Story** with Hepburn once more, **My Favorite Wife** and **Penny Serenade** (1941), again with Dunne, Hitchcock's **Suspicion** and Capra's **Arsenic and Old Lace** (1944).

A serious role in **None But the Lonely Heart** was a mistake, as was **Night and Day** (1946), in which he played Cole Porter, but Grant was back on target with Hitchcock's **Notorious, The Bachelor and the Bobby Soxer** (1947), **Mr Blandings Builds His Dream House** (1948), **I Was a Male War**

Bride (1949), **Crisis** (1950) and **People Will Talk** (1951). The last two, however, were not box-office successes, and Grant's career went through a lean period before Hitchcock revived it with **To Catch a Thief** (1955). From then until his retirement there was an almost unbroken run of successes: **An Affair to Remember** (1957), **Indiscreet** (1958), **Houseboat** with Sophia Loren, Hitchcock's **North by Northwest** (1959), **Operation Petticoat, That Touch of Mink** (1962), with Doris Day, and **Charade** (1963), with Audrey Hepburn.

Now graying at the temples, he successfully wooed yet another generation of the screen's leading ladies, finally moving into the upper-age bracket in **Walk Don't Run** (1966), leaving the romance to others. He hasn't filmed since. Instead he has devoted his energies to a cosmetics company.

Jean Harlow

🎥 In her slinky, loose-fitting but revealing gowns, Jean Harlow meant sexuality to one generation. She spoke it too, inasmuch as she let certain lucky men know that she wanted them, most memorably Clark Gable, and she always had a wisecrack to top one of his.

She was born in Kansas City in 1911 and became a movie extra when her parents moved to California. She had a line or two in Laurel and Hardy's **Double Whoopee** (1928), and a supporting role in **The Saturday Night Kid** (1929). In refashioning **Hell's Angels** (1930) as a Talkie, Howard Hughes had to sack Greta Nissen, because of her strong Norwegian accent. Harlow's acting was no better, but her blatant seduction of Ben Lyon wowed audiences. Several parts on loan-out included the title role in Capra's **Platinum Blonde** (1931) and she was then signed by MGM.

▲ *MGM were quick to promote Jean Harlow – the platinum blonde – issuing publicity stills like the one shown here.*

Harlow was a very un-MGM kind of star, but this was the era of gangster's molls and loose ladies, which she played in **The Beast of the City** (1932) and **Red-Headed Woman** respectively. Her gifts as a comedienne were revealed in **Red Dust** and **Hold Your Man** (1933), both with Gable, and further in the all-star **Dinner at Eight** and a witty satire about a movie queen, **Bombshell.** After the tightening of the Production Code (which now prevented the "frank" dialogue Harlow had been given) and **Reckless** (1935), MGM began to soften Harlow's image, but she still had Gable to sass in **China Seas.** A last quintet included the amusing **Libeled Lady** (1936) and, with Gable, **Saratoga** (1937) but she died during shooting and it was completed with a double.

♥ Married: Charles McGrew (1927-30), but the marriage didn't last that long; producer Paul Bern (1932), who committed suicide under mysterious circumstances; and cinematographer Hal Rossen (1933), but that was also brief. Lovers include Clark Gable and co-star William Powell, whom she was expected to marry at the time of her death.

❝ She chatted gaily, 'The news-papers sure have loused me up, calling me a sex-pot! Where'd they ever get such a screwy idea?' One look at Harlow and whether you were male or female you could get no other idea; she was the Scylla and Charybdis of sex, from her provoca-tive come-hither expression to the flowing lines of her beautifully pro-portioned body." – *Frances Marion.* "She didn't want to be famous. She wanted to be happy." – *Clark Gable.* "A square shooter if ever there was one." – *Spencer Tracy.*

Rita Hayworth

🎥◁ They called her "The Love Goddess". She was ravishing to look at, sometimes a formidable screen presence and always a glamor-ous one. Her life has been more tragic than any of the plots of her films.

Rita Hayworth was born in Brooklyn in 1918, into a family of dancers. An executive of Fox saw her dancing and gave her a contract. She made her début in **Under the Pampas Moon** (1935) but had only small roles until she played the second female lead in **Only Angels Have Wings** (1939). By this time she was at Columbia, who now gave her star roles, but it was at Warners with **The Strawberry Blonde** (1941) that she first revealed that warm,

seductive quality; and it was another loan-out, for **Blood and Sand,** that first showed how Technicolor en-hanced her appearance. She danced with Fred Astaire in **You'll Never Get Rich** and **You Were Never Lovelier** (1942) and sang (though dubbed) in **My Gal Sal** and **Cover Girl** (1944).

The latter and the melodrama **Gilda** (1946) were the zenith of Hayworth's career. From there, it was downhill all the way, through Welles' **The Lady from Shanghai** (1948), **The Loves of Carmen, Salome** (1953), **Miss Sadie Thompson** and **Pal Joey** (1957), in which she appeared with Kim Novak, who had replaced her as the studio's biggest star. She also appeared in **Separate Tables** (1958), produced by her then husband, but few of her subsequent films are notable; the last to date is **The Wrath of God** (1972).

▼ *"There never was a woman like Gilda!" read the ads for* **Gilda** *(1946), and here is Rita Hayworth at her most Gildaesque. The backing song is "Put the Blame on Mame".*

Connecticut, in 1907, into a wealthy family. She became an actress and was a minor Broadway star when RKO signed her to play in **A Bill of Divorcement** (1932). She won an Oscar with her third film, **Morning Glory** (1933), as an aspiring actress, and gave intelligent performances as Jo in **Little Women** and in **Alice Adams** (1935). Perhaps she was equally good in **Sylvia Scarlett** (in drag), **Mary of Scotland** (1936) and **Quality Street** (1937), both in period costume, but the public rejected them so decisively that two fine comedies, **Stage Door** and **Bringing Up Baby** (1938), did much less well than expected.

She has been directed by some of Hollywood's finest craftsmen, including George Stevens and George Cukor, who was to remain her friend for life and with whom she made **Holiday** (1938) at Columbia, at less than her usual salary but, stigmatized as "box-office poison", she returned to Broadway. The play she made, "The Philadelphia Story", was so successful that MGM was happy enough to acquire her along with the rights; the film (1940), directed by Cukor, started her on a second film career and, with **Woman of the Year** (1942), an MGM contract.

Her co-star was Spencer Tracy, and though her other movies were poor, those she did with him varied from the interesting to the magnificent: **Keeper of the Flame, Without Love** (1945), **The Sea of Grass** (1947), Capra's **State of the Union** (1948), **Adam's Rib** (1949) – which may be the best of them – and **Pat and Mike** (1952). Her career received a further boost from her performance as a prissy but fusty spinster in **The African Queen** (1951) opposite Humphrey Bogart. She had not dissimilar roles in **Summertime** (1955), made in Britain (but set in Venice), and **The Rainmaker** (1956) with Burt Lancaster. **The Iron Petticoat,** made in Britain, was an unfortunate teaming with Bob Hope, but happily **Desk Set** (1957) was a somewhat better one with Tracy. After playing a dead gay man's mother in **Suddenly Last Summer** (1959) and a drug-addicted one in **Long Day's Journey Into Night** (1962) – from plays by Tennessee Williams and Eugene O'Neill respectively – she was off the screen till **Guess Who's Coming to Dinner?** (1967), her last

♥ Married: Edward Judson (1937-43); Orson Welles (1943-7); Prince Aly Khan (1949-51) – a publicist's dream for her studio, except that marriage kept her off-screen; singer Dick Haymes (1953-5); producer James Hill (1958-61). Lovers include Victor Mature.

❝ Few women have more willingly and deftly submitted to becoming the passive material out of which a myth can be created, and this fact, added to her rather remarkable qualifications, goes a long way toward explaining her success." – *Winthrop Sargent.*
"High in the hierachy of stars who don't even have to pretend to act is Rita Hayworth, who might be called the Betty Grable of the intellectuals. She sways her scattered millions of fans by remote emotional-erotic control; and no such thing as a story is ever allowed to interfere [in **Gilda**]." – *Richard Winnington.*
"Every man I've known has fallen in love with Gilda and wakened with me." – *Rita Hayworth.*

▲ *It's not difficult to understand why Rita Hayworth was known as "The Love Goddess", but her career – like that of many other Hollywood beauties – ended in sad decline.*

"Rita Hayworth is not an actress of great depth. She was a dancer, a glamorous personality and a sex symbol. These qualities are such that they can carry her no further professionally." – *Gene Ringgold.*

Katharine Hepburn

🎥 It has often been touch and go in Hepburn's long career; at first her forthright, self-confident personality was refreshing but later she chose unpopular material thought to be too elitist. Fortunately she developed into a sparkling light comedienne while deepening her range of emotional drama.

Hepburn was born in Hartford,

Bob Hope

That American institution, that aged man who tells jokes on TV, was once one of the funniest comics in movies, having created a vain and cowardly character which was most ingratiating.

He was born in the London suburb of Eltham in 1903, but was raised in Cleveland, Ohio. He entered show-business as a patter comic and singer, and was a Broadway star in his early thirties; Paramount signed him for **The Big Broadcast of 1938,** and, singing "Thanks for the Memory" got his film career off to a fine start; he was also a star of radio. His popularity was boosted by two comedy-thrillers, **The Cat and the Canary** (1939) and **The Ghost Breakers** (1940), and by his teaming with Bing Crosby in **Road to Singapore,** which led to many hugely successful sequels. **My Favorite Blonde** (1942) with Madeleine Carroll, **My Favorite Brunette** (1947) with Dorothy Lamour and **Where There's Life** proved Hope adept at escaping from spies, crooks and other baddies, while he was equally funny in spoofs – **The Princess and the Pirate** (1944), **Monsieur Beaucaire** (1946) and **The Paleface** (1948).

His enormous popularity remained through two Damon Runyon adapta-

film with Tracy and another mother role, as one whose daughter (Katharine Houghton) wants to marry a Negro.

She received an Oscar for this film and another for her performance as Eleanor of Aquitaine in **The Lion in Winter** (1968). There followed a fourth for **On Golden Pond** (1981), creating a record among actors, but many may have felt that, like most of her recent appearances (in films for TV and cinemas), there was much self-indulgence and an over-reliance on her trade-marked "radiance". Her most recent film is **The Ultimate Solution of Grace Quigley** (1984).

♥ Married: Ludlow Ogden Smith (1928-34), but the marriage lasted only some months. Her love affair with Spencer Tracy, from 1942 to his death, became one of *the* pieces of Hollywood folklore.

❝ This dame is terrific – and expert in her craft and so electrifying on set that if you don't watch out, you're likely to wind up as part of the scenery." – *Bob Hope.*
"She is divine – no other word for it." – *Hugh Walpole.*
"I think the nicest thing that has happened to me this summer has been getting to know Kate much

▲ *Humphrey Bogart and Katharine Hepburn deciding how to blow up the German battleship in a scene from* **The African Queen** *(1951), one of the most fondly recalled of all movies.*

better. She has great quality and I am devoted to her." – *Cole Porter.*
"Well, we just got used to working together. She butts in, and I don't mind, and I pick it up when she leaves off. We just got used to working together, that's all." – *Spencer Tracy.*

▼ *Bob Hope in the* **Road to Morocco** *(1942), rightly looking apprehensive since Dorothy Lamour seldom preferred him to Bing.*

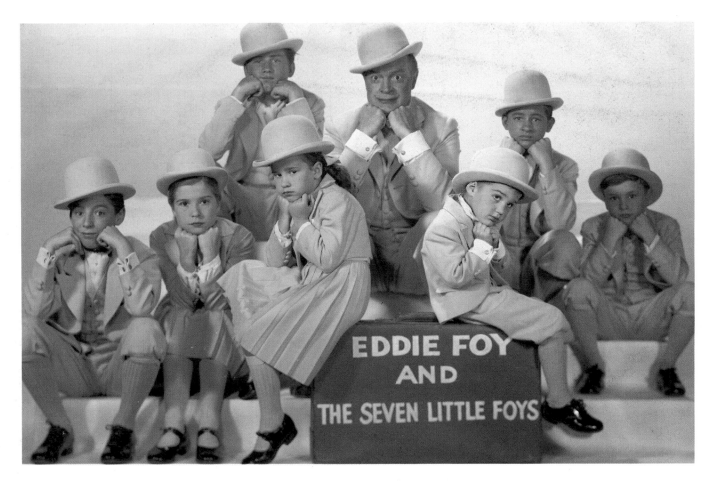

EDDIE FOY
AND
THE SEVEN LITTLE FOYS

▲ *Bob Hope in* **The Seven Little Foys** *(1955). Hope's screen career stretches back to the late thirties, during which time he has won five "special" Academy Awards.*

tions, **Sorrowful Jones** (1949) and **The Lemon Drop Kid** (1951), and through **The Great Lover** (1949) and **My Favorite Spy** (1951); but **Son of Paleface** (1952) and **Road to Bali** were only shadows of the originals. He tried a more serious image with **Beau James** (1957), which marked the end of his association with Paramount, and made only two more good films, **Alias Jesse James** (1959) and **The Facts of Life** (1960), though he continued in movies for another decade.

♥ Married: singer Dolores Reade (1933).

❝ The film character that Hope generally chooses for himself in films is, when we meet this real-life counterpart, usually unlikable. He is mean, avaricious, cocky, and a thorough coward. Yet in Hope's hands we love him, because although on the surface he is a smart Aleck he invari-

ably gets the sticky end of the lollipop, and very rarely the girl." — *Veronica Hitchcock.*
"Bob Hope is one of the funniest men alive. He can double you up with bright quips and dazzling sallies. But how many of his jokes can you recall five minutes after 'The Bob Hope Show' goes off the air." — *Buster Keaton.*
"It's not enough just to get laughs. The audience has to love you, and Bob gets love as well as laughs from his audiences." — *Jack Benny.*
"I had more pleasure looking at Hope's films than making any film I've ever made. I think he's just a great, huge talent. Part of what I like about him is that flippant, Californian, obsessed-with-golf striding through life. His not caring about the serious side at all. That's very seductive to me." — *Woody Allen.*

Leslie Howard

🎬 Soft-spoken, mild of manner but able to suggest both soulfulness and lightheartedness, Leslie Howard was considered the "typical" Englishman, though of Hungarian-

Jewish extraction. He was, however, born in London, in 1893. Invalided in the First World War, he took up acting and moved from amateur to professional; he made five movies at this time, starting with **The Happy Warrior** (1917) but didn't return to the cinema until he was an international star with **Outward Bound** (1930), **A Free Soul** (1931) and **Smilin' Through** (1932) with Norma Shearer, **Berkeley Square**

▼ *Leslie Howard in* **Intermezzo: A Love Story** *(1939), the last film he made in Hollywood.*

(1933), **Of Human Bondage** (1934) and, in Britain, **The Scarlet Pimpernel** (1935).

Howard remained in great demand at every studio, and continued to be fastidious in choice: **The Petrified Forest** (1936), **Romeo and Juliet** with Shearer, **It's Love I'm After** (1937) and, in Britain, **Pygmalion** (1938), which he co-directed. After a pair for David Selznick, **Gone With the Wind** (1939) and **Intermezzo**, he returned to Britain, making movies to help the war effort, **Pimpernel Smith** (1941), **The 49th Parallel** and **The First of the Few** (1942). While flying from Portugal in 1943 his plane was shot down by the Germans.

 Married: Ruth Martin (1916).

❝ Leslie Howard was a darling flirt. He'd be caressing your eyes and have his hand on someone else's leg at the same time. He was adorable. He was a little devil and just wanted his hands on every woman around . . . . He just loved ladies." — *Joan Blondell.*

"Leslie Howard was wonderful. He'd come on the set, have a quiet walk through in rehearsal and then he would repeat a shot again and again — even his eyelashes would be in the same place at any given moment, yet his performance was never mechanical. He had the most wonderfully controlled technique I have ever seen." — *Anthony Asquith.*

"Howard was more than just a popular actor. Since the war he has become something of a symbol to the British people." — *C.A. Lejeune.*

"It is amazing how hopelessly wrong

▲ *Bette Davis and Leslie Howard in* **Of Human Bondage** *(1934), in which he played the medical student infatuated by her beauty.*

Leslie is [in **Pygmalion**]. However, the public will like him and probably want him to marry Eliza, which is just what I don't want." — *Bernard Shaw.*

Al Jolson

Al Jolson's place in history is secure as the first man to speak from the screen. His emotional manner of selling a song was carried over to his acting: these factors, plus his bounding vitality and self-confidence made him popular, at least with audiences. However, the com-

▼ *What a way to start the Talkies . . . Al Jolson hams it up for "Mammy" in his film autobiography, the still very popular* **The Jazz Singer** *(1927).*

bination, added to vanity and several forms of meanness, did not endear him to colleagues backstage.

He was born in St Petersburg, Russia, in 1886 and brought to the US as a boy. His parents intended him to be a cantor but he ran away to join a vaudeville tour — the plot of **The Jazz Singer** (1927). To restore its flagging fortunes, Warner Brothers decided to use one of the Sound systems then being peddled to the studios: this system synchronized the picture with a record of Jolson singing six songs, at intervals. He spoke a sentence ("You ain't heard nothing yet!") between two of them, and thus doomed the Silent movie.

A part-Talkie, **The Singing Fool** (1928), was even more sensationally popular, but Jolson and Warners taxed audience patience with the equally maudlin films that followed, in most of which he also sang in blackface. After a failure for United Artists, **Hallelujah I'm a Bum** (1933), Jolson returned to Warners for **Wonder Bar** (1934), **Go Into Your Dance** (1936) and **The Singing Kid** (1936). He sang medleys of his old songs in a supporting role in **Rose of Washington Square** (1939) and he remained at 20th Century-Fox to make **Swanee River** (1940). He was almost unknown to that generation of moviegoers when he ghosted Larry Parks in **The Jolson Story** (1946), which was so successful that it generated **Jolson Sings Again** (1949). Plans were afoot for Jolson himself to film again when he died in 1950.

❤ Married: Henrietta Keller (1906-19); Ethel Delmar (1922-6); dancer and actress Ruby Keeler (1928-39), who has never

so on his home ground in **Anchors Aweigh** (1945) and showed prowess as a swashbuckler in **The Pirate** (1948) with Garland, and **The Three Musketeers**. **Take Me Out to the Ball Game** (1949) showed a lot of nice youngsters having fun, and that led to the innovative **On the Town**, directed by Kelly and Donen. That was followed by two further triumphs, Minnelli's **An American in Paris** (1951), for which Kelly won a special Oscar, and his own and Donen's **Singin' in the Rain** (1952).

Since that is most people's favorite musical, it is sad that nothing went right for Kelly after that — including Minnelli's **Brigadoon** (1954) and his own **It's Always Fair Weather** (1955) and **Invitation to the Dance** (1956). These were part of the reason Hollywood lost faith in musicals, and Kelly's last role as an actor was **Les Girls** (1957). Since then he has directed movies, but his film appearances have not been memorable and the last two — **Viva Knievel** (1977) and **Xanadu** (1980) — were mistakes.

▼ *Gene Kelly and Vera-Ellen in the trail-blazing musical* **On the Town** *(1949) which Kelly also co-directed. He played one of three sailors seeing New York on a 24-hour pass.*

▲ *Al Jolson was already a vaudeville topliner when he carved his way into movie history by becoming the first man to speak on the screen. In films as on stage he sang sentimental songs, accompanied by flamboyant gestures to attract large audiences.*

publicly discussed the marriage other than to refer to it as "a long mistake"; and Erle Galbraith (1945), who outlived him.

❝ Al Jolson, for instance, was a great instinctive artist with magic and vitality. He was the most impressive entertainer on the American stage . . . . Whatever he sang, he brought you up or down to his level; even his ridiculous song 'Mammy' enthralled everyone. Only a shadow of himself appeared in films." — *Charlie Chaplin.*
"The screen didn't give him enough space to project in. I remember as a kid seeing him on stage, and I think to this day there have been two great

performers in the world: one is Jolson and the other is Judy Garland. They had some kind of magic in front of people that no one could surpass — they were sheer, magnificent talents beyond belief. I get chills when I think of them." — *Joan Blondell.*

Gene Kelly

Other men danced on the screen besides Fred Astaire, but only one other stepped his way to immortality — and Gene Kelly did it with verve. He was born in 1912 in Pittsburgh and, after several jobs, taught dancing. His first job in New York was in the chorus, but two years later he starred in "Pal Joey": that sent him to Hollywood and he began his long association with MGM in **For Me and My Gal** (1942) opposite Judy Garland, but it was on loan that he first showed his individuality as a hoofer, in **Cover Girl** (1944). He did

▲ *Younger Kelly playing a sailor seeing Hollywood, with Frank Sinatra (left), in* **Anchors Aweigh** *(1945). Their freewheeling antics lead to greater triumphs in 1949.*

 Married: actress Betsy Blair (1940-57); and Jeanne Coyne (1960, widowed 1973).

❝ For me, Gene Kelly has been the single most important influence on the musical cinema, as a conceptualizer, director and, of course, as a musical performer." — *Francis Ford Coppola.*
"He is the long-distance dancer who kept up the pace long after he helped set it." — *Peter Evans.*
"The American film musical at its best, we shall see if we live so long, was a genuine art form with all the necessary qualifications like conviction and originality, durability of appeal and universality, and at the heart of the best of the genre was Gene Kelly." — *John Sandilands.*
"It would be hard to express the elation of a man who has won his

heart's desire more eloquently than does Kelly in his literal interpretation of the title number, 'Singin' in the Rain' . . . . You are left feeling that nothing could be more cheering than the rain." — *Catherine de la Roche.*

Alan Ladd

🎥 Alan Ladd was a lucky find for Paramount, who found in him an ideal tough hero, taciturn and trench-coated, for the *films noirs* of the forties and early fifties.
He was born in Hot Springs, Arkansas, in 1913 and did a variety of jobs before Universal decided that his college-boy looks made him star material, but they dropped him after a bit in **Once in a Lifetime** (1932). Occasionally he played extra roles, especially after meeting agent and former star Sue Carol; and after Paramount saw him in **Joan of Paris** (1942) they put him in **This Gun for Hire,** which swept him to stardom.
He made a couple of films a year for the studio, but few are worth noting:

▲ *Alan Ladd, as tough and as dead pan as ever, in the 1949 movie* **After Midnight.** *Ladd built his reputation on roles such as this.*

The Glass Key, The Blue Dahlia (1946), **Two Years Before the Mast** and **The Great Gatsby** (1949). He was working for other studios when he had his biggest success with Paramount, the Western **Shane** (1953), and that was the end of the association. **Hell on Frisco Bay** (1955), **Boy on a Dolphin** (1957) and **The Proud Rebel** (1958) are perhaps the best of his subsequent films until **The Carpetbaggers** (1964), a "come-back", for it was his first movie in two years and the first to be much noticed in a while.

 Married: Marjorie Jane Farnsworth (widowed); Sue Carol (1942), who outlived him. Sheila Graham reports an affair with co-star June Allyson in the mid-fifties.

❝ He was awfully good in putting across what he had, in looks and in manner; he had something very attractive — a definite film personality which he had worked very hard to perfect." — *Deborah Kerr.*
"Alan Ladd was a marvelous person in his simplicity. In so many ways we were kindred spirits. We both were professionally conceived through Hollywood's search for box-office and the *types* to insure that box-office. And we were both little people. Alan wasn't as short as most people believe. It was true that, in certain films

▲ *Alan Ladd with Dianne Foster in* **The Deep Six** *(1958) one of the rather undistinguished action movies which ended his career.*

in which his leading lady was on the tallish side, Alan would climb a small platform or the girl worked in a slit trench. We had no such problems together." — *Veronica Lake.*

"By a curious chemistry of film Alan had a great following, but it has nothing to do with acting. So you are surprised to find, when you play opposite him, that he is a very good actor just the same." — *Edmund O'Brien.*

Veronica Lake

◁Looking out from behind her fringe, Veronica Lake had a silky, insolent little-girl quality which made a superb foil to Alan Ladd's sullen, boyish tough guy. Without the fringe or Ladd she was merely little — both of stature and screen presence.

She was born in Brooklyn in 1919 and entered showbusiness via beauty contests and extra work in **Sorority House** (1939). An agent got her a leading role in **I Wanted Wings** (1941) at Paramount, who immediately starred her in Sturges' **Sullivan's Travels,** followed by two with Ladd, **This Gun for Hire** (1942) and **The Glass Key.** Clair's **I Married a Witch,** opposite Fredric March, was followed by the one with the new hairstyle, **So Proudly We Hail**

(1943). Her popularity began to wane at the same time, and Paramount did little to reverse the trend, apart from **The Blue Dahlia** (1946) and **Saigon** (1948), reunions with Ladd.

Her other movies were quickly-forgotten comedies and musicals. At 20th Century-Fox she did **Slattery's Hurricane** (1949), but there were no more Hollywood offers, though she did do **Stronghold** (1952) in Mexico. In 1962 she was discovered as a cocktail waitress in New York, which resulted in some stage offers and a low-budget Canadian effort, **Footsteps in the Snow** (1966). She died from hepatitis in 1973.

♥ Married: John Detlie (1940-3); director Andre de Toth (1944-52); Joseph McCarthy (1955-9); Ron House (1962-70); an English naval captain (1972), but it lasted only a few months. Her autobiography suggests several lovers, including producer William Dozier.

❝ Miss Lake is supposed to be a *femme fatale* and to that end it was arranged that her truly splendid bosom should be unconfined and draped ever so slightly in a manner to make the current crop of sweater girls prigs by comparison. Such to-do has been made over doing justice to those attributes of Miss Lake that everything else about her has been thrown out of focus. The effect is too uncanny." — *Cecilia Ager.*
"She's one of the little people. Like Mary Pickford, Douglas Fairbanks and Freddie Bartholomew when he started, who take hold of an audience immediately. She's nothing much in real life — a quiet, rather timid little

▶ *Veronica Lake in a characteristic Hollywood pose in* **Ramrod** *(1947).*

▼ *Ladd again, this time with Veronica Lake, who was never as good with other male partners. There was a screen chemistry between the two, apparent in a number of features, the first being* **This Gun for Hire** *(1942).*

thing. But the screen transforms, electrifies and brings her to life." — *Preston Sturges*.

"**The Blue Dahlia** wasn't a topnotch film by any means, largely because Veronica Lake couldn't play the love scenes and too much had to be discarded." — *Raymond Chandler*.

Dorothy Lamour

Remembered now as the girl in a sarong and the one fought over by Hope and Crosby in the "Road" films, Dorothy Lamour was also a sympathetic actress in her own right.

She was born in New Orleans in 1914; wanted to be a singer and auditioned successfully for bandleader Herbie Kay. Paramount tested her and put her into **The Jungle Princess** (1936), and after some supporting roles she was back in a sarong in **The Hurricane** (1937). She donned it again for **Road to Singapore** (1940), and the sequels that followed turned just another pretty star into a box-office attraction; she was particularly good with Bob Hope in **Caught in the Draft** (1941), **They Got Me Covered** (1943) and **My Favorite Brunette** (1947).

► *Dorothy Lamour single-handedly – or perhaps we should say single-bodily – made the sarong famous. She yearned to make more serious films than the jungle epics, but in later life admitted that she owed much, if not her whole career, to the garment.*
▼ *Dorothy as she was about ten years later, in 1948.*

Although impressive on loan in two dramatic movies, **Johnny Apollo** (1940) and **Chad Hanna,** she proved not to be box-office at her home studio in similar films, such as **A Medal for Benny** (1945), so apart from the "Road" films and the sarong epics she was in such musicals as **The Fleet's In** (1942) and **And the Angels Sing** (1943). There was little interest after she was dropped in 1947 by Paramount, but the studio welcomed her back for a guest spot in **The Greatest Show on Earth** (1952) and **Road to Bali.** She was offscreen till the next, last and worst of the "Road" films, **The Road to Hong Kong** (1962), though ceding her leading role to Joan Collins, and made just two more movies, the last of which is **Pajama Party** (1964).

♥ Married: Herbie Kay (1935-9); William Howard (1943, but widowed in 1978).

❝ Dottie was fearless. She stands there before the camera and ad libs with Crosby and me, fully knowing, the way the script's written, she'll come off second or third best." — *Bob Hope*.
"When they toast your wonderful career, count us in; when they mention your unparalleled contribution to this nation in World War II, we agree wholeheartedly; and when they applaud one of the brightest stars to ever shine in the Hollywood firmament, ours will be the loudest clapping you hear." — *Ronald and Nancy Reagan*.

In 1937 the duo took to the West. ▲

Laurel & Hardy

The two-reel comedies were supposedly ephemeral, forgotten as soon as the main feature came on. At the time Laurel and Hardy met on the Hal Roach lot both Talkies and television were unknown — they would not, then, have thought that their modest little cut-ups were to provide their road to immortality.

Stan Laurel, the driving force behind the partnership, was born in 1890 in Ulverston, Lancashire; in 1903 he joined a troupe of juvenile clowns and later traveled to the US in the same music-hall company as Charlie Chaplin. Oliver Hardy was born in Atlanta, Georgia, in 1892 and had drifted into films, as an extra, by the time he was 21. Laurel made the move from vaudeville to movies in 1918, but he wasn't immediately successful and had had several bosses

before joining Roach. By that time Hardy had made a small reputation as a villain in two-reel comedies.

In the early twenties both were members of Roach's "Comedy All-Stars" and had appeared in many films together without being paired. That happened in **Putting Pants on Philip** (1927), but it was not until **The Second Hundred Years** that they found their personae as a team: well-meaning, timid, flustered Stan and magnanimous, busybodying and monstrous Ollie, both equally maladroit. Their third teaming, **The Battle of the Century,** featured one of those full-scale climactic battles of destruction which were such a feature of their Silents, of which the best are **From Soup to Nuts** (1928), **You're Darn Tootin', Their Purple Moment, Liberty** (1929) and **Big**

Business. They made the transition to Sound in that year and continued to make some excellent shorts, including **The Perfect Day, Laughing Gravy** (1931), **County Hospital** (1932) and **The Music Box,** which was awarded an Oscar.

The quality began to diminish and from an average of eight a year they went to half that number, making their last short, **Thicker than Water,** in 1935.

Roach released through MGM, who engaged the team to brighten up a tedious operetta already completed, **The Rogue Song** (1930), which thus became their first feature. They made others, including **Sons of the Desert** (1933), **Bonnie Scotland** (1935), **Our Relations** (1936) and **Way Out West** (1937). Laurel's bitter relations with Roach led to a

▲ *"Another fine mess you've got me into!": Ollie to Stan, as usual, in this scene from a Laurel & Hardy short.*

complete break in 1940, but he was allowed almost no creative control on the subsequent half-dozen B pictures made for MGM and 20th Century-Fox, concluding with **The Bull Fighters** (1945). They returned to the stage and in 1951 made their last film in France, **Atoll K,** a failure. Both died in 1965, five years after being awarded an honorary Oscar.

♥ Stan Laurel married Lois Neilson (divorced 1934), Virginia Ruth (1934-6) and Ida Kitaeva (1946). Oliver Hardy married Myrtle Reeves (1921-37) and Lucille Jones (1940). Their last wives outlived them.

❝ A joke of Laurel and Hardy's is no transient thing. It is sniffed and savored before use, then used, squeezed dry and squeezed again; smoothed out, folded up with care and put away ready for the next time." – *David Robinson.*

"The magic of Laurel and Hardy is their love for each other. Bud Abbott ditches Lou Costello in a second when the chips are down. Groucho Marx gleefully cheats Chico and Harpo – and vice versa. And there is no doubt that Dean Martin clearly thinks Jerry Lewis is a moron. But between Laurel and Hardy there is a loyalty

that transcends all their trials. While it often seems that other comedy teams are together purely out of convenience, Stan and Ollie are an organic whole from the first frame of every picture. You never question their oneness." – *John Landis.*

"Speaking for myself, I cannot like anyone who does not like Laurel and Hardy, nor love anyone who does not love them. In 104 films they never ran out of comic ideas, insane invention, charming conceits." – *Garson Kanin.*

Vivien Leigh

She was Scarlett O'Hara and that would be enough. She was also entrancingly beautiful, ambitious and married to the greatest actor of his time, Laurence Olivier.

Vivien Leigh was born in Darjeeling, India, in 1913, to British parents who had her educated in Europe. She studied to be an actress, married, and had some minor movie roles – the first was in **Things Are Looking Up** (1934) – before becoming a success on the West End stage. Alexander Korda cast her as Olivier's romantic interest in **Fire Over England** (1937) and she starred in a handful of British movies before being selected by David Selznick to play Scarlett in **Gone With the Wind** (1939) while visiting Olivier in Hollywood; the role won her an Oscar, as well as parts in **Waterloo Bridge** (1940) and, with Olivier, **That Hamilton Woman** (1941).

She returned to Britain to join him at the outbreak of war but because of illness and the war made only one film, **Caesar and Cleopatra** (1945), based on Shaw's play, with Claude

▼ *Vivien Leigh on the set of* **Gone With the Wind** *(1939). The role of Scarlett O'Hara brought in her first Academy Award.*

tury (1934), in which she played a temperamental movie queen opposite John Barrymore, is reckoned to be the first of the "screwball" comedies and Lombard was in some of the choicest: **Hands Across the Table** (1935), **Love Before Breakfast** (1936), **My Man Godfrey,** with William Powell, **True Confession** (1937) and **Nothing Sacred**.

Carole Lombard also proved her skill as a dramatic actress in **Swing High Swing Low** and **Made for Each Other** (1939). During her last years she was under contract to Selznick and RKO, but only one outstanding movie emerged: Lubitsch's **To Be or Not To Be** (1942), which was released posthumously. Earlier that year she was killed in an air-crash.

Married: William Powell (1931-3); Clark Gable (1939). Lovers include Howard Hughes.

" She was breathtakingly beautiful in a day which demanded plastic beauty of its heroes and heroines. What would, I think, have led her on to still greater stardom were the interior qualities, of wit and unaffected worldly wisdom, untrammeled spirits, honesty, directness, and her apparent awareness that freedom is not necessarily the same thing as being alone and that the truest freedom is within a secure love." — *Charlie Chaplin.*

"I never dreamed that Lombard had such a performance in her. Her work

Rains. She appeared in only five more movies: **Anna Karenina** (1948), produced by Korda; **A Streetcar Named Desire** (1951), in Hollywood, gaining a second Oscar for her portrayal of a schizophrenic, a role she had played on the London stage, and one much more like her real self than anyone could have thought at the time; **The Deep Blue Sea** (1955); and, after the break-up of her marriage to Olivier, **The Roman Spring of Mrs Stone** (1961) and **Ship of Fools** (1965). During the latter part of her life her stage work took precedence; she died in 1967 of tuberculosis.

Married: lawyer Herbert Holman (1932-40); Laurence Olivier (1940-60). Reputedly had various lovers, including the actor Peter Finch, Olivier's protégé. The affair began in 1948, caused her a breakdown in 1953 and resulted in pregnancy two years later.

" I first set eyes upon the possessor of this wondrous unimagined beauty on the stage of the Ambassadors' Theatre . . . Apart from her looks, which were magical, she possessed beautiful poise; her neck looked almost too fragile to support her head and bore it with a sense of surprise, and something of the pride of the master juggler who can make a brilliant maneuver appear almost accidental. She also had something else: an attraction of the most

▲ *Vivien Leigh, seen here with Lee Marvin in* **Ship of Fools** *(1965) playing one of the rather masochistic roles she assumed after separating from Laurence Olivier.*

perturbing nature I had ever encountered." — *Laurence Olivier.*
"She, a stunner whose ravishing beauty often tended to obscure her staggering achievements as an actress. Great beauties are infrequently great actresses, simply because they do not need to be. Vivien was different; ambitious, persevering, serious, often inspired." — *Garson Kanin.*

Carole Lombard

No one has any right to be as talented and gifted as Carole Lombard, who was not only stunningly beautiful but one of the most delicious comediennes who ever graced the screen.

She was born in 1908 in Fort Wayne, Indiana, and moved as a child to Los Angeles, where she was spotted by the director Allan Dwan, who was looking for a lively teenager to play in **A Perfect Crime** (1921). Four years later she began to appear regularly in movies, including some Max Sennett shorts. With **Safety in Numbers** (1930) she began a time at Paramount, but was not impressive until **No Man of Her Own** (1932) with Clark Gable. **Twentieth Cen-**

▼ *Carole Lombard, the beautiful and talented comedienne, whose films are justifiably as popular as ever.*

is superb. Her art in this picture is compelling, understanding and convincing." — *John Barrymore*.

"It is always a pleasure to watch those hollow Garbo features, those neurotic elbows and bewildered hands, and her voice has the same odd beauty a street musician discovers in old iron, scraping out heartbreaking and nostalgic melodies. But you will be well advised to wait for another occasion [than **Fools for Scandal**] before serving at her shrine." — *Graham Greene*.

Myrna Loy

Miss Loy was known as the screen's "perfect wife", which rather overlooks the fact that when she first played wives she was often a rather gamey one. The sobriquet ignores the fact that she played vamps, often Oriental ones, and it gives no indication that she was a skilled comedienne and a dramatic actress of much sensitivity.

She was born in Helena, Montana, in 1905, and moved to Los Angeles, where she became a dancer. Her looks attracted so much attention that she was given a role in **What Price Beauty?** (1925), after which she averaged a dozen movies a year, in parts great and small (but her best chances didn't come till the Sound era), as sinister Orientals in **The Black Watch** (1929) and **The Mask of Fu Manchu** (1932), and as "the other woman" in **Consolation Marriage** (1931) and **Arrowsmith.**

MGM decided to groom her for stardom and, thinking that she had "clicked" with William Powell in **Manhattan Melodrama** (1934), reteamed them in **The Thin Man,** as a hard-drinking, bantering, elegant couple who did amateur sleuthing. The wildly successful result brought half a dozen sequels, the last in 1947, as well as other films with Powell, including **The Great Ziegfeld** (1936),

Libeled Lady, Double Wedding (1937) and **Love Crazy** (1941). She was a good foil to Clark Gable in **Too Hot to Handle** (1938) and **Test Pilot** and an adulterous wife in **The Rains Came** (1939).

She retired during the Second World War to work with the Red Cross and after it was involved in UNESCO. Freelancing, she began to play "mother" roles, notably in the very popular **The Best Years of Our Lives** (1946) opposite Fredric March and **Cheaper by the Dozen** (1950) with Clifton Webb. Her teamings with Cary Grant in **The Bachelor and the Bobby Soxer** (1947) and **Mr Blandings Builds His Dreamhouse** (1948) were much appreciated; after **Belles on Their Toes** (1952), a sequel to the Webb movie, she retired, returning as a supporting actress in **The Ambassador's Daughter** (1956).

▼ *Kissing in confidence.*

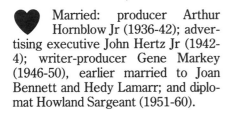 *Although remembered as a fine light comedienne and "the screen's perfect wife", Myrna Loy had an earlier existence playing slinky and often evil Orientals, as seen here in* **The Mask of Fu Manchu** *(1932).*

There have been other supporting roles, most recently in **Just Tell Me What You Want** (1980), but she has preferred to work on the stage or in television.

♥ Married: producer Arthur Hornblow Jr (1936-42); advertising executive John Hertz Jr (1942-4); writer-producer Gene Markey (1946-50), earlier married to Joan Bennett and Hedy Lamarr; and diplomat Howland Sargeant (1951-60).

❝ The MGM studio experts soon streamlined her image and made her high fashion: elegantly gowned and coiffured, she was every bit as smart as the ladies in the illustrations of *Vogue* and *Vanity Fair*. But there was nothing stiff or artificial about Loy; she viewed herself and the world around her with great good humor." – *Gary Carey.*
"[**Belles on Their Toes**] conveys the definitive Loy image: a totally modern woman – indeed a feminist sympathizer – who, ironically, remains an old-fashioned perfect wife." – *Karyn Kay.*
"Myrna Loy, what a joy!" – *Lillian Gish.*
"I'm an irrationally devoted fan. – *Lauren Bacall.*

Jeanette MacDonald

🎥◁ Jeanette MacDonald sang the airs of operetta throughout a movie career that had two phases: first, in a series of deliciously saucy farces with Maurice Chevalier, matching his roguish charm with a dimpling smile, and second, a series of classic musicals with Nelson Eddy, whose somewhat heavy screen personality was lightened by that same delightful smile.

She was born in Philadelphia in 1907 and became a dancer, but it was as a singer that she became a Broadway star. Lubitsch engaged her to partner Chevalier in **The Love Parade** (1929), and among the other films she made for him is **Monte Carlo** (1930) in which Jack Buchanan replaced Chevalier; but the Paramount bosses never liked her and dropped her a second time after **One Hour with You** (1932) and **Love Me Tonight.** MGM took her on for **The Cat and the Fiddle** (1934), which was followed by a reunion of the old team for **The Merry Widow.** She first co-starred

▼ *Jeanette MacDonald prepares to take on the saucy doctor in* **Love Me Tonight** *(1932).*

▲ *The young, soulful Jeanette MacDonald revealing signs of a more serious future singing operettas, opposite Nelson Eddy.*

with Eddy in **Naughty Marietta** (1935), which was followed by **Rose Marie** (1936), **Maytime** (1937), **The Girl of the Golden West** (1938), **Sweethearts, New Moon** (1940), **Bitter Sweet** and **I Married an Angel** (1942); the other highlights are **San Francisco** (1936), in which Clark Gable loved her, and **The Firefly** (1937).

At one time she had been Louis B. Mayer's favorite star, but it is believed that he wanted to drop her after a quarrel. The popularity of the MacDonald-Eddy films had fallen away only minutely but MGM was interested in neither star so their film careers were virtually at a finish. Producer Joe Pasternak got her back to that studio for **Three Daring Daughters** (1948) and **The Sun Comes Up** (1949), in which her earlier vivacity had been replaced by a certain crispness. She went into semi-retirement and died of a heart attack in 1965.

♥ Married: movie star Gene Raymond (1937), who outlived her. In 1964, Chevalier reported that they had had a close relationship during the time they made the Lubitsch films.

66 **The Merry Widow** marked the end of what many consider the most interesting part of Jeanette MacDonald's career, when she was the only singer in pictures who could sing with her tongue in the cheek." — *Clive Hirschhorn.*
"Jeanette MacDonald and Nelson Eddy were my fellow musicians as well as my close friends. They had certain personal characteristics in common, which involved almost

story-book qualities: unremitting fealty to their profession, loyalty to their associates, and 'no compromises' in the matter of doing justice to their talents. Unflaggingly did they accept the virtually unlimited demands their careers constantly made upon them. Their particular niche in showbusiness annals is secure for all time to come." — *Meredith Willson.*

Marx Brothers

There were originally five, but they were four by the time they arrived in films: Zeppo (born in 1901 in New York, where the rest also came from), the straight man, who opted out in 1933, leaving Groucho (born 1895), of the loping walk and false mustache, insulting everyone at crackerjack speed and especially the stately, loving Margaret Dumont; Harpo (born 1893), of the blond curls and larcenous disposition, who couldn't speak at all; and Chico (born 1891), who spoke fractured English and was devious at every turn — as were they all.

Their mother had showbusiness connections and pushed them into vaudeville at an early age. By the mid-twenties they were Broadway stars, and their first two films were based on shows they had done, **The Cocoanuts** (1929) and **Animal Crackers** (1930); at Paramount they also did **Monkey Business** (1931), **Horse Feathers** (1932) and the best and most anarchic of their comedies,

▼ *The Mad Marxes not long after arriving at MGM. From top to bottom: Harpo, Chico and Groucho.*

▲ *The second of the MGM Marx Brothers' movies and the last prepared under the aegis of studio chief and "genius" Irving Thalberg. After his death the studio's lack of enthusiasm for the team showed in their less effective films.*

Duck Soup (1933). The quality was maintained when they moved to MGM for **A Night at the Opera** (1935) but it began to decline after **A Day at the Races** (1937), if reversed somewhat with their last MGM film, **The Big Store** (1941).

They came out of retirement for **A Night in Casablanca** (1946) and Groucho did a small but key role in **Love Happy** (1949), planned as a star vehicle for the other two. He made some solo appearances in movies, and − for the record − they were all in an odd venture, **The Story of Mankind** (1957). Chico died in 1961, Harpo in 1964, Groucho in 1977 and Zeppo in 1979.

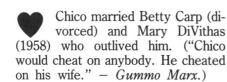 Chico married Betty Carp (divorced) and Mary DiVithas (1958) who outlived him. ("Chico would cheat on anybody. He cheated on his wife." − *Gummo Marx*.)

Harpo married Susan Fleming (1936), who outlived him.
Groucho married Ruth Johnson (1920-42), Catherine Gorcey (1945-51) and Eden Hartford (1954), from whom he was separated. Erin Fleming, the companion of his last years, sued the estate unsuccessfully for "palimony".
Zeppo married Marion Benda (1927) but they divorced.

“ These men were not motivated by greed, ambition, or lechery. Their zaniness sprang from pure hearts: hearts so clean, in fact, so undefiled by the world that the brothers were free to do what they wanted. And they did. Clipping ties off stuffed shirts at a banquet, setting an orchestra adrift on a large raft, confounding everyone with Groucho's cloudy logic − the Marx Brothers scampered through their films like a horde of impetuous children. The strictures of society and the unwritten law to behave by conforming had no meaning for the Marx Brothers except as targets." − *William Kuhns*.
"If you ever eat at the round table at the Hillcrest Country Club and Groucho is there you'll find that he'll

make you laugh in the same way he does on screen. Chico, I would say, loved women and gambling, period. Harpo was probably the sweetest man you would ever want to meet." − *Jack Benny*.

James Mason

Solid gold: whether as romantic leading man or, later, supporting actor, James Mason had style, presence and versatility. He never had the career he merited, as he himself admitted, but he was a star in demand for almost 50 years.

He was born in Huddersfield in 1909 and became an actor after leaving Cambridge; he had acquired a small West End reputation when he made his film début in a quota quickie, **Late Extra** (1935). He was usually in supporting roles until **The Man in Grey** (1943), when his portrayal of a Regency rake made him not only a star, but Britain's biggest box-office attraction. He was equally evil in **Fanny by Gaslight** (1944), **They Were Sisters** (1945) and **The Wicked Lady,** but his romantic appeal was best exemplified by **The Seventh Veil**, where he beat Ann

Todd but got her in the last reel. With **Odd Man Out** (1947) he had a good film for a change and after **The Upturned Glass** he went to Hollywood.

Attempting to get away from typecasting, he played sympathetic roles in some not too interesting films, but he did two with the director Max Ophuls, **Caught** (1949) and **The Reckless Moment,** though he did not really make his mark in the US until **The Desert Fox** (1951), as Rommel, and **Five Fingers** (1952). Also admired were his Brutus in **Julius Caesar** (1953), his fading movie star in **A Star Is Born** (1954) and his Captain Nemo in **20,000 Leagues Under the Sea.** Except for Hitchcock's **North by Northwest** (1959), **Journey to the Center of the Earth** and Kubrick's **Lolita** (1962), his films of this period are an undistinguished batch, and he soon settled into supporting, or character roles, though never losing star billing: **The Pumpkin Eater** (1964), **Lord Jim** (1965), **Georgy Girl** (1966), Lumet's **The Deadly Affair** and **The Seagull** (1968), **Child's Play** (1972), **Cross of Iron** (1977), **Heaven Can Wait** (1978) and **The Verdict** (1982), among many. He died in 1984; **The Shooting Party** and **The Assisi Underground** were released posthumously.

 Married: actress Pamela Kellino (1939-64); actress Clarissa Kaye (1971).

" He was a punctilious man, beautifully mannered, quiet, generous and amusing. I never heard him say a vicious or bitter thing about anything or anyone." – *John Gielgud.*
"By creating characters that command attention, he gives the other characters in the films importance they do not deserve under the circumstances. For some time I'd been thinking that Mason was becoming a better, more interesting actor with the passage of time. Having recently reseen **Lolita, North by North-**

◄ *After his years as a romantic and sometimes sinister leading man, James Mason eased himself into some varied supporting roles in which he was always value for money – even if the films were not.*

west and **Georgy Girl** it now occurs to me that he has always been superb. He is, in fact, one of the few actors worth taking the trouble to see, even when the film that encases him is so much cement." – *Vincent Canby.*
"He was one of the closest friends I ever had. A wonderful actor, and a humble and wonderful man." – *Stewart Granger.*

Robert Mitchum

As a young actor, Robert Mitchum did so little that many – colleagues and critics – thought him lazy: he already understood that screen acting has more to do with presence than business. Then, he spoke little and was quick with his fists. He has hardly varied his appearance or approach, but he can play a wide spectrum of roles with conviction. He is one of the industry's most respected actors, despite the

fact that he has made many less memorable films than, say, Humphrey Bogart or Gary Cooper.

He was born in Bridgeport, Connecticut, in 1917, and among many other jobs was once a prizefighter; he was a studio writer and then an extra, beginning with **Hoppy Serves a Writ** (1943). He progressed to leading parts in B movies and became a star when William Wellman chose him for one of two chief roles in **The Story of G.I. Joe** (1945).

While he was under contract to RKO his pictures included **Crossfire** (1947), **Out of the Past, Blood on the Moon** (1948), **The Red Pony** (1949) and **Angel Face** (1952); he also went to jail for smoking marijuana, which some considered might finish his career. Of his films since, the best are: **River of No Return** (1954), Charles Laughton's **The**

▼ *Robert Mitchum with Jane Greer, an under-rated screen team, in* **The Big Steal** *(1949).*

▲ *Robert Mitchum came to prominence in* **The Story of G.I. Joe** *(1945), being nominated as best supporting actor. He was typecast as a man of action, and is here seen in the 1958 drama* **The Hunters.**

Night of the Hunter (1955), **Heaven Knows Mr Allison** (1957), **Home From the Hill** (1960), **The Sundowners, Cape Fear** (1962), **Two for the See-Saw, El Dorado** (1967), **Ryan's Daughter** (1970), in which his understated work almost salvaged the inflated enterprise, **The Friends of Eddie Coyle** (1973), **The Yakuza** (1975) and **Farewell My Lovely.** He has recently made some films for TV; his last cinema film to date is **Maria's Lovers** (1984).

 Married: Dorothy Spence (1940).

❝ He is, in fact, a consummate actor, no matter how unconcerned he may appear. He has what many of the great thirties and forties actors who are today's cult heroes had: a capacity to retain and even expand their dignity, their image, their self-possession, even in the midst of the worst possible material." — *Roger Ebert.*
"You're the biggest fraud I ever met. You pretend you don't care a damn thing about a scene, and you're the hardest working so-and-so I've ever known." — *Howard Hawks.*
"Bob is one of the best actors in the world. All his hip talk is a blind. He's a very fine man with wonderful manners and he speaks beautifully when

he wants to. He won't thank you for destroying the tough image he's built up as a defense. In fact he's a very tender man and a very great gentleman." — *Charles Laughton.*

Laurence Olivier

🎬◀ The man commonly regarded as the century's greatest actor always preferred the stage, but his legacy to cinema is nearly as great.

He was born in Dorking, Surrey, in 1907 and studied for the stage. He was a West End lead when he made his first feature, **The Temporary Widow** (1930), in Germany. An RKO contract and three Hollywood movies soured him on filming, so he spent the thirties establishing himself as one of Britain's leading Shakespearian actors, though his athleticism and dynamism were seen to advantage in **Moscow Nights** (1935) and **Fire Over England** (1937). A second Hollywood sojourn found him playing the romantic hero of four films constantly revived: **Wuthering Heights** (1939), **Rebecca** (1940), **Pride and Prejudice** and **That Hamilton Woman** (1941).

In Britain he was in **The 49th**

▼ *The first time Shakespeare was successfully filmed:* **Henry V** *(1944). Olivier also produced and directed.*

▲ *Not exactly an even matching of talent: Olivier and Merle Oberon in William Wyler's* **Wuthering Heights** *(1939). Oberon did not invoke much passion as one of the doomed lovers, but Olivier more than made up for her.*

Parallel and **The Demi-Paradise** (1943), before producing, directing and starring in **Henry V** (1944). Two further Shakespeare films were also greatly admired: **Hamlet** (1948), which also won Oscars for Best Actor and Best Picture, and **Richard III** (1955). His only other films during this period are **The Magic Box** (1951), **Carrie** (1952), **The Beggar's Opera** (1953), **The Prince**

and the Showgirl** (1957), which he also directed, and **The Devil's Disciple** (1959). **The Entertainer** (1960) is based on one of his greatest stage successes.

Olivier was knighted in 1947 and created a baron in 1970, the first of his profession to be so honored; in 1963 he became the first head of the British National Theatre, often taking time out to play cameo roles in movies, but he also had the leading parts in **Bunny Lake Is Missing** (1965) and **Sleuth** (1972). After

▼ *Olivier's energy and versatility in his later film roles often impress more than the films themselves. This is a shot from* **Marathon Man** *(1976).*

being forced to give up the theater, he again took leading roles in films, for the money (almost all earlier fees had been ploughed into his theater companies); and if he works non-stop it may be because his prodigious energy is undimmed by old age and many illnesses which might have killed another man. His last cinema film to date is **The Bounty** (1984). He was awarded a special Oscar in 1978.

♥ Married: actress Jill Esmond (1930-40); actress Vivien Leigh (1940-60); actress Joan Plowright (1961).

❝ I think that when Sir Laurence went into the theater, motion pictures lost one of the great romantic stars of our time." – *Alfred Hitchcock.*
"Olivier is the greatest actor in the world." – *Anthony Quinn.*
"Sir Laurence Olivier is one of the most disciplined, prepared, able and intelligent and cooperative actors I have ever worked with. This may well be because he is also a director, and a very good one." – *William Wyler.*
"I consider him, in common with my colleagues, the greatest actor alive." – *Charlton Heston.*

Gregory Peck

🎥 In his time, Gregory Peck was the foremost among his generation of movie stars, in demand at every studio and constantly praised by the press. That was 30 years ago, and he has never lost stardom: but it was clear after a while that he was really only capable of one role.

He was born in La Jolla, California, in 1916, and became an actor after leaving college. The screenwriter Casey Robinson brought him from Broadway to play a Russian guerrilla in **Days of Glory** (1944), but it was Peck's role as a priest in **The Keys of the Kingdom** which made him a star. He had a very good run: **The Valley of Decision** (1945), **Spellbound, The Yearling** (1946), **Duel in the Sun, Gentlemen's Agreement** (1947), **Yellow Sky** (1948), **Twelve O'Clock High** (1949), **The Gunfighter** (1950), in which he gave his best performance,

▲ *Gregory Peck was one of the first stars in the postwar era to cross the Atlantic for a British film, though it has to be acknowledged that* **Captain Horatio Hornblower** *(1951) was produced by the Warner Bros.*

Captain Horatio Hornblower (1951), **David and Bathshebam, The Snows of Kilimanjaro** (1952) and Wyler's **Roman Holiday** (1953).

He received huge fees from Rank, still trying to break into the US market, for two British films, **The Million Pound Note** (1954) and **The Purple Plain**.

Returning to Hollywood, he played, inadequately, Ahab in Huston's **Moby Dick** (1956). He was heavy in a comedy, **Designing Woman** (1957), miscast as Scott Fitzgerald in **Beloved Infidel** (1959), but had big successes with a Western he co-produced with William Wyler (an

association which ended in bitterness), **The Big Country** (1958), and a war movie, **The Guns of Navarone** (1961). He won an Oscar for his portrayal of a liberal lawyer in **To Kill a Mockingbird** (1962), but in the late sixties and seventies was in an almost unbroken run of failures. That was presumably why he made a horror film, **The Omen** (1976), which was a big success. And perhaps it was desperation which made him play his first out-and-out villain, in **The Boys from Brazil** (1978).

♥ Married: Greta Rice (1942-54); French journalist Véronique Passani (1955).

❝ Of all the actors who have been on the screen since movies began I think the three whose faces most express the American ethos are Gary Cooper, Henry Fonda

and Gregory Peck." – *Jeanne Stein.* "I had asked him what he thought of the film [**Beloved Infidel**] and this was his answer: 'I thought I was splendid!'" – *Sheilah Graham.* "But to become a star and to maintain that status over many years are two different things; and to appraise his assets that have made the latter possible is to take a look at the man himself. Solid, kindly, dignified, likable, and somewhat self-effacing, he is at his best in roles that match these qualities. When miscast, he has gone down with a dull thud." – *Casey Robinson.*

Tyrone Power

Tyrone Power was so handsome in youth that it was immaterial whether or not he could act. As he aged his looks began to leave him and the question, unfortunately, began to be asked.

He was born in Cincinnati, Ohio, in 1913 to a theatrical family, and accompanied his father to Hollywood when he was offered film parts; he himself made his movie début in **Tom Brown of Culver** (1932) but got nowhere and went to Broadway. After a test, 20th Century-Fox put him in **Girls' Dormitory** (1936) and he became a star with **Lloyd's of London.** Two films with Alice Faye and Don Ameche consolidated his popularity, **In Old Chicago** (1938) and **Alexander's Ragtime Band;** and although he played in all genres, few of them were demanding: **Marie**

▼ *Fop by day, righter-of-wrongs by night – when masked, that is. Tyrone Power in* **The Mark of Zorro** *(1940).*

Edward G. Robinson

Without conventionally handsome leading-man looks, Edward G. Robinson had only a precarious hold on stardom. The fact that he lasted so long is due to his dynamism, to talent, and probably to the fact that the public sensed a kind man, even under the egregious bad men that he so often played.

He was born in Bucharest, Romania, in 1893 and came to the US as a boy. He studied acting and became a respected stage actor. Apart from **The Bright Shawl** (1923), he made no movies till Talkies caused the demand for trained players. He was the villain in **The Hole in the Wall** (1929) but it wasn't till **Little Caesar** (1930) that everyone sat up: his thinly disguised portrait of gangster Al Capone made him one of the biggest stars on the Warner lot.

He made **Five Star Final** (1931), **Two Seconds** (1932) and **Little Giant** (1933), while in **The Whole Town's Talking** (1935) he had a dual role essaying the two sides of the Robinson screen persona — the vain, bragging gangster and the meek, kindly "little" man. **Bullets or Ballots** (1936), **Kid Galahad** (1937) and a wonderful black comedy, **A Slight Case of Murder** (1938), showed him in familiar style, but he had more challenging roles in **Confessions of a Nazi Spy** (1939), **Dr Ehrlich's Magic Bullet** (1940) and **The Sea Wolf** (1941). Billy Wilder's **Double**

▲ *Tyrone Power and Mai Zetterling in* **Seven Waves Away** *(1957), US title* **Abandon Ship!**

Antoinette, Jesse James (1939), The Rains Came, Johnny Apollo (1940), The Mark of Zorro, Blood and Sand (1941), A Yank in the RAF and The Black Swan (1942).

He spent the war years in the Marines, returning in two serious roles, in **The Razor's Edge** (1946) and **Nightmare Alley** (1947), but it now became imperative to find roles which would hide his limitations; and although he continued to film for Fox till **The Sun Also Rises** (1957) he seldom was assigned the plum roles — and indeed was allowed to do stage work and film elsewhere. Of his late films only **The Eddy Duchin Story** (1956) was very successful, though he was effective in **Witness for the Prosecution** (1958). He died of a heart attack while making **Solomon and Sheba** in 1958.

♥ Married: co-star Annabella (1939-48); Linda Christian (1949-55); Deborah Minardos (1958), who outlived him. Lovers include Sonja Henie, Lana Turner, Judy Garland, Mai Zetterling, Anita Ekberg and others.

“ He quickly matured into a leading man of the classic type — exuding a kind of generalized sex appeal while suggesting no strongly personal traits. He could thus play any part — Western, urban, comic, dramatic — without becoming automatically typed. Yet, because he was a man of intelligence and some sensitivity, he occasionally rose above being a mere leading man and did a bit of acting, notably in **Nightmare Alley.** He had intelligence, adaptability and energy that other leading men — equally reliable — lacked." — *Richard Schickel.*

"A lovely gentleman with a great quality of imagination." — *Myrna Loy.*

▼ *Edward G. as the public preferred him: mobster in* **Little Caesar** *(1930).*

Indemnity (1944), Fritz Lang's **The Woman in the Window** and **Scarlet Street** (1945), Orson Welles' **The Stranger** (1946), John Huston's **Key Largo** (1948) and Wolf Mankiewicz's **House of Strangers** (1949) all found Robinson working with the best directors, but good offers dried up during the Communist witch hunt, although Robinson was cleared of involvement.

Although he appeared with such stars as Alan Ladd, Barbara Stanwyck and Ginger Rogers over the next few years, he himself regarded De Mille's **The Ten Commandments** (1956) as his return to major movies, but despite some good roles — Capra's **A Hole in the Head** (1959), **The Cincinnati Kid** (1965) — the parts began to diminish in importance, though he starred in some undistinguished European films. In 1973 he was awarded an honorary Oscar just a few days after he died; **Soylent Green** was released posthumously.

▼ *Older, wiser and bearded. Edward G. Robinson in his last film,* **Soylent Green** *(1973).*

♥ Married: Gladys Lloyd (1927-56); Jane Adler (1958), who outlived him.

❝ I had the pleasure of directing Mr Robinson in **Little Caesar** and we have been great friends for many years. He is one of the finest actors living, and one of the finest gentlemen it has been my good fortune to know. I cannot say enough about him as an actor or as a person." — *Mervyn LeRoy.*

"I will never forget the pleasure and instruction I derived from working with a true master of his art, such as Edward G. Robinson was — and is. In today's theatrical world, the number of actors who are seriously dedicated are few and far between, and the excellence of an artist of Mr Robinson's stature stands out more than ever. Surely his record for versatility, studied characterization — ranging from the modern colloquial to the classics — and artistic integrity is unsurpassed. Furthermore, everyone who has worked with him recalls with pleasure his considerable personal charm." — *Douglas Fairbanks Jr.*

▲ *The early style Ginger Rogers before she became a star. The movie is* **Young Man of Manhattan** *(1930).*

Ginger Rogers

Sassy, wise-cracking Ginger, Fred Astaire's most famous partner, was born in 1911 in Independence, Missouri, to a mother who pushed her into showbusiness at every opportunity; she became a dancer and was noticed on Broadway by Paramount, who gave her a supporting role in **Young Man of Manhattan** (1930). She was soon freelancing, notably in **42nd Street** (1933) and **Gold Diggers of 1933,** in both as wised-up showgirls. After receiving star billing in **Professional Sweetheart** at RKO, where she remained for a decade, she had only second lead in **Flying Down to Rio,** but she did get to dance with Fred Astaire — and thus achieved real stardom. She made many more movies than he, including some good ones such as **Vivacious Lady** (1938), **Bachelor Mother** (1939), and **Fifth Avenue Girl,** all of which were comedies.

After winning an Oscar for her portrayal of a working-class girl in **Kitty Foyle** (1940) she played more dramatic roles, some at Paramount, where she made **The Major and the Minor** (1942) and **Lady in the Dark** (1944), both with Ray Milland.

Few of her postwar movies were of sufficient caliber to prevent her popularity from fading, but she was boosted by a reunion with Astaire at MGM, **The Barkleys of Broadway** (1949), replacing Judy Garland, who was sick. Later she had some more comedy chances — **We're Not Married** (1952), **Dreamboat** and **The First Traveling Saleslady** (1956), while another, **Oh, Men! Oh, Women!** (1957) finished her screen career. Between appearances on the stage she made two movies hardly ever seen — **Quick, Let's Get Married** (1964, released 1971) with Ray Milland, which her then-husband produced and, replacing Garland, **Harlow** (the Videotape version), as that lady's mother.

▼ *Ginger posing for a publicity shot.*

♥ Married: dancing partner Jack Culpepper (1929-31), but it lasted less than a year; movie star Lew Ayres (1934-41); Marine private Jack Briggs (1943-9); Jacques Bergerac (1953-7), a Frenchman 20 years her junior, whom she turned into an actor; and actor William Marshall (1961) who had earlier been married to French stars Michèle Morgan and Micheline Presle.

The marriage seems to have finished in 1971 and since 1976 Ginger's companion has been Greek-born actor-dancer George Pan, who is about 40 years younger. In the thirties, she had affairs with Howard Hughes and director George Stevens; her name was also linked with Cary Grant, James Stewart, Alfred Gwynne Vanderbilt, Burgess Meredith and lawyer Gregg Bautzer.

“ An impudent young thing, Ginger Rogers, who carries youth and humor to the point where they are completely charming." — *Brooks Atkinson.*

"Ginger was wonderful in that she came to rehearsals, and was agreeable, and she would work hard. She'd do anything you would tell her — until it came time for her to put on the dress. She used to wear dresses that were full of bugle beads that would whip around and smack [Astaire] in the face." — *Hermes Pan.*

Randolph Scott

◄📽 Sunny of countenance and disposition, Randolph Scott was for a while the all-purpose leading man — and one who kept his career alive by specializing in Westerns, where his ease in a saddle or with a gun was pleasing to see: he didn't always smile at the villain but he always routed him.

He was born in Orange County, Virginia, in 1903 and studied engineering, but abandoned it for acting. A chance meeting with Howard Hughes led to a bit role in **The Far Call** (1929) and he was soon playing leads in the B Westerns Paramont made. He was kept as a threat to Gary Cooper and got his best chances romancing Irene Dunne in **Roberta** (1935) and **High, Wide and Handsome** (1937). Starring roles in these and **The Texans** (1938) led to nothing better than playing second fiddle to the likes of Shirley Temple — in **Rebecca of Sunnybrook Farm** — at 20th Century-Fox.

At this studio his best starring roles were in **Western Union** (1941) and

▼ *Randolph Scott in action in one of his innumerable Westerns,* **The Bounty Hunter** *(1954).*

▲ *To begin with Randolph Scott was a leading all-round action man, but later he concentrated on Westerns.*

Norma Shearer

To her millions of fans she was the epitome of chic and, by virtue of her marriage to one of the movies' most powerful moguls, the uncrowned Queen of Hollywood. Her regality should not, however, blind us to the fact that she was an actress of range and sensitivity.

She was born in Montreal in 1904, to a "stage" mother who pushed her towards modeling and extra work in New York. Her first important role was in **The Stealers** (1920) and she played leads and second leads before **He Who Gets Slapped** (1924), which persuaded MGM, who held her contract, that she was star material. In 1927 she married the studio's production chief, Irving Thalberg, who expertly guided her through the Talkie revolution and continued to cast her alternatively as glamorous *femmes du monde* and dewy heroines, in melodramas like **A Free Soul** (1931) and such comedies as **Private Lives.** She won an Oscar for **The Divorcee** (1930).

As "The First Lady of the Screen" it was appropriate that her sometimes

Belle Starr, after which he was teamed with Dietrich and Wayne in **The Spoilers** (1942) and **Pittsburgh,** for Universal. He was excellent in **Corvette K-225** (1943) and **Gung Ho!,** after which, except for **Christmas Eve** (1947), he concentrated on Westerns, chiefly at RKO, Warners and Columbia. His last film was Sam Peckinpah's **Ride the High Country** (1962), in which he played an aging gunman and teamed with Joel McCrea, whose career had paralleled Scott's, except that he was a bigger name before confining himself to Westerns. Another coincidence: they were, due to investments, among the movies' richest men.

♥ Married: Marianna du Pont Somerville (1936-44); Pat Stillman (1944).

❝ Randy Scott is a complete anachronism. He's a gentleman. And so far he's the only one I've met in this business full of self-promoting sons-of-bitches." — *Michael Curtiz.*

"But everything [on **High, Wide and Handsome**] became a little brighter when I got to know Randolph Scott, one of the finest men in Hollywood . . . . Now a retired millionaire, he's still as handsome as he was in 1937, totally charming and loads of fun." — *Dorothy Lamour.*

Norma Shearer, ▼ *sultry and sexy and the happy outdoor girl* ▶. *Her fans adored her sophisticated look.*

PHOTOPLAY

JANUARY
1/6

NORMA SHEARER

THE STORY BEHIND THE
STANWYCK-FAY BREAK-UP
A Great Human Document
By Adela Rogers St. Johns

PERFECT CAMERA FACE
BY DOROTHY SPEARE
A Revealing Novel About
A Star You'll Recognize

rare films were prestige affairs, second only to Garbo's: **Riptide** (1934), **The Barretts of Wimpole Street, Romeo and Juliet** (1936), **Marie Antoinette** (1938), **Idiot's Delight** (1939), **The Women** and **Escape** (1940). Thalberg's death in 1936 had left her in an uneasy situation at the studio and she retired after two successive failures, **We Were Dancing** (1942) and **Her Cardboard Lover.** She died in 1983.

♥ Married: Irving Thalberg (1927) and Martin Arrouge (1942). In 1940 she had been expected to marry George Raft.

❝ **Romeo and Juliet** was very moving — largely due to the acting of Shearer, who turned in a superb potion and death scene. Shearer was no comedienne, but she could reach tragic heights. She did again in **Marie Antoinette.** She enjoyed playing anguish; it exercised all her faculties. She could perform a scene over and over — pouring tears, her eyes like taps .... And she began to pour afresh as she ran back under the hot lights and bathed her face in spouting salt with the vigor of a kill at the tennis court." — *Agnes De Mille.*

"She is an idol, with her talent, her beauty, her glamor, and, more important, her warmth and love as a person. She was responsible for my discovery, she made it possible for me to have a chance: she opened a whole new world for me. I love her." — *Janet Leigh.*

Ann Sheridan

🎥 Ann Sheridan's greatest quality was her warmth. She was publicized as "The Oomph Girl", which hardly admitted her talent, equally at ease in comedy, drama and musicals. She only made a few musicals, which is a pity, since she sang superbly.

She was born in Denton, Texas, in 1915, and arrived at Paramount via a beauty contest, named for her first film, **Search for Beauty** (1934). She had a dozen or so bit parts before Paramount let her go; Warners thought she had something, and in her first films for them she proved she

had the stuff stars are made of, but important movies and/or roles eluded her till she played opposite Cagney in **Angels with Dirty Faces** (1938). Then she made **Torrid Zone** (1940) with him, **They Drive by Night, City for Conquest, King's Row** (1941) and, singing, **Thank Your Lucky Stars** (1943) and **Shine on Harvest Moon** (1944). Not long after carrying two fine melodramas, **Nora Prentiss** (1947) and **The Unfaithful,** she left Warners.

Freelancing began well, with **Good Sam** (1948) opposite Gary Cooper and **I Was a Male War Bride** (1949) with Cary Grant, but her star

The two sides of Ann Sheridan. ▲ *Hollywood style and* ▲ *"sending up" the image in* **The Man Who Came to Dinner** *(1942).*

appeal began to dim quite quickly. She made a half-dozen more films, of which the best was **Come Next Spring** (1956) and the last **Woman and the Hunter** (1957). She died of cancer in 1967.

♥ Married: actors Edward Norris (1936-9); George Brent (1942-3); Scott McKay (1966), who survived her.

"Ann Sheridan, Oomph girl supreme, was also a whoppingly good comedienne, a frequently fine actress and a terrific personality." – *Ray Hagen.*

"The leading lady of **Angels with Dirty Faces** was that lovely, talented gal, Ann Sheridan. So much to offer – and a three-pack-a-day smoker . . . . Years later when the lung cancer hit, she didn't have much of a chance, and what a powerful shame that was. A mighty nice gal, Annie." – *James Cagney.*

"Great . . . . And she outlived some of the worst pictures you've ever known and became good. People liked her. They made her a star in spite of the bad pictures . . . . Oh, she was quick and good and everything." – *Howard Hawks.*

Barbara Stanwyck

Most of the stars of the thirties had their careers nurtured by one studio, but Barbara Stanwyck either freelanced or had commitments with several at the same time. With that independent attitude you had to be both strong and popular to have a long career. Stanwyck was recognized as both – by film-makers, who adored working with her, and cinemagoers, who admired the character she brought to all genres of film.

She was born in Brooklyn in 1907 and became a dancer, which is what she played in "Burlesque", the show that made her a star. She had a supporting role in **Broadway Nights** (1927) and made her Talkie début in her second film, **The Locked Door**

▲ *Barbara Stanwyck, one of the screen's greatest actresses. "Under her sullen shyness smoldered the emotional fires of a young Duse or a Bernhardt."*

(1929). She attained screen stardom playing working women, in Capra's **Ladies of Leisure** (1930), **Ten Cents a Dance** (1931), Capra's **The Miracle Woman, Night Nurse,** Capra's **Forbidden** (1932) and **The Bitter Tea of General Yen** (1933) and **Baby Face.** She settled into a rut until she played **Stella Dallas** (1937), and had further good movies with **The Mad Miss Manton** (1938), **Union Pacific** (1939), **Golden Boy, Remember the Night** (1940), Sturges' **The Lady Eve** (1941) and Capra's **Meet John Doe.**

After magnificent performances as slangy showgirls in **Ball of Fire** (1942) and **Lady of Burlesque** (1943) she was even better as the adulterous wife in **Double Indemnity** (1944), for which she should have won the Oscar. Her best postwar films were mostly meaty melodramas: **The Strange Love of Martha Ivers** (1946), **Sorry Wrong Number**

◄ *Stanwyck's screen career was not enhanced by some B Westerns:* **Cattle Queen of Montana** *(1954), with the man who became President Reagan.*

(1948), **The File on Thelma Jordan** (1949), **The Furies** (1950) and **Clash by Night** (1952). A couple of years later the good offers stopped coming, and she made programmers and minor Westerns, usually yanking them up to her level. After **The Night Walker** (1965) she went into TV, where she found new popularity.

♥ Married: stage star Frank Fay (1928-35); film star Robert Taylor (1939-52).

❝ Destined to be beloved by all directors, actors, crews, and extras. In a Hollywood popularity contest she would win first prize hands down . . . . Under her sullen shyness smoldered the emotional fires of a young Duse or a Bernhardt. Naïve, unsophisticated, caring nothing about makeup, or hairdos, this chorus girl could grab your heart and tear it to pieces. She knew nothing about camera tricks. She just turned it on — and everything else on the stage stopped." – *Frank Capra*.
"I have never worked with an actress who was more cooperative, less temperamental, and a better workman, to use my term of highest compliment, than Barbara Stanwyck. When I count over those [actresses] of whom my memories are unmarred by any unpleasant recollection of friction on the set, or unwillingness to do whatever the role required, or squalls of temperament or temper, Barbara's is the first name that comes to mind." – *Cecil B. De Mille*.

James Stewart

At first, James Stewart was considered a surrogate Gary Cooper, silent and laconic. He quickly developed into a pleasing light comedian because, like Cooper, he gave his lines a distinctive reading. He was very much his own man, which is why he had such a long career — for no player ever really succeeded who was much like another.

He was born in Indiana, Pennsylvania, in 1908, and was studying at Princeton when he met Joshua Logan, who introduced him to summer stock, from whence he moved to Broadway. MGM signed him and he made his feature début in **The Murder Man** (1935). He played

▲ *James Stewart, Cary Grant and Katharine Hepburn in* **The Philadelphia Story** *(1940), for which Stewart won a Best Actor Oscar: it was thought that the award was compensation for not having won with* **Mr Smith Goes to Washington** *(1939).*

second leads until **Born to Dance** (1936), in which he sang "Easy to Love", and then began to get into some excellent films: **Of Human Hearts** (1938), **Vivacious Lady**, Frank Capra's **You Can't Take It With You, Made for Each Other** (1939) and **It's a Wonderful World**. A second film with Capra, **Mr Smith Goes to Washington,** put him into what we would later call the "superstar" bracket, and it was followed by three fine comedies, **Destry Rides Again, The Shop Around the Corner** (1940) and **The Philadelphia Story,** for which he won an Oscar.

Returning from war service he freelanced, starting with his own favorite among his films, Capra's **It's a Wonderful Life** (1947). Other highlights include **Call Northside 777** (1948), Hitchcock's **Rope, Winchester '73** (1950), **Harvey, The Greatest Show on Earth** (1952), **The Glenn Miller Story,** Alfred Hitchcock's **Rear Window** (1954) and **The Man Who Knew Too Much** (1956) and Wilder's **The**

Spirit of St Louis (1957). The latter was unsuccessful, proving that the popularity of the others was only partly due to Stewart's participation. He continued his career by making Westerns and family comedies until a couple of failures sent him into semi-retirement, from which he emerged to make some guest appearances, starting with **The Shootist** (1976).

♥ Married: Gloria McLean (1949).

❝ I adored working with Jimmy. He's such an endearing character, a perfectionist at his job, but with a droll sense of humor and a shy way of watching you to see if you react to that humor." – *Joan Crawford*.
"I sensed the character and rockribbed honesty of a Gary Cooper, plus the breeding and intelligence of an ivy league idealist. One could believe that young Stewart [in **You Can't Take It With You**] could reject his father's patrimony — a kingdom on Wall Street." – *Frank Capra*.

▶ *Stewart in late middle-age, one of the most beloved survivors of Hollywood's golden age. In 1985 he received a second Oscar, in this case in recognition of his long and splendid career – a star for over sixty years.*

◀ *Margaret Sullavan with Richard Carlson in* **Back Street** *(1941). She successfully matched the fine performance by Irene Dunne in the 1932 version.*

Margaret Sullavan

Though Margaret Sullavan's screen personality appealed to everyone — and especially critics — hers could not be considered a successful career: but since she made a high number of fine movies it remains surprising — in these days of re-evaluations — that this delightful and captivating actress is not better known than she is.

She was born in Norfolk, Virginia, in 1911 and after acting at college studied drama. Director John M. Stahl saw her on Broadway and offered her a role in **Only Yesterday** (1933), which typed her as a suffering heroine, but she played these ladies with both lightheartedness and asperity. She was in Frank Borzage's **Little Man What Now?** (1934), William Wyler's **The Good Fairy** (1935) and King Vidor's **So Red the Rose** before making a commitment to MGM, which resulted in Borzage's **Three Comrades** (1938) and **The Mortal Storm** (1940), as well as Ernst Lubitsch's enchanting comedy **The Shop Around the Corner**. If anything, her acting had acquired even more delicacy and grace. After **So Ends Our Night** (1941), **Back Street** and **Cry Havoc** (1943) she returned yet again to the stage, making only one more film, **No Sad Songs for Me** (1950).

Her dislike of Hollywood and filming had caused her to be labeled temperamental, and there were perhaps few movie offers again. In 1960 she committed suicide, probably because deafness prevented her from continuing her career — though her daughter's memoir emphasized that that was always secondary to her home life.

♥ Married: Henry Fonda (1931-3); William Wyler (1934-6); agent and producer Leland Hayward (1936-47), by whom she had three children, including Brooke, who wrote a book on the disintegrating marriage; British businessman Kenneth Wagg (1950), who outlived her.

❝ A special dream princess." — *Herman J. Mankiewicz.* "With those enormous moonstone gray eyes, the enchanting, guileless smile, darkish blonde hair, and that voice murmuring in the lower register and then breaking crazily in the middle register, she projected a certain vitality from the screen, a rare ability to impart flesh to a role, a fascinating image. Star quality. You could place Maggie, who exuded a rare kind of sensuous innocence, in the category with Janet Gaynor, Jean Arthur, Olivia de Havilland, Grace Kelly." — *Maurice Zolotow.*

▼ *Sullavan the enchantress. Although she made comparatively few movies, many of them are among the treasures of cinema history.*

Robert Taylor

Even more than Errol Flynn and Tyrone Power — his rivals at other studios — Robert Taylor found that his looks were his passport to fame and fortune. Like them, he had a certain buoyancy in youth, but as he aged he was duller.

He was born in Filley, Nebraska, in 1911, and after acting as an amateur, began to study drama; an MGM talent scout saw him on the stage and brought him to the studio where he would remain for two decades, although his movie début was in **Handy Andy** (1934), while on loan to Fox. Another loan-out, for **Magnificent Obsession** (1935), made him a star, and then MGM featured him opposite most of their leading women stars, including Garbo in **Camille** (1936) and Margaret

▶ *Magazines such as* Photoplay *featured stars like Jean Harlow for their avid readers. They also adored Robert Taylor, her co-star in* **Personal Property** *(1937).* ▼ *Here he is later, in* **The Law and Jake Wade** *(1958) with Richard Widmark.*

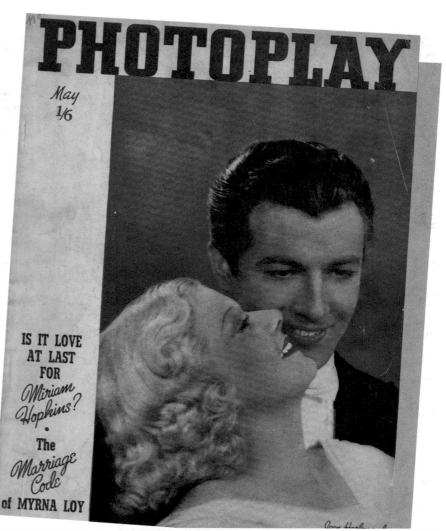

PHOTOPLAY

May 1/6

IS IT LOVE AT LAST FOR *Miriam Hopkins?*

The *Marriage Code* of MYRNA LOY

Sullavan in **Three Comrades** (1938). **Waterloo Bridge** (1940), with Vivien Leigh, was his own favorite film.

Like Power, he did not project a deeply virile image, and male spectators did not overly care for him in **Billy the Kid** (1941), **Johnny Eager, Stand By for Action** (1943) and **Bataan**. After **Song of Russia** (1944) he went off to fight, returning to the screen in **Undercurrent** (1946) opposite Katharine Hepburn, in his first "villainous" role. Two epics, **Quo Vadis** (1951) and **Ivanhoe** (1952), somewhat shored up his diminishing box-office luster, and MGM continued to give him top production values; but apart from **The Adventures of Quentin Durward** (1955) the films are not memorable.

His career had been prolonged (like many others) by making Westerns: after **Saddle the Wind** (1958) and **The Law and Jake Wade** there was another gangster thriller, **Party Girl,** after which MGM let him go. It was cold outside, and after some program movies Taylor was reduced to making routine action movies in Europe. He died of cancer in 1969, aged 58.

♥ Married: Barbara Stanwyck (1939-52); actress Ursula Theiss (1954), who outlived him.

❝ I had no trouble at all with him. He did everything I asked him to; he was wonderful . . . . I have never gotten along with actors. Oh, Joel McCrea was all right. And, like I said, Bob Taylor I was very fond of." — *William A. Wellman.*

Shirley Temple

The little moppet was not to everyone's taste and she herself has hinted that her stardom was an aberration — that the audiences of the Depression years found new hope in this optimistic tot. There were other child stars more talented, but few with so robust a personality. Those who adored her did so to a phenomenal degree, and there were millions of them, for she outstripped even Clark Gable's drawing power for a while.

She was born in 1928 in Santa Monica, to a mother determined that she should be in movies, and so she was, not too long after she could walk. She starred in several shorts, and once in the casting books began to get work in features, the first of which seems to have been **The Red-Haired Alibi** (1932); she attracted attention with her one song in **Stand Up and Cheer** (1934) at Fox, which put her under contract. **Little Miss Marker,** at Paramount, gave her a large role, and **Bright Eyes,** in which she sang "On the Good Ship Lollipop", made her a star.

Her vehicles were chiefly sentimental, and often concerned with showbusiness so that she could display her very ordinary talents as singer and dancer: the best of them

Shirley Temple was one of the few bright spots of the Depression years.
▲ **The Littlest Rebel** *(1935) and* **The Sound of Laughter** ▶ *were two of her greatest movie releases. She left show-business to pursue a successful political career and remains a popular celebrity.* ▶

are **Stowaway** (1936), **Wee Willie Winkie** (1937), **Heidi, Rebecca of Sunnybrook Farm** (1938) and **The Little Princess** (1939). Her boss, Darryl F. Zanuck, refused to loan her to MGM for **The Wizard of Oz,** and then tried to out-wizard the wizard with **The Blue Bird** (1940). It was a box-office failure, as was **Young People.**

The public's swift desertion of Temple may be due to the fact that as she approached adolescence she simply wasn't in the same league as Judy Garland and Deanna Durbin. Zanuck let Temple go, so she did minor films for MGM and United Artists; Selznick launched her as a teenager in **Since You Went Away** (1944), but she retired when that contract ended, with **The Story of Seabiscuit** (1949). She had retained star billing, but when she played the lead the films were uninteresting; otherwise she supported other players, as in **The Bachelor and the Bobby Soxer** (1947) and **Fort Apache** (1948). Ten years later she appeared in some TV series before turning to politics.

♥ Married: John Agar (1945-9); Charles Black (1950).

66 Shirley Temple was difficult. I used to have to go down to Palm Beach to coach her, and she'd get involved in a badminton game with me, and her father would call her and she'd say 'I'm not ready and *I'll* tell you when I'm ready. *I* earn all the money in this household'. Of course she's a different type of person now." – *Jule Styne*.

"As frequently as I have seen little Miss Temple, I find myself still unreconciled upon approaching her latest vehicle. Yet so amazing is the talent and persuasiveness of the most famous of baby actresses that each time I am slowly won over by her remarkable expertness and filled with admiration." – *Richard Watts Jr.*

Spencer Tracy

 The adulation accorded Tracy by his peers and reviewers is due to a screen presence that was massive but not due to obvious tricks or techniques. The greatness of Laurence Olivier and Charles Laughton as screen performers is due in part to their chameleon-like ability to change temperament and appearance, but Tracy attained his always-high reputation while being much the same – a decent working man, with streaks of rueful humor and Irish stubbornness in his character.

He was born in Milwaukee, Wisconsin, in 1900 and studied acting

after college. Though a Broadway star by 1929, no studio thought him film material until director John Ford put him into **Up the River** (1930) at Fox, which recognized his potential but didn't know what to do with him, so they made him a gangster in **Quick Millions** (1931). Although he had the firm personality of Cagney and Gable, he lacked their sex appeal, and his unsatisfying Fox period includes few grade A movies: **Me and My Gal** (1932) as a cop; **20,000 Years in Sing Sing** (1932) at Warners, as a convict; **The Power and the Glory** (1933) as a tycoon;

▲ *Spencer Tracy in the first of his teamings with Katharine Hepburn,* **Woman of the Year** *(1942).*
▲ *Tracy was much admired by his peers. This is his last film* **Guess Who's Coming to Dinner?** *(1967).*

Man's Castle at Columbia, as a derelict. Fox then dropped him and he went to MGM, playing opposite Jean Harlow in **Riff Raff** (1935).

His career took off with Fritz Lang's **Fury** (1936), **San Francisco,** the comedy **Libeled Lady** and **Captains Courageous**

(1937), for which his portrayal of a Portuguese fisherman won him his first Oscar. He won another for **Boys' Town** (1938), playing a priest; and made impressive appearances in **Stanley and Livingstone** (1939), **Northwest Passage** (1940), **Edison the Man** and **Dr Jekyll and Mr Hyde** (1941). Apart from Zinnemann's **The Seventh Cross** (1944) and Vincente Minnelli's **Father of the Bride** (1950), his other good movies of this time were all with Katharine Hepburn, when their contrasting personalities clashed, but harmoniously: the best of these were George Stevens' **Woman of the Year** (1942), Frank Capra's **State of the Union** (1948) and George Cukor's **Adam's Rib** (1949). Cukor also directed **The Actress** (1953) which, with John Sturges' **Bad Day at Black Rock** (1955), make up the two outstanding movies of Tracy's last MGM years.

MGM found him increasingly un-reasonable and he was fired from **Tribute to a Bad Man;** freelancing, he did a wonderful job in Ford's **The Last Hurrah** (1958), and gave impeccable performances for producer-director Stanley Kramer in four movies, two of which are halfway decent: **Judgment at Nuremberg** (1961) and **Guess Who's Coming to Dinner?** (1967), which was released posthumously.

 Married: Louise Treadwell (1928), but they separated in 1934 when he fell in love with movie star Loretta Young; as Catholics they never divorced. His friendship with Katharine Hepburn began in 1941.

" If I am to be remembered for anything I have done in this profession, I would like it to be for the four films in which I directed Spencer Tracy." – *Stanley Kramer.*
"Spencer does it, that's all. Feels it. Says it. Talks. Listens. He means what he says when he says it, and if you think that's easy, try it." – *Humphrey Bogart.*
"You know, Spence was a great artist. I think I'm a good artist. But he was in a class almost by himself. A consummate artist, his criticism was always brilliant." – *Katharine Hepburn.*

Lana Turner

Lana Turner's love life, if we are to believe the tabloids, has been colorful, which is more than can be said for her presence on screen, though as a young woman she had blonde good looks and a certain teas-ing quality which made her an ideal partner for Clark Gable. Had she been at some lesser studio, they would probably have put her, dubbed, into undemanding musicals, but MGM had enough talented singers: at times, in drama, her limitations were cruelly exposed, yet at the same time MGM's expertise in showcasing their glamorous ladies – and they had no one else at this time quite so sexy – was so sure that she remained a star, even after that essential youthful bloom had faded.

▶ *Who could ever forget Lana when she looked like this?*

She was born in Wallace, Idaho, in 1921, and as a teenager living in Los Angeles got a series of interviews which led to the director Mervyn Le Roy, who made her the murder victim in **They Won't Forget** (1937). He took her with him when he moved from Warners to MGM, who gave her progressively larger roles, until she starred in **Ziegfeld Girl** (1941) and **Dr Jekyll and Mr Hyde.** She appeared opposite Gable in **Honky Tonk** and **Somewhere I'll Find You** (1942), Robert Taylor in **Johnny Eager** (1941), John Garfield in **The Postman Always Rings Twice** (1946) and Spencer Tracy in **Cass Timberlane** (1947), but she did not distinguish herself as Milady in **The Three Musketeers** (1948) or as the new **The Merry Widow** (1952). Indeed, MGM found few takers for her talents if her co-star wasn't right,

▲ *Lana Turner and John Garfield in* **The Postman Always Rings Twice** *(1946), perhaps the best of her not very memorable films.*

John Wayne

 The screen's great cowboy was far more versatile than he often seemed. We all have an image of John Wayne — a leathery individualist, courteous towards women, scornful of fools, slow to anger but quick to action when roused, good humored: but to this basic character he could, when required, add arrogance, fanaticism, sarcasm and obtuseness. And we still loved him, to the extent that he was a bigger box-office draw, and for longer, than anyone else.

He was born in Winterset, Iowa, in 1907 and entered movies as a prop man at Fox. Almost immediately, director John Ford gave him a walk-on in **Hangman's House** (1928) and after a few more small roles Ford recommended him for the lead in **The Big Trail** (1930), but its failure condemned Wayne to several years of supporting roles or starring in B Westerns until Ford made one of the few big-budget Westerns of the time, **Stagecoach** (1939). For Ford, Wayne did **The Long Voyage Home** (1940) and **They Were Expendable** (1945), for De Mille **Reap the Wild Wind** (1942), and he teamed well with Dietrich in **Seven Sinners** (1940), **The Spoilers** (1942) and **Pittsburgh;** but Wayne's other movies, chiefly Westerns and war tales, usually for RKO and Republic, did not create much stir.

He became a box-office star with Hawks' **Red River** (1948) and with

and she left them after **Diane** (1956).

As a freelance she was in three soap opera successes, **Peyton Place** (1957) as a frigid mother, **Imitation of Life** (1959) and **Portrait in Black** (1960), but few of her subsequent films rated much attention, including the last to date, **Bittersweet Love** (1976). In recent years she has done stage work.

♥ Married: bandleader Artie Shaw (1940-1), after they had appeared in the same film; Stephen Crane (1942-4); Bob Topping (1948-52); actor Lex Barker (1953-7); Fred May (1960-2); Robert Eaton (1965-9), 10 years her junior, "after five husbands and a few lovers, I finally experienced passion for the first time"; hypnotist Ronald Dante

(1969), but it lasted for only a few months.

Lovers include lawyer Greg Bautzer; Howard Hughes; actor Turhan Bey; Tyrone Power; John Alden Talbot Jr (whose wife named her as co-respondent); actor Fernando Lamas (who married two other Metro ladies, Arlene Dahl and Esther Williams); gangster Johnny Stompanato, who was stabbed to death in 1958 by Lana's daughter Cheryl.

❝ The real Lana Turner everyone knows about. She always wanted to be a Movie Star, and loved being one. Her personal life and her Movie Star life are one." – *Adela Rogers St Johns.*
"Even her admirers would admit that she can't act her way out of a paper bag." – *David Shipman.*

▼ *John Wayne in* **Stagecoach** *(1939), which made him a star after years of playing the lead in low-budget Westerns.*

Sands of Iwo Jima (1949); the association with Ford was renewed with **Fort Apache** (1948), **Three Godfathers, She Wore a Yellow Ribbon** (1949), **Rio Grande** (1950) and **The Quiet Man** (1952) – all classics, though only the last-named was greatly successful at the time.

Wayne signed a non-exclusive deal and was his own producer for many subsequent films: **Hondo** (1953), **The High and the Mighty** (1954), Ford's **The Searchers** (1956) and **Wings of Eagles** (1957), Huston's **The Barbarian and the Geisha** (1958), **The Alamo** (1960), which Wayne also directed, Hathaway's **The Sons of Katie Elder** (1965) and Hawks' **El Dorado** (1967). Wayne won an Oscar for his grand performance of the "ornery" one-eyed sheriff in **True Grit** (1969), by now a mythic figure in American cinema. Mark Rydell cleverly used him as such in **The Cowboys** (1972), but most of Wayne's movies were formula action stuff, and they eventually began to fail at the box office. The obvious wig and the paunch didn't help; but he played a man of his own age in his last film **The Shootist** (1976), as a cowboy dying of cancer, as he was himself. He died in 1979.

♥ Married: Josephine Saenz (1933-44); Esperanza Baur (1946-53); Pilar Pallette (1954), but this marriage didn't last. All were from south of the border. Baur named the actress Gail Russell in her divorce suit; one of his secretaries wrote a book claiming a seven-year relationship.

❝ A recent poll showed that more people recognized John Wayne's name and face than any other man in US history except Abraham Lincoln." – *Jim Beaver.*
"Wayne endures and is here to stay whether he is wanted or not; a dubious American hero but undoubtedly a remarkable screen presence." – *Graham Fuller.*
"How can I hate John Wayne upholding Goldwater and yet love him tenderly when abruptly he takes

▶ *Wayne is associated with the Western more than any other leading player. He is seen here in one of the best of his late Westerns,* **The Sons of Katie Elder** *(1965).*

Natalie Wood into his arms in the last reel of **The Searchers**?" — *Jean-Luc Godard*.

"He is as tough as an old nut and as soft as a yellow ribbon." — *Elizabeth Taylor*.

Orson Welles

Orson Welles directed two magnificent films at the start of his screen career and was an actor of force and subtlety, but at some point he decided to take the money and run. That's all very well, but not only were the films he appeared in seldom up to much, his own performances were also decidedly amateur. As he said himself, he started at the top and worked his way down.

He was born in Kenosha, Wisconsin, in 1915 and in 1931 bluffed his way into acting at the Gate Theatre, Dublin; in New York he made such a name for himself in radio and theater that RKO gave him a *carte blanche* contract, in the hope that he would come up with something equally sensational. He did: **Citizen Kane** (1941), with himself as a press tycoon

▲ *Orson Welles, seen here with Everett Sloane and Joseph Cotten, in* **Citizen Kane** *(1941).*

based on William Randolph Hearst. The RKO agreement did not work out, and after directing **The Magnificent Ambersons** (1942) and appearing in his own production **Journey into Fear** (1943) he was a powerful Mr Rochester in **Jane Eyre**

(1944) for 20th Century-Fox. He appeared in **Tomorrow Is Forever** (1946) and directed and starred in three movies with uneven results: **The Stranger, The Lady from Shanghai** (1948) and a dreadful **Macbeth**.

▼ *The genius and the beauty; Orson Welles and his then wife, Rita Hayworth, in 1948.*

He retreated to Europe – and Africa – to make **Othello** (1952), which was partly financed from his earnings from acting, as were **Confidential Report** (1955) and the best of the later films he directed, **Chimes at Midnight** (as Falstaff) (1966); a number of other projects were abandoned when funds were not forthcoming, and he also directed **Touch of Evil** (1958). His Harry Lime in Reed's **The Third Man** (1949) is his most polished screen acting after **Kane,** but perhaps the only other Welles films to see are **Prince of Foxes,** Hathaway's **The Black Rose** (1950), **Moby Dick** (1956), **The Long Hot Summer** (1958), **Compulsion** (1959), **Is Paris Burning?** (1966), **A Man for All Seasons** and **Catch-22** (1970). Much of his work has been in Europe; his last film to date is **Voyage of the Damned** (1976).

Married: Virginia Nicholson (1934-40); Rita Hayworth (1943-7); Paola Mori (1956). Lovers include Dolores del Rio (c. 1940).

It's like meeting God without dying." – *Dorothy Parker.*
"It never occurs to him that there is any solution other than his own. Despite yourself, you find yourself accepting this notion." – *Herman J. Mankiewicz.*
"Awesome Orson, the self-styled genius." – *Louella Parsons.*
"An active loafer, a wise madman." – *Jean Cocteau.*

Mae West

Mae West didn't invent sex, she re-invented it. She was not the first female movie star to show an overwhelming yen for men, but she was the first to do it so blatantly and with a sense of humor – speaking lines she had written for herself. If we regard her sexual witticisms and innuendos, her hourglass figure, her way of walking and surveying men – the *tout ensemble* – we may say that she invented herself.

▶ *Mae West in* **I'm No Angel** *(1933) with Cary Grant, who obviously has not thought twice about coming up to see her.*

She was born in 1892 in Brooklyn, New York, and had so much aplomb as a child that she was a seasoned stage performer before she reached her teens. She gained such notoriety as both actress and dramatist that Hollywood looked askance until George Raft asked Paramount to put her into **Night After Night** (1932). Under contract, she made **She Done Him Wrong** (1933), based on her play "Diamond Lil", and the receipts saved the studio from bankruptcy. After, and because of, **I'm No Angel,** the Production Code was tightened, and the dialogue she wrote was progressively less risqué through **Belle of the Nineties** (1934), **Going to Town** (1935) and **Klondike Annie** (1936).

Two last movies for the studio are poor, and there is little to be said for **My Little Chickadee** (1940), despite the teaming with W. C. Fields, or **The Heat's On** (1943). Hollywood had finished with Mae, but appearances in the flesh kept her very famous: she deigned to return in **Myra Breckinridge** (1970), but playing a bride in **Sextette** (1978) was a mistake. She died in 1980.

Married: Frank Wallace (1911-43), but it lasted only weeks. Although in her memoir she boasted innumerable lovers, one biographer suggested that she actually hated to be even touched. Longtime companions were legal advisor James A. Timony, for 30 years, and muscleman Paul Novak, for the last 26 years of her life.

She is an earthquake, a tornado, an admirable scourge, a sky-rocket, a liberating explosion." – *Ado Kyrou.*
"Only Charlie Chaplin and Mae West in Hollywood dare to directly attack with their mockery the graying morals and manners of a dreary world." – *Hugh Walpole.*
"No doubt she observed the female impersonator and, spontaneously imitating him, extracted for herself all his comedy, leaving him to his pathos. In effect, she expunged the *burlesque* quality from his active masquerade of the female sex." – *Parker Tyler.*
"Is it not time Congress did something about Mae West?" – *William Randolph Hearst.*

The Studios' Last Stars

Although European cinema experienced a new boom in the postwar years, this was not so in Hollywood. Despite the determination of war veterans in the industry to make more responsible films, somehow — with one exception, **The Best Years of Our Lives** (1946) — these were never made. But what they wanted above all was a change in the old Hollywood system towards greater independence for themselves. After all, the three greatest-ever box-office hits, **Gone With the Wind** (1939), **The Best Years of Our Lives** and **The Bells of St Mary's** (1945), were made independently of the big studios.

Breaking the studio system

The new attitude was shared by different branches of the film world. David O. Selznick, the producer of **Gone With the Wind**, had a number of stars under contract whom he didn't use since he produced so few films; instead he hired them out at a profit. For example, from the $200 000 he might receive for loaning out Ingrid Bergman, he would pay her the contracted fee of $70 000 — and pocket the remainder himself.

Stars, too, had begun to demand greater freedom. When James Stewart returned from the war he abandoned MGM, where he had risen to stardom, in favor of a freelance career. And when one studio, Universal, was unable to pay his full fee, Stewart negotiated with them a profit-sharing deal. This was not the first example of such an arrangement,

Jean Simmons and Marlon Brando in the musical **Guys and Dolls** *(1955). Famous now, it received only reasonable reviews on release.*

but it did set a noticeable trend. Stars wanted more choice in the roles they accepted and the studios they worked for, especially if this meant higher earnings.

Crisis for Hollywood

Universal and RKO welcomed independents inside their studios; United Artists, which — by virtue of its charter to help directors make their own films — should have done also, was instead caught up helplessly in the fighting between its administrators, Mary Pickford and Charlie Chaplin. The remaining major studios were simply determined to grant as little freedom as possible.

Of the new postwar companies which attempted to allow greater independence (including Enterprise, which had looked set to become a major studio) almost all failed and had to close. The studio executives had been proved right — but they could not afford to sit back and relax. The film business was soon facing its worst crisis since the coming of the Talkies. The studios could no longer enforce the showing of their films in their own cinema chains. Profits dropped and consequently the Hollywood companies were forced to look more closely at their overheads.

Star salaries and contracts appeared in a new light. What was the point of employing one actress at $7000 a week if the studio could pay a freelancer a single lump sum of $150 000 for a whole movie, especially if the freelancer was a much better known box-office star?

TV threat

The rise of television, however, was much more threatening than the loss of guaranteed bookings and rising overheads. At first the industry

▲ *Surrounded by the kind of mystique not witnessed since after the death of Valentino, James Dean, in a career which spanned only three films, became the personification of a generation.*

refused to take the new medium seriously, but by the early fifties it had to face up to the fact that the public preferred to stay at home watching lousy television instead of venturing out to watch movies.

The film moguls resorted to new technical devices to lure back the missing crowds. Oddly enough, the audiences of the thirties had disliked the early Technicolor feature films, which had been slow to catch on, but by the fifties musicals and costume epics, and soon Westerns and comedies, were all being shown in glorious Technicolor.

Typically, MGM was among the last of the studios to abandon faith in the old star system. It snapped up Glenn Ford and Doris Day when they were free, and was still fashioning star films for them and for its own Debbie Reynolds as late as the early sixties. Universal also kept a stable of promising players until 1960, when it, too, finally changed its policy.

During the early sixties, scripts with good roles for actresses were offered successively to a handful of stars — Marilyn Monroe, Shirley MacLaine, Audrey Hepburn and Elizabeth Taylor — since the female field had virtually narrowed down to these few. The studios preferred using home-bred stars to some of the European actresses imported to America after achieving fame in their own countries. As a result, most foreign actresses returned home after just one film. It seemed, after all, that

opportunities were often greater in Germany, France and Italy than in America, where TV now reigned.

The sixties also saw American companies beginning to film overseas. Although most retained their studio premises, location shooting became the custom, breathing new life into the flagging industry.

New directions

American film acting received a much-needed shot in the arm with the advent of Marlon Brando, but film plots and filming techniques were still lagging behind European cinema, which was much more sophisticated. But gradually, methods of filming and story-telling were influenced by France's New Wave. France also boasted a new and potent attraction in Brigitte Bardot, who proved that sex appeal didn't need the backing of English-speaking studios to hit the box-office jackpot.

The lifting of America's Production Code enabled Hollywood to join the bandwagon and produce "sexploitation" movies. When in 1968 the Code was finally abandoned, there was a spate of sexually explicit films.

The period of transition

Few of the fifties film stars, like their predecessors of the thirties, had any extensive experience of the stage or of drama school. But unlike the older generation, these players had not had the opportunity to learn how to act in front of the camera before they became stars. Only a few, therefore, had any real staying power, which is why this section omits Glenn Ford, Debbie Reynolds, William Holden and other box-office stars of the time who have since lost our affection.

However, a number of stars are included in the following pages — the "executive" stars, including Kirk Douglas and Burt Lancaster, who became their own producers and extended their careers by getting first-rate film makers to fashion star vehicles for them. Even today, some are still making valuable contributions to films. They arrived in Hollywood when the big studios prevailed, and proved themselves stronger than the system.

▶ *The one and only Brigitte Bardot who, single-handedly, was responsible for the popularization of the French movie.*

▲ *The "sex kitten" Brigitte Bardot starring as a revolutionary in the much publicized* **Viva Maria!** *(1965), set in Central America.*

Brigitte Bardot

France's sex kitten, pouting, giggling and displaying her neat little body, did more than anyone else to open the US market to foreign-language films; and as an early example of the new permissiveness she was influential in Hollywood throwing out its old censorship rules.

Brigitte Bardot was born in Paris in 1934 and was modeling when she married Roger Vadim, assistant to director Marc Allégret. She made her début in **Crazy for Love** (1952) and slowly advanced to stardom: the film that made her was a vehicle Vadim constructed for her, a steamy tale set in St Tropez, **And God Created Woman** (1956). She became the most famous woman in France, but **The Truth** (1960) did not, as anticipated, establish her as a serious actress.

The most successful of her other movies in the international market were the cruelly autobiographical **A Very Private Affair** (1962) and the much-publicized co-starring stint with France's other sex symbol, Jeanne Moreau, in **Viva Maria!** (1965), both directed by Louis Malle. She turned down many American offers, but played herself in cameo in a James Stewart vehicle, **Dear Brigitte;** and as Bardolatry was dying, made **Shalako** (1968), with Sean Connery. She had not enjoyed her career and

Anne Bancroft

Anne Bancroft, a stylish and elegant actress, reversed the standard movie pattern by going from failure to success. She was born in the Bronx, New York, in 1931, and studied acting. A TV appearance brought a contract from 20th Century-Fox, who featured her in **Don't Bother to Knock** (1952). She had leads in another dozen movies of little distinction, and eventually returned to New York, where she became a star in two plays by William Gibson, "Two for the Seesaw" and "The Miracle Worker" — in the latter as Helen Keller's teacher. She won an Oscar for her repeat in the movie version (1962) and has filmed occasionally since, appearing most notably in: **The Pumpkin Eater** (1964), **The Slender Thread** (1965), **The Graduate** (1967), **The Prisoner of Second Avenue** (1975), **The Turning Point** (1977), **The Elephant Man** (1979) and **To Be or Not to Be**

▲ *Anne Bancroft is a fine actress first, a star second. Her greatest roles have been in* **The Pumpkin Eater** *(1962),* **The Turning Point** *(1977) and here as Mrs Robinson in* **The Graduate** *(1967).*

(1983), co-starring in the last-named with her husband Mel Brooks.

♥ Married: real-estate man Martin May (1953-7); screenwriter, director and actor Mel Brooks (1964).

❝ Anne Bancroft burns with a black flame as Mrs Robinson [in **The Graduate**], and succeeds in making this outré Fury nearly human and believable." *— John Simon.*
"Anne Bancroft is a great screen actress, one of the very best, yet she has not become a major movie star because she has chosen to remain a character actress rather than a personality." *— Ken Wlaschin.*

there was at least one suicide attempt; and she refused all offers after **L'Histoire Très Bonne et Très Joyeuse de Colinot Trousse-Chemise** (1973), to devote herself to animal causes.

♥ Married: director Roger Vadim (1952-7); actor Jacques Charrier (1959-62); German executive Gunther Sachs von Opel (1966-9). Lovers include actor Jean-Louis Trintignant, actor Sami Frey (c.1961), Alain Carré, actor Gustavo Rojo, singer Gilbert Bécaud, tennis-player Jean-Noel Grinda, singer Sacha Distel, nightclub owner Luigi Rizzi, Bob Zaguri, Mike Sarne, Patrick Gilles, publisher Michel Engel, part-time barman/ski instructor Christian Kalt, Laurent Vergez and artist Miroslav Brozek.

❝ Her attitude toward sex (both in films and out) was said to be symptomatic and symbolic of the times. Marilyn Monroe was merely a tease, it was suggested, while Brigitte Bardot was the real thing. *She* frankly enjoyed sex, and no double standard for her either." – *Hollis Alpert.*
"In France today, we have too many Bardots. We have big Bardots and small Bardots, fat Bardots and thin Bardots — and they all pout. But still there is only one Bardot. She has something of her own. She was born Bardot." – *Françoise Rosay.*
"She eats when she is hungry and she makes love in the same matter-of-fact manner." – *Simone de Beauvoir.*

Marlon Brando

Marlon Brando changed the course of American acting. It wasn't merely that for a while he played slobs or rebels, but that he played different sorts of slobs and rebels, with infinite shadings and an ability to change moods more quickly and completely than any actor before him. Like Olivier, he *dared,* but it

▲ *Brando, Mark I: rebel and outsider. Here he is as the motor-cycle gang leader in* **The Wild One** *(1954).*

could not be said that all of his later attempts at versatility were entirely successful.

He was born in Omaha, Nebraska, in 1924, studied at the Actors' Studio and became its most famous alumnus. After several Broadway roles he made his reputation under Elia Kazan's direction in Tennessee Williams' "A Streetcar Named Desire", and they reprised the role on screen in 1951; Brando had already

made his screen début as a paraplegic veteran in Zinnemann's **The Men** (1950). For a while everything he undertook was memorable: Kazan's **Viva Zapata!** (1952), Mankiewicz's **Julius Caesar** (1953) as Mark Antony, and Kazan's **On the Waterfront** (1954). He was Napoleon in **Desirée** (1954), a singing Runyon type in **Guys and Dolls** (1955), a Japanese villager in **The Teahouse of the August Moon** (1956), an American officer in **Sayonara** (1957), a German one in **The Young Lions** (1958) and one of Williams' drifters in **The Fugitive Kind** (1960).

Brando directed himself in a Western, **One-Eyed Jacks** (1961), and gained a reputation for temperament and extravagance while making **Mutiny on the Bounty** (1962), though not all admired his foppish Fletcher Christian. His best work during the next decade was as the closet homosexual in Huston's **Reflections in a Golden Eye** (1967), and he was badly in need of a success when he played the title role in Coppola's **The Godfather** (1972), for which he was voted a second Oscar (the first was for **On the**

▼ *Brando, Mark II: Oscar-lauded and Establishment actor as the Mafia leader in* **The Godfather** *(1972).*

Waterfront). In his subsequent films his performances have been needlessly self-indulgent: **Last Tango in Paris** (1972), **The Missouri Breaks** (1976), **Superman** (1978), **Apocalypse Now** (1979) and **The Formula** (1980).

♥ Married: Anna Kashfi (1957-9); Movita Castenada (1960-8); has two children (1961, 1970) by Taritatumi Terripia. Has admitted to affairs with men.

66 Their [method actors] godhead, the remarkably gifted Marlon Brando, may bring (as all true stars do) his own personal magnetism to every part, but his scope and projection are unarguable. He has always transcended the techniques he was taught. His consequent glamor and style have nothing to do with self-involvement but rather radiation." − *Bette Davis.*
"Marlon Brando is an exceptionally good actor. He has a quality, a personality that is indefinable. You talk to him − great charm. Great naïveté, I think. Talent coming out of the seams. There were a lot of things he did that I didn't like − but, you know, they came off one hundred per cent." − *Charlie Chaplin.*
"I thought Brando's performance as Fletcher Christian was horrible. I've only seen him act once, and that was on Broadway in "A Streetcar Named Desire", a marvelous performance. But he was never an actor before and hasn't been one since." − *Lewis Milestone.*
"The pressure was incredible. Paramount acted like **The Godfather** was the first movie ever being made. And do you know who was the greatest tension reliever of all? Brando. The guy was fantastic." − *James Caan.*

Richard Burton

Whether it was the booze, fame or his love life, Richard Burton did little actual acting on screen. He had presence, he had a magnificent voice and, when young, looks, but he never troubled to stun us with either versatility or the likable personality of a Gable or Cooper.

He was born in Pontrhydfen, Wales in 1925, into a mining family, but a

▲ *Richard Burton as the centurion with Jean Simmons in* **The Robe** *(1953), the first film made in CinemaScope.*

teacher directed him towards a stage career. His first appearance was in a play by Emlyn Williams, who later gave Burton his first film chance, **The Last Days of Dolwyn** (1949). He was making a reputation as a classical actor when 20th Century-Fox took him to Hollywood to play opposite Olivia de Havilland in **My Cousin Rachel** (1952), but the films which followed, including the first in CinemaScope, **The Robe** (1953), were poor. He was **Alexander the Great** (1956) and Jimmy Porter in his best film, **Look Back in Anger** (1959), in Britain.

His movie following was minute when Fox asked him back to play Mark Antony opposite Elizabeth Taylor's **Cleopatra** (1963) and their consequent love affair made him a box-office star: **The VIPs, Becket** (1964), **The Night of the Iguana, The Spy Who Came in From the Cold** (1965), **Who's Afraid of Virginia Woolf?** (1966) and **The Taming of the Shrew** (1967) provided an interesting run, but some

disasters followed, and the situation was compounded by the high, and absurd, profile carried by Burton and Taylor. The enormous salary demands tapered off after he played Henry VIII in **Anne of the Thousand Days** (1969), the last of his films to enjoy much success, apart from **The Wild Geese** (1978). His

▼ *Burton once again in ancient Rome, but promoted to general – Mark Antony in* **Cleopatra** *(1963), with Elizabeth Taylor.*

last film was **1984,** made in that year, just before his death.

♥ Married: Sybil Williams (1949-63); Elizabeth Taylor (1964-74 and 1975, for a matter of months); Susan Hunt (1976-82); Sally Hay (1983), who survived him. Boasted of seducing all his leading ladies, but at least one — Olivia de Havilland — disliked him.

❝ Richard Burton tends to give cleverly externalized performances in which a nice overlay of melancholy is shot through by flashes of something or other. Here [in **The Taming of the Shrew**] we are treated to the obverse: instead of the customarily weary and sullen Burton, we get an infantile, bellowing, guffawing boor, a cross between Jack the Ripper and Jack the Giant Killer." — *John Simon.*

"Richard Burton plays Henry [in **Anne of the Thousand Days**] like a man who has promised to buy another diamond before Easter, using himself like an acting machine that will, if flogged, produce another million dollars." — *Penelope Mortimer.*

Montgomery Clift

Sadly, Montgomery Clift never fulfilled his early promise. He was born in Omaha, Nebraska, in 1920 and became an actor at the age of 14. Modest stardom on Broadway brought Hollywood offers, and cinemagoers first experienced his sensitivity and air of conviction in Fred

Zinnemann's **The Search** (1948), which was followed by a role in a John Wayne Western. Of the many offers he accepted few: **The Heiress** (1949), **The Big Lift** (1950), **A Place in the Sun** (1951), opposite Elizabeth Taylor, Alfred Hitchcock's **I Confess** (1953), Zinnemann's **From Here to Eternity** and De Sica's **Indiscretion of an American Wife** (1954), with Jennifer Jones.

While making **Raintree County** (1957) he was in an automobile accident: that and a diffident offscreen personality led to an increase in promiscuity and an intake of booze and narcotics that eventually affected his acting: **The Young Lions** (1958), **Lonelyhearts** (1959), **Suddenly Last Summer,** Kazan's **Wild River** (1960) and Huston's **The Misfits** (1961). After a cameo in **Judgment at Nuremberg** he played the title role in Huston's **Freud** (1962).

He made one last film, **The Defector** (1966), the only one of these unworthy of his immense talent. He died in 1966 and it was released posthumously.

 He never married.

66 He had so much power, so much concentration. Clift was a complicated man, there's no question about it . . . . He was a sweet man, Monty, very emotional." – *Burt Lancaster.*

"The best compliment that he got for his acting in **The Search** came when someone said to me 'Where did you find a soldier who could act?' He

▲ *Montgomery Clift in* **From Here to Eternity** *(1953) with Donna Reed, who won a Best Supporting Oscar.*

maintained the same authenticity as the children." – *Fred Zinnemann.*
"Monty is the most emotional actor I have ever worked with. And it is contagious." – *Elizabeth Taylor.*
"Mr Montgomery Clift gives the performance of his career [in **A Place in the Sun**], which is not saying a great deal, since he had already demonstrated in **The Heiress** that he didn't belong on the same screen with first-class actors." – *Raymond Chandler.*

Tony Curtis

As a young actor, Tony Curtis had a bullet-headed cockiness and jauntiness which set him apart from the other teenage heroes. He was born in the Bronx in 1925 and became an actor after navy service. Universal gave him a contract and he had a bit part in **Criss Cross** (1948). His roles rose in prominence until he starred in **The Prince Who Was a Thief** (1951), but two outside films with Burt Lancaster, **Trapeze** (1956) and especially **Sweet Smell of Success** (1957), were the first to bring critical acclaim.

He was in **The Vikings** (1958) and **The Defiant Ones,** during these years of peak demand; and in drag in **Some Like It Hot** (1959), his biggest success, doing his Cary Grant

impersonation. Curtis acted with Cary Grant in **Operation Petticoat** (1959), which affected all his subsequent comedy performances, until his Grantish delivery became tiresome. His popularity began to drift away after **The Great Race** (1965), and in the seventies he was either starring in minor movies or doing supporting stints in others, such as **Little Miss Marker** (1980). His last film to date is **Insignificance** (1985).

▼ *Unrecognizable in drag; Tony Curtis tries to be casual in* **Some Like It Hot** *(1959).*

♥ Married: film star Janet Leigh (1951-62), mother of their daughter Jamie Lee Curtis; German starlet Christine Kaufmann (1963-8); Leslie Allen (1968-82). A supposed fourth marriage in 1984 was a publicity stunt.

" The stars had this neurosis which goes right to the edge. You have somehow to use this to get performances from these deep-sea monsters. There was this enormous difference between [Lancaster] and Tony Curtis. Tony has a fantastic vanity, but no ego. He could act Burt off the screen, but he will never be a star. He hasn't this granite quality of the ego." – *Alexander Mackendrick.*
"A curious combination of the sheikh and the sixties style of star." – *Peter Evans.*
"Tony Curtis is the white rabbit of showbusiness: always in a hurry." – *Roderick Mann.*

Doris Day

🎥 Doris Day looked happy and sang happily, and she made audiences feel the same way. She quickly proved her natural ability as a serious actress, and when musicals died out she took to comedy with the same ease.

She was born in Cincinnati, Ohio, in 1924 and began singing on local radio; she was on the national networks when Warner Brothers tested her for one of the four leads in **Romance on the High Seas** (1948). Stardom

▼ *And here is Doris in the tomboy title role of perhaps her most enjoyable musical, and certainly her favorite film,* **Calamity Jane** *(1953).*

▲ *Miss Day, at an amazingly fit 40 plus, in a novelty number in one of her films,* **The Glass-Bottom Boat** *(1966).*

came immediately, and she was in some good light-hearted films: **Young Man With a Horn** (1950), **Tea for Two, Storm Warning** (the serious role), **Lullaby of Broadway** (1951), **I'll See You in My Dreams** (1952) and especially **Calamity Jane** (1953), where she broke out of the mold to give a fighting performance as a tomboy and sang "Secret Love". She returned to Warners for another fine musical, **The Pajama Game** (1957), but her best moment was, perhaps, as singer Ruth Etting in **Love Me or Leave Me** (1955), made under a pact with MGM. In Alfred Hitchcock's **The Man Who Knew Too Much** (1956) she sang her other great hit, "Que Sera Sera". **It Happened to Jane** (1959), with Jack Lemmon, was a delightful comedy but not a hit; **Pillow Talk,** with Rock Hudson, caused Day to restrict herself to similar comedies.

She was box-office queen, but the public was losing interest by the time she had made her last film, **With Six You Get Eggroll** (1969). Her husband had already committed her to her own TV show and, as soon as she could get free, she retired.

♥ Married: musician Al Jorden (1941-3); George Weidler (1946-9); agent Marty Melcher (1951, widowed 1969). After his death Day discovered that he had turned all her money over to attorney Jerome Rosenthal, whom she successfully sued for $22 million. She remarried in 1976 to Barry Comden, but it didn't last.

❝❝ Doris is a joy to work with. She was never a minute late, always good-humored, and always solicitous of the people around her. They were her family and she cared about them, not for appearance's sake, but she *cared*. In her performance Doris has an unerring instinct as to her moves, motives and impact . . . . She also has impeccable comedic timing, which is the quality I most admire in a performer. To play with her is elevating. She makes you want to give all you've got to a scene, to rise to her level. I also feel that Doris has an enticing sexual quality that is there but subliminal." — *Jack Lemmon.*
"When I think about all the performers I've been associated with over the course of my 50-odd years [in showbusiness], when I think about *natural talent,* I'd have to rate ladies at the forefront — Doris Day and Judy Garland." — *Bob Hope.*

James Dean

🎥 Movie-star mythology works very well for James Dean, whose face still decorates T-shirts three decades after his untimely death — and that has much to do with the Dean cult; also in his three starring films he played the loner, the loser, the outsider, the rebel, and one young enough for adolescents to relate to.

He had a certain intensity, but it is difficult to say whether he would have had a long career.

He was born in Marion, Indiana, in 1931 and while at UCLA belonged to a drama group run by James Whitmore, a contact that enabled him to get extra work on **Fixed Bayonets** (1951) and two other movies. Other contacts got him jobs on Broadway: Elia Kazan saw him in one play and signed him for **East of Eden** (1955), the only Dean film

released before he was killed while driving at 115 mph in a new Porsche. **Rebel Without a Cause** and **Giant** (1956) were released posthumously.

♥ He never married.

❝❝ James Dean's unusual sexual preferences won him the nickname 'the human ashtray'." — *Penny Stallings.*
"A cult following . . . developed for James Dean, whose actual stardom lasted — from the première of **East of Eden** to his fatal car-crash — only 5 months and 20 days." — *Harry Haun.*
"A tremendous influence on me! I was very, very affected by James Dean and the fact that he was communicating to me and others in the audience. And I said 'That's it! That's what I want to do.' Dean was so *real.* I believed he was the real person, that he wasn't acting . . . . See, I never thought Rock Hudson was real, or any of the guys in the forefront then — Gregory Peck, Paul Newman and them." — *Bruce Dern.*
"I had realized that, for a successful

▲ *A moody portrait of James Dean, who has managed to become a legendary figure on the strength of only three movies.*

collaboration, he needed a special kind of climate. He needed reassurance, tolerance, understanding." — *Nicholas Ray.*

Kirk Douglas

🎥 Dimple-chinned Kirk Douglas has been a forceful screen presence for 40 years — too forceful, perhaps, for he played a weakling in his first film, and he has since denied us versatility: but the powerful, egotistical half-heel heroes he often plays — much like himself in life, it seems — have engaged us during all this time.

He was born in Amsterdam, New York in 1916 and worked his way through college and acting school: Hal B. Wallis saw him on Broadway and gave him a large role in **The Strange Love of Martha Ivers** (1946). After **A Letter to Three Wives,** made in

▲ *Kirk Douglas with the Italian star Sylva Koscina in the 1968 thriller* **A Lovely Way to Die,** *in which he plays a former cop who has taken up the profession of private eye.*

1949, he was the **Champion,** which made him in demand at every studio. **Young Man With a Horn** (1950), **The Glass Menagerie,** Wilder's **Ace in the Hole** (1951), Wyler's **Detective Story,** Vincente Minnelli's **The Bad and the Beautiful** (1952) in the role of a film producer, and **Lust for Life** (1956) as Van Gogh followed. **20,000 Leagues Under the Sea** (1954), **Gunfight at the OK Corral** (1957), **The Vikings** (1958) and **Lonely Are the Brave** (1962) are excellent action films, while **Paths of Glory** (1957) is an outstanding war drama. Stanley Kubrick directed the last, and, acknowledging Douglas' enormous talent, then helmed **Spartacus** (1960), the most expensive of Douglas' own productions.

Douglas continued in such films as **Seven Days in May** (1964), **In Harm's Way** (1965), Kazan's **The Arrangement** (1969) and **There Was a Crooked Man** (1970). He has continued to command star roles until this day, but only devoted fans could name the films. The last of them to date is **Eddie Macon's Run** (1982).

♥ Married: Diana Hill (1943-51), mother of their son, produceractor Michael Douglas; and Anna Buydens (1954).

❝ Kirk was civil to me and that's about all. But then Kirk never makes much of an effort toward anyone else. He's pretty wrapped up in himself." – *Doris Day.*
"A lithe, barrel-chested six-footer who impressed me enormously. He had a jauntiness, a self-confident grace that commanded attention . . . . I went backstage to talk to him. I found him quiet, soft spoken, but bursting with energy and animal magnetism." – *Hal B. Wallis.*
"We both came from, sort of, well, shall we say, humble beginnings. We were both young, brash, cocky,

▼ *Douglas relentless and angry as the ruthless newspaperman in Billy Wilder's* **Ace in the Hole** *(1951).*

arrogant. We knew everything, were highly opinionated. We were invincible. Nobody liked us." — *Burt Lancaster.*

Ava Gardner

She is one of the greatest-looking women ever to make movies, but she had no confidence in herself or liking for the industry. She is highly intelligent, which may be why she breathes life into some undemanding roles: many of her performances are burnt into all our memories.

Ava Gardner was born in Smithfield, North Carolina, in 1922: while visiting her sister in New York some pictures were taken of her and seen by an MGM employee. She made her movie début in **We Were Dancing** (1942) but neither then nor later did MGM have confidence in her star potential. She continued to have small roles until loaned out for

Whistle Stop (1946) and **The Killers,** which made her a star. Though she had some scenes with Gable in **The Hucksters** (1947), her biggest roles were at other studios: **Pandora and the Flying Dutchman** (1951) and **My Forbidden Past. Show Boat** and two with Gable, **Lone Star** (1952) and **Mogambo** (1953), finally established her. She had fine chances elsewhere with **The Snows of Kilimanjaro** (1952), **The Barefoot Contessa** (1954) and, at MGM, with **Bhowani Junction** (1956).

Although she had battled for better material she has made few good movies as a freelance: **Seven Days in May** (1964), **The Night of the Iguana, The Bible** (1966). Her last to date is **Regina,** made in 1982 but still unreleased by 1985.

▼ *One of the screen's great beauties, Ava Gardner, in one of the costumes she wore in* **55 Days at Peking** *(1963).*

♥ Married: actor Mickey Rooney (1942-3); bandleader Artie Shaw (1945-6); actor/singer Frank Sinatra (1951-7). Since then her name has been linked to Matador Dominguin, Italian actor Walter Chiari and George C. Scott.

❝ That darling Ava! What a woman!" — *Stewart Granger.* "Ava has been completely victimized by the kind of life she has led, and as a result has become the kind of person she is today." — *Artie Shaw.* "Ava herself was charming. She's a real movie queen, really exciting; lovely looking, too, with marvelous legs. When she crosses the screen, you're bound to follow her." — *George Cukor.* "She was her customary self, as amiable as an adder . . . . Both Elizabeth Taylor and Ava are as spoiled as medieval queens. They expect men to fall at their feet, and they are accustomed to being catered to and having everything done for them." — *Helen Lawrenson.*

Audrey Hepburn

The very special Audrey Hepburn, whose keen, elegant looks and voice cadences cap-

▼ *Audrey Hepburn ("Not since Garbo has there been anything like it, with the possible exception of Bergman") and* ▶ *appearing as Holly Golightly in* **Breakfast at Tiffany's** *(1961).*

Afternoon (1957), Fred Zinnemann for **The Nun's Story** (1958), John Huston for **The Unforgiven** (1960) and Wyler again, off-form, for two films in the sixties, when she also made **Charade** (1963), **My Fair Lady** (1964) and **Two for the Road** (1966). She retired after **Wait Until Dark** (1967) to bring up her family, but returned to make **Robin and Marian** (1976), **Bloodline** (1979) and **They All Laughed** (1981), all failures, despite her customary excellent notices.

♥ Married: actor Mel Ferrer (1954-68), who directed her worst film, **Green Mansions** (1958); Dr Andrea Dotti (1969).

" . . . Not since Garbo has there been anything like it, with the possible exception of Bergman. It's the kind of thing where the director plans 16 close-ups throughout the picture with that dame − that curious, ugly face of that dame." − *Billy Wilder.*
"As a result of her enormous success, she has acquired that extra incandescent glow which comes as a result of being acclaimed. Her voice is peculiarly personal. With its sing-song cadence that develops into a flat drawl ending in a child-like query, it has a quality of heartbreak." − *Cecil Beaton.*
"I knew that Audrey wanted to make the picture and that sooner or later they would come round − because Audrey is a lady who gets her way. So, I told my agents to forget all other projects for me. I was waiting for Audrey Hepburn. She asked for me, and I was ready. This could be the last and only opportunity I'd have to work with the great and lovely Audrey . . . ." − *Fred Astaire.*

Charlton Heston

The epic hero. Every time they needed someone to play one of the great leaders of men, noble and preferably saintly, they sent for Heston: tall, deep-voiced, chiseled-featured and broad-chested − an attribute he always gave us an opportunity to admire.

He was born in Evanston, Illinois, in 1923 and made his movie début while at college in an amateur version

tured the hearts of every young man who saw her, was an enchantress in both comedy and drama.

She was born in 1929 in Brussels, to Irish-Dutch parents who sent her to study dance in Britain. She made her movie début in a Dutch film, **Nederland in 7 Lessen** (1948), and was much touted as the next British screen star after some London appearances, but played only supporting roles until Hollywood's gain proved Britain's loss when she played

the runaway princess in William Wyler's **Roman Holiday** (1953), which won her an Oscar.

By a complicated agreement with her British studio, Paramount had the use of her services in Billy Wilder's **Sabrina** (1954), **War and Peace** (1956), **Funny Face** (1957), dancing with Fred Astaire, and **Breakfast at Tiffany's** (1961), where she was the lightest of loose ladies. She worked for Hollywood's best directors: Wilder again for **Love in the**

▲ *Charlton Heston with the whip hand and, as we used to see him, heroic and noble. Here he is in the title-role of the box-office hit* **Ben-Hur** *(1959), for which he won an Academy Award as Best Actor.*

▲ *Judy Holliday in* **Adam's Rib** *(1949), the first film in which she demonstrated her exceptional gifts as a comedienne. The tale hinges round a court case in which she is accused of the attempted murder of her husband's mistress.*

of **Peer Gynt** (1941). Producer Hal Wallis later saw him acting on TV and signed him to a contract, starting with **Dark City** (1950). De Mille used him for **The Greatest Show on Earth** (1952) in which he was just another good-looking piece of screen furniture until he played Moses for the same director in the biblical epic **The Ten Commandments** (1956).

He played a Mexican in Orson Welles' **Touch of Evil** (1958) and the pacifist in Wyler's **The Big Country**, after which came the heroic roles: Wyler's **Ben-Hur** (1959), which won Heston an Oscar; **El Cid** (1961); **55 Days at Peking** (1963); **The Greatest Story Ever Told** (1965) as John the Baptist; **Major Dundee**; **The Agony and the Ecstasy** as Michelangelo; **The War Lord** (1965), perhaps his best film; and **Will Penny** (1968). A sci-fi tale, **Planet of the Apes,** was so successful that Heston did more in this genre, but only a handful of his subsequent films

were well received. He directed himself in Shakespeare's **Antony and Cleopatra** (1972) to disastrous notices. His most recent film is **Mother Lode** (1982).

♥ Married: Lydia Clark (1944).

❝ The cold, piercing blue eyes, the strong jaw, and tall and muscular carved figure, equipped Heston with the ideal monumental look for roles in epics.❞ – *Ronald Bergan.*

Judy Holliday

🎥◁ Whether she was a subtle comedienne or a great clown didn't matter, she could be very funny. She played dumb or at least lovable blondes, with the emphasis on the word "lovable".

She was born in New York in 1922 and made a name there as a revue artist alongside Betty Comden and Adolph Green. Darryl F. Zanuck signed her and gave her a role in **Winged Victory** (1944), but dropped her after she declined to accompany him on the casting-room couch.

She became a star when she replaced an ailing Jean Arthur in Garson Kanin's play "Born Yesterday" and won an Oscar for the film version (1950) directed by George Cukor. Kanin, Cukor, Katharine Hepburn and Spencer Tracy all conspired to ensure that she and no one else did the film by showcasing her supporting role in **Adam's Rib** (1949).

After two more splendid films with Kanin and Cukor, **The Marrying Kind** (1952) and **It Should Happen to You** (1954), she made only four more: **Phffft!**, **The Solid Gold Cadillac** (1956), **Full of Life** and the musical **Bells are Ringing** (1960), written for her by Comden and Green and which she had done on Broadway. Ill health dogged her until she died of cancer in 1965.

♥ Married: David Oppenheim (1948-58). Lovers include Broadway co-star Sydney Chaplin (c. 1958) and musician Gerry Mulligan, with whom she lived during her last few years.

❝ Even at their daffiest, Holliday's actions carried pathos and vulnerability – a yearning quality that went right to your heart. Like all great comediennes, she was a great actress. Dumb blondes are, by definition, shallow: Judy gave them depth. She did it with right-on-the-money timing and attention to detail. She was a surpassingly intelligent woman (as was Monroe) and therein lies the clue: one has to be smart to play dumb." – *Douglas Marshall.*

Rock Hudson

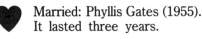

Rock Hudson was one of a bevy of beefcake stars of the fifties, some with daft first names (invented by their "discoverer", the agent Henry Willson), and virtually the only one to survive. He did that by being likable as well as personable, but with luck too, it has to be admitted: he had some very big hits.

Hudson was born in Winnetka, Illinois, in 1925, and was a postman until Willson introduced him to director Raoul Walsh, who put him into **Fighter Squadron** (1948). But he was soon tranferred to Universal, in their stable of oddly named young He died of AIDS in October 1985.

▼ *After a run in a series of comedies Rock Hudson returned to action. This is* **The Hornet's Nest** *(1969).*

men, and the studio began to groom him for stardom, which finally came when he played opposite Jane Wyman in the sentimental remake of **Magnificent Obsession** (1954). Universal moved him from action tales to soap operas, and though at the time George Stevens' **Giant** (1956, on loan-out) seemed more than that, it doesn't now. Another loan-out, for **A Farewell to Arms** (1957), further boosted his career, as did a comedy with Doris Day, **Pillow Talk** (1959).

He returned to action tales, alternating them with a series of rather salacious comedies which kept him a box-office draw in the early sixties, but he plummeted badly in the last years of the decade and turned to TV.

♥ Married: Phyllis Gates (1955). It lasted three years.

❝ Reams of copy have been written about Hudson to explain his appeal and success, but none of them has touched on the vital point

– that he is a traditional Romantic Hero in an era when such types are exceedingly rare . . . . The archetype in silent films was John Gilbert and in sound films was Tyrone Power; their successor is Rock Hudson." – *Jimmie Hicks.*

"I thought I saw something. So I arranged to meet him, and he seemed to be not too much to the eye, except very handsome. But the camera sees with its own eye . . . . I put him into **Has Anybody Seen My Gal?** [1952]. Within a few years he became a number one box-office star in America." – *Douglas Sirk.*

"He had size, good looks, strength and a certain shyness that I thought would make him a star like Gable. He had the kind of personal charm that makes you think you'd enjoy sitting down and spending time with him." – *Henry Willson.*

"Rock Hudson, of all people, emerged from **The Last Sunset** [1961] more creditably than anyone. Most people don't consider him a very accomplished actor, but I found him to be terribly hard-working, dedicated and very serious . . . . If everyone on the

picture, from producer to writer to other actors, had approached it with the same dedication, it would have been a lot better." – *Robert Aldrich.*

Howard Keel

When MGM stopped making musicals they released Howard Keel, whose movie career then went to pieces. But his lusty, cheery presence was one of the reasons those films are constantly revived, and the soundtrack recordings have never stopped selling, due again to him or, rather, his rich baritone voice.

He was born in Gillespie, Illinois, in 1919 and had such a good singing voice that he was introduced to Oscar

▼ **Kismet** *(1955) was not one of the most successful Broadway musicals to be transferred to film, but as singer and actor Howard Keel (here with Mike Mazurki) gave a powerful performance.*

Hammerstein, who sent him to London to star in "Oklahoma!". This led to a role as a convict in a British film, **The Small Voice** (1948), and the male lead in **Annie Get Your Gun** (1950), opposite Betty Hutton. Although he was clearly a talented actor, MGM did poorly by him in straight films, but he was in some of their glorious musicals: **Pagan Love Song, Show Boat** (1951), **Lovely to Look At** (1952), **Calamity Jane** (1953) at Warners, **Kiss Me Kate,** where he did particularly well by Cole Porter's score, and **Seven Brides for Seven Brothers** (1954). He had nothing whatsoever to do with the failures of **Jupiter's Darling** (1955) and **Kismet,** being the best thing about both.

He starred in some undistinguished movies for other studios and left the screen after a starring role in a supporting Western, **Arizona Bushwackers** (1968). He continued to be an attraction on stage and TV, so it's ironic that a non-singing role in TV's **Dallas** has brought him undreamed-of popularity on concert tours.

♥ Married: Rosemary Cooper (1943-8); dancer Helen Anderson (1949-72); former air stewardess Judy Magamoll (1972).

❝ Howard Keel, of course, is a rare talent . . . an actor and singer. A bass of near opera quality." – *Clifford Davis.*
"There is a lot of Keel. He stands 6ft 4in and his shoulders are still as broad as a barn door." – *James Green.*

Grace Kelly

She was the girl who had everything – looks, style, a sense of humor, class (at a time when it was in short supply) and a delightful screen presence. Not to mention all of Hollywood at her feet.

She was born in Philadelphia in 1929 into a wealthy family; she studied acting and was spotted on TV by Hollywood. After a small role in **Fourteen Hours** (1951), she played Gary Cooper's wife in **High Noon** (1952), but MGM signed her as a result of a test and gave her the second lead in **Mogambo** (1953). Alfred Hitchcock's **Dial M for Murder** (1954) made her a star and **Rear Window** made her a superstar; these, plus **The Bridges of Toko-Ri, The Country Girl,** which won her an Oscar, and Hitchcock's **To Catch a Thief** (1955) were all made at outside studios.

Kelly's one MGM movie, **Green Fire,** was so undistinguished that it was shaming – and she was prepared to go on suspension rather than do another like it; but of the expensive projects then lined up for her she did only **The Swan** (1956) and **High Society,** before retiring when she married. In 1982 she suffered a stroke while driving and was killed.

♥ Married: Prince Rainier III of Monaco (1956).

❝ I have dressed thousands of actors, actresses and animals, but whenever I'm asked which star is my personal favorite, I answer 'Grace Kelly'. She is a charming lady, a most gifted actress and, to me, a valued friend." – *Edith Head.*
"Grace Kelly was a Dresden doll, I

▲ *"Mind If I Make Love To You?" Frank Sinatra sings to Grace Kelly in* **High Society** *(1956).*

thought, with a kind of platinum beneath the delicate porcelain, a beautiful girl who I felt was always in control of her world." – *Maurice Chevalier.*

"She was very serious about her work . . . had her eyes and ears open. She was trying to learn, you could see that. You can tell if a person really wants to be an actress. She was one of those people you could get that feeling about, and she was very pretty. It didn't surprise me when she was a big success." – *Gary Cooper.*

Burt Lancaster

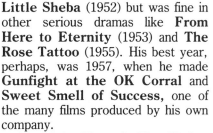Burt Lancaster is one of the screen's great, if variable, all-rounders. He began as a rather glum tough guy and then became an insistently smiling action hero; given his weighty screen presence he might have had a long career in either persona, but instead he decided to stretch his talents – admittedly with uncertain results.

He was born in New York in 1913 and was briefly part of an acrobatic act before army service. Afterwards, he managed to get a role on Broadway and his agent later won him a contract with Hal Wallis. He made his movie début in **The Killers** (1946), and among the thrillers that followed are **Sorry Wrong Number** (1948) and **Criss Cross** (1949); the best of his action films is a swashbuckler, **The**

Crimson Pirate (1952), followed by **Vera Cruz** (1953) and **Apache** (1954). He directed, unsuccessfully, another Western, **The Kentuckian** (1955). He didn't do well as an aging alcoholic doctor in **Come Back**

▼ *The articulate and increasingly craggy features of Burt Lancaster have dominated many an action adventure.* **The Train,** *made in 1965, was one of the more serious ones.*

Little Sheba (1952) but was fine in other serious dramas like **From Here to Eternity** (1953) and **The Rose Tattoo** (1955). His best year, perhaps, was 1957, when he made **Gunfight at the OK Corral** and **Sweet Smell of Success,** one of the many films produced by his own company.

After John Huston's **The Unforgiven,** he won an Oscar for **Elmer Gantry** (1960) and kept his career at full throttle by working with the best talent and taking on challenging projects: **Bird Man of Alcatraz** (1962), **A Child is Waiting** (1963), Visconti's **The Leopard, Seven Days in May** (1964), **The Professionals** (1966), **The Gypsy Moths** (1969) and **Airport** (1970), one of his biggest successes. Throughout the seventies he played authoritarian figures with practiced ease, but few of the films were interesting. Eventually his aging gangster in the film **Atlantic City** (1981)

renewed interest in him. His last film to date is **The Osterman Weekend** (1983).

♥ Married: Norma Anderson (1946-69). Former hairdresser Jackie Bone has been his companion for 17 years. Lovers include Shelley Winters (c. 1955).

❝ Burt Lancaster is a talented actor. He has the 'punch' to play tough guys, but at the same time he has an extraordinary sensibility." – *Kirk Douglas.*
"The Prince [in **The Leopard**] was a very complex character – at times autocratic, rude, strong – at times romantic, good, understanding – and sometimes even stupid, and above all, mysterious. Burt is all these things too. I sometimes think Burt the most perfectly mysterious man I have ever met in my life." – *Luchino Visconti.*
"You have to give him a reason for everything. Once you do he's easy to handle." – *Robert Siodmak.*
"There is only one man worse than me for telling directors what to do, and that's Burt." – *Kirk Douglas.*

Jack Lemmon

He has spent his career in a welter of superlatives – the best/finest/greatest/most polished comedian/light comedian of his generation/era/time. There'll be no argument here, though it should be added that he's pretty good in drama, too.

He was born in Boston, in 1925, and studied at Harvard: performing claimed him there, and he was later seen on TV by Columbia and offered the lead opposite Judy Holliday in **It Should Happen to You** (1954). His Columbia contract required him to do some inferior movies but it also encompassed **My Sister Eileen, Mister Roberts** (1955) on loan, for which he won the Best Supporting Oscar, **Operation Mad Ball** (1957) and **It Happened to Jane** (1959). His association with Billy Wilder, whose favorite interpreter he is, began with **Some Like It Hot,** and continued triumphantly through **The Apartment** (1960), **The Fortune Cookie** (1966), **Avanti!** (1972) and others; he teamed with Walter Matthau on the third of these and equally felicitously in **The Odd Couple** (1968).

His fine serious performances are in **Days of Wine and Roses** (1962),

▶ *Jack Lemmon giving a typically resourceful comic performance as a* flic *in* **Irma La Douce** *(1963).*

▼ *Lemmon in* **The Odd Couple** *(1968), in which he was felicitously teamed with his friend Walter Matthau.*

Save the Tiger (1972), which won him a second Oscar, **The China Syndrome** (1979) and **Missing** (1982). His last film to date is **Mass Appeal** (1984).

 Married: actress Cynthia Stone (1950-7) and Felicia Farr (1962).

" What Felicia saw in Jack Lemmon was the vulnerability behind the extrovert front. Whatever the parts he played on screen, inside he was still very closed up." – *David Lewin.*

"He has the greatest rapport with an audience since Chaplin. Just by looking at him people can tell what goes on in his heart." – *Billy Wilder.*

"And the plant supervisor [in **The China Syndrome**] in his agonizing dilemma very nearly becomes a genuine tragic hero. Jack Lemmon trenchantly portrays this unspectacular man's rise to great moral heights as well as his ultimate collapse: no one man can convey specious cheerfulness better than Lemmon or make you feel more clammily sweaty under the collar." – *John Simon.*

"He has extraordinary instinct. He's almost infallible." – *Lee Remick.*

Gina Lollobrigida

 Busty, sultry Gina Lollobrigida was one of the first European sex bombs. She was born in 1928 in Subiaco, near Rome, where she was noticed by director Mario Costa, who offered her a role in **Elisir d'Amore** (1946) starring Tito Gobbi. Within two years she had advanced to stardom and in 1950 she made a British movie, **A Tale of Five Cities.**

Howard Hughes signed her, but after sitting around in Hollywood doing nothing she returned to Europe, making her first dent in the international market in two films co-starring Gérard Philipe, **Fanfan la Tulipe** (1951) and **Night Beauties** (1952). After playing Humphrey Bogart's wife in **Beat the Devil** (1953), she was in one of her biggest successes, **Pane, Amore e Fantasie** (1954), opposite Vittorio de Sica. She did the sequel, but not the next in the series (at one point she was involved in seven simultaneous lawsuits over contracts): Sophia Loren replaced her, and although Lollobrigida preceded her in making films in English it was soon clear that Loren was getting better offers – which may be why Lollobrigida gave up filming for photography in 1972. Until that time she worked in the US, Britain, France, Spain and Italy.

▲ *Gina Lollobrigida after she had received the glossy MGM glamor treatment. The film she was making at the time was* **Go Naked in the World** *(1961).*

The best-known of her English-language features are: **Trapeze** (1956), **Solomon and Sheba** (1959), **Woman of Straw** (1964) and **Buona Sera Mrs Campbell** (1968). The last film in which she appeared was the Italian **The Lonely Woman** (1975), but she returned to showbusiness when Loren's fee for TV's "Falcon Crest" was too high.

 Married: Dr Milko Skofic (1949-68).

" Lollofrigidaire." – *Humphrey Bogart.*

"At 40 she looks even more beautiful, more serene, more enchanting and so much more radiant than when she was 20." – *Ken Johns.*

"The personality is somewhat lackluster. She switches from comedy to drama without varying her approach. Her sex-appeal is basically that of an advertisement-hoarding." – *David Shipman.*

Sophia Loren

 She's still around because, unlike many sex bombs, she *knows* how to act. She isn't a Sarah Bernhardt, but she has vivacity and – like all the great stars – a very individual voice.

Sophia Loren was born illegitimate in Rome in 1934 to a mother who took her back to Rome from Naples after Sophia had won a beauty contest: she was determined to get the girl into films and did – as an extra, starting with **Cuori sul Mare** (1950). Sophia met the producer Carlo Ponti and became his mistress; he ensured that

▼ *Italy's other great export. Sophia Loren won her first beauty competition aged 14 and was a star before she was 20.*

◀ Sophia Loren, who had arrived in
Hollywood in 1958 accompanied by an
enormous publicity campaign.

she received bigger roles and consequently was seen in two films bound
to find attention in the international
market, **Attila** (1954) with Anthony
Quinn and De Sica's **Gold of Naples.**
She was a star in her next film,
Woman of the River, and soon
important enough to be sought by
Hollywood for **The Pride and
the Passion** (1957). Except for
Houseboat (1958), opposite Cary
Grant, few of her Hollywood films
attracted much attention, though she
herself was seen to advantage in
Heller in Pink Tights (1960) and,
with Clark Gable, **It Started in
Naples.**

Returning to Italy, she won an
Oscar for De Sica's **Two Women**
(1960); and while she looked lovely in
El Cid, it did less for her than
Yesterday, Today and Tomorrow
(1963) and **Marriage Italian Style,**
both directed by De Sica and both
co-starring Marcello Mastroianni.
Since then she has continued to work
in Italy and abroad, sometimes in
unfortunate material such as **A
Countess from Hong Kong** (1967)
and **Man of La Mancha** (1972).
Indeed, few of her later vehicles have
been worthy of her. In 1980 she
played herself and her mother in a TV
film of her autobiography and her
most recent film, **Blood Feud,** dates
from that year.

♥ Married: Carlo Ponti in 1966,
in France, after years of his
vainly trying to divorce his wife in
Italy. In 1980 they were reported as
estranged, with Sophia living with a
French businessman in Paris. Her
book implies an open marriage with
Ponti and speaks of a love affair with
Cary Grant (c. 1957). Peter Sellers
was in love with her when they made
The Millionairess.

❝ She is as beautiful as an erotic
dream . . . . Tall and extremely large bosomed. Tremendously long legs. They go up to her
shoulders, practically. Beautifully
brown eyes, set in a marvelously
vulpine, almost satanic, face." —
Richard Burton.
"That's a *real* working woman. Not
like those teenage tots who think

once they've been in a picture,
they're too important to be gracious
to their colleagues by being on time."
— *Trevor Howard.*

Shirley MacLaine

🎥◁ She started as a kooky comedienne, became an actress of
power and subtlety, and on the way
showed us that she was a terrific
song-and-dance girl. Unfortunately
she came at a time when no one was
much interested in making vehicles
for the female stars.

She was born in Richmond,
Virginia, in 1934 and was trained as a
dancer: Hal B. Wallis saw her when
she went on for second lead Carol
Haney in "The Pajama Game" on
Broadway and offered her a contract.
He loaned her to Alfred Hitchcock for
The Trouble with Harry (1955).
Despite warm notices for this and the
films which followed, the one that
really got her noticed was **Some
Came Running** (1959), in which she
played a hooker. Offered the choice of
roles, she made several poor films.
Among the better ones were: **Ask
Any Girl** (1959), **The Apartment**
(1960), felicitously teamed with Jack
Lemmon, and **Two for the Seesaw**
(1962). A big musical, **Sweet**

▼ *MacLaine here with Jack
Nicholson in* **Terms of
Endearment** *(1983), for which she
finally won an Oscar award.*

▲ *Shirley MacLaine's dancing and
singing were the highlights of the
otherwise unremarkable* **Sweet
Charity** *(1969).*

Charity (1969), was not successful,
nor was a co-starring stint with Clint
Eastwood, **Two Mules for Sister
Sara** (1970). She put together her
own act, which triumphed on
Broadway and elsewhere, making
only occasional movies, including **The
Turning Point** (1977), **Being**

There (1979) and **Terms of Endearment** (1983), for which she won an Oscar. Her last film to date is **Cannonball Run II** (1984), in a guest appearance.

♥ Married: Steve Parker (1954), and the publicity line on their marriage was that it worked because she lived in the US and he in Japan. Her series of memoirs names several lovers by their Christian names only, including a married British MP called "Gerry". Admits to a long romance with journalist Pete Hamill.

❝ She hated rehearsals and had a bad habit of ad-libbing, which didn't set well with Billy Wilder. But we got used to each other, because mainly she's a helluva girl." – *Jack Lemmon.*
"We always had lots of laughs, and we've shared a few sorrows, too. But I'd never worked with her. I heard she was a tough nut. [**Terms of Endearment**] was an important movie, and the work was tough. But tough and interesting. And playing with Shirl – like in the love scenes, which are funny but also touching – was great." – *Jack Nicholson.*

Lee Marvin

🎥◁ Lee Marvin made his living from violence. Though sympathetic in his roles as the hero's best friend, he was more often sneering cheerfully before socking him in the jaw; and when this swift, icy villain eventually found stardom he inevitably played very tough cookies.

He was born in New York City in 1924 into comfortable circumstances and took up acting after serving in the Marines. Director Henry Hathaway saw him on TV and gave him a small role in **You're in the Navy Now** (1951). Marvin was soon into evil, notably in **The Big Heat** (1953), **The Wild One** (1954), **Bad Day at Black Rock, The Comancheros** (1961) and **The Man Who Shot Liberty Valance** (1962), the last two opposite John Wayne, plus **The Killers** (1964), in which he was top-billed. After a sympathetic part in **Ship of Fools** (1965), he won an Oscar for his dual role in **Cat Ballou. The Professionals** (1966) and especially **The Dirty Dozen** (1967) were

very popular, but Marvin's box-office value declined in an even batch of movies. He was at his best in **Paint Your Wagon** (1969), **Monte Walsh** (1970), **Pocket Money** (1972) and **Gorky Park** (1983). The latest to date is **Dog Day** (1984), made in France.

♥ Married: Betty Edeling (1952-65) and Pamela Freeley (1970). In 1979 Michelle Triola sued him successfully for "palimony". Lovers include Jeanne Moreau.

❝ Look, this feller is a pretty good boozer, he's got a short fuse, but he can be handled okay." – *Robert Aldrich.*
"Lee Marvin is more male than anyone I have ever acted with. He is the greatest man's man I have ever met and that includes all the European stars I have worked with." – *Jeanne Moreau.*
"Not since Attila the Hun swept across Europe leaving 500 years of total blackness has there been a man like Lee Marvin." – *Joshua Logan.*

Marcello Mastroianni

🎥◁ Marcello Mastroianni had been a star for a long while before finding fame in the international market as a somewhat jaded Latin lover – a role which didn't exactly suit him, since both before and since he has been much more sprightly as a character actor.

He was born in Fontana Liri, Frosinone, Italy, in 1926 and was acting as an amateur when Luchino Visconti persuaded him to turn professional. His first film was **I Miserabili** (1947), after which he made three or more films every year, but hardly became known outside Italy before **White Nights** (1958), directed by

▼ *As a supporting actor, Lee Marvin was a villain in Westerns, but as a star he was the hero, as in* **Monte Walsh** *(1970).*

▲ *Marcello Mastroianni numbers among his conquests a beautiful Indonesian airline hostess in Joseph E. Levine's hilarious comedy* **Casanova 70** *(1965).*

Visconti, and **Big Deal on Madonna Street.** He became very famous by being world weary in Fellini's **La Dolce Vita** (1960) and Antonioni's **La Notte** (1961); and gave a masterly performance in **Divorce Italian Style.** Two teamings with Sophia Loren, **Yesterday, Today and Tomorrow** (1963) and **Marriage Italian Style,** confirmed his popularity, but he was unlucky with all the English-language films he chose to do. The best of his subsequent Italian films are Visconti's **The Stranger** (1967), **A Special Day** (1977), as a gay man seduced by Loren, and **Wifemistress.** His last film to date is **Enrico IV** (1984).

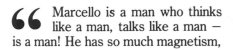 Married: Flora Carabella (1948), enduringly. Lovers include co-stars Faye Dunaway (c. 1969), and Catherine Deneuve, mother of his child.

❝ Marcello is a man who thinks like a man, talks like a man — is a man! He has so much magnetism, he brings out the very soul in a woman." — *Sophia Loren.*
"I could fall in love with Marcello even though he is older than my father." — *Nastassia Kinski.*

Walter Matthau

Lugubrious, skeptical, grouchy but given to rare and cunning grins, Walter Matthau has provided some of the screen's funniest performances, often as an erring or disgruntled husband. His looks qualify him for a degree of over-reacting which he does to perfection being a subtle and expert exponent.

He was born in New York in 1920 and, after war service, studied drama. He was playing leads on Broadway when co-opted to oppose Burt Lancaster in **The Kentuckian** (1955). Although he played a romantic role of sorts in **A Face in the Crowd** (1957), he was known chiefly as the heavy from **Strangers When We Meet** (1960) and **Charade**

▼ *Walter Matthau puts on a disguise before robbing a bank in* **Charley Varrick** *(1973).*

(1963). In 1965, he starred on Broadway in Neil Simon's "The Odd Couple", as a slob, and repeated the role in the film (1968) with Jack Lemmon; in the meantime he had received a Best Supporting Oscar for Billy Wilder's **The Fortune Cookie** (1966) and starred in **A Guide for the Married Man** (1967).

He starred in **The Secret Life of an American Wife** (1968), **Hello, Dolly!** (1969), **Cactus Flower, A New Leaf** (1970), **Kotch** (1971), directed by Lemmon, **Pete 'n' Tillie** (1972), **Charley Varrick** (1973),

The Taking of Pelham 1, 2, 3 (1974), **The Front Page** with Lemmon, **The Sunshine Boys** (1975) and **The Bad News Bears** (1976). After that his box-office standing faltered, but he has continued to make good movies, including **California Suite** (1978).

▼ *Walter Matthau in somber mood. This still may be associated with one of his serious roles, though he managed to look like this in most of his screen comedies.*

♥ Married: Grace Johnson (1948-58); Carol Marcus Saroyan (1959).

❝ Conceivably the best character actor in America." — *Kenneth Tynan.*
"He was an absolute delight and a professional in every sense of the word." — *Carol Burnett.*
"We have great rapport — we're very close friends — and it's very exciting to work with him: if in the middle of a scene someone gets an idea, there's no hesitation. We just do it." — *Jack Lemmon.*
"He has talent that still hasn't been tapped. Films haven't yet touched on his depth." — *Jack Lemmon.*

▲ *Steve McQueen caught up in* **The Great Escape** *(1963) (from a PoW camp), one of his best remembered pictures.*

Steve McQueen

Cool, jaunty, bullet-headed, casual and insolent, Steve McQueen was a cat that walked by himself, anti-Establishment even when playing the cop in **Bullitt** (1968), the film that more than any other embodies his star quality.

He was born in Slater, Missouri, in 1930 and did a number of manual jobs before a chance meeting got him into acting. He was an extra in **Somebody Up There Likes Me** (1956) and, after some Broadway and TV work, had a featured role in **Never Love a Stranger** (1958). He progressed to stardom in **Never So Few** (1959), **The Magnificent Seven** (1960) and **The Great**

132

▲ *Towards the end of his career there was a hiatus in Steve McQueen's screen work, partly because his fee was so high and partly because he wanted more challenging roles. He eventually made two conventional movies and this is one of them:* **Tom Horn** *(1979).*

Escape (1963). Other notable milestones include **Love With the Proper Stranger, The Cincinnati Kid** (1965), **The Sand Pebbles** (1966), **The Thomas Crown Affair** (1968), **Bullitt, The Reivers** (1970), Sam Peckinpah's **Junior Bonner** (1972) and **The Getaway, Papillon** (1973) and **The Towering Inferno** (1974). By this time his fee was so huge that the studios refused to meet it: in response he produced himself in Ibsen's **An Enemy of the People** (1978), but no one wanted to show it. He was already dying of cancer when he made **Tom Horn** (1979) and **The Hunter** (1980). He died on 7 November 1980.

♥ Married: actress/dancer Neile Adams (1955-72); co-star Ali McGraw (1973-8); Barbara Minty (1979), who outlived him.

❝ More versatile than Caan or Newman, but lacking their coat-hanger appeal; rangier than Hackman, but without his coiled-wire urban intensity; no personality to match Marvin's; lacking the urbanity of Coburn; of far greater range than Eastwood but without his immediate screen impact. Looked at closely, McQueen was the thorough outsider . . . ." − *Derek Elley.*
"He walked around with the attitude that the burden of preserving the integrity of the picture was on his shoulders and all the rest of us were company men ready to sell out, grind out an inferior picture for a few bucks and the bosses. One day I told him that his attitude bored me, that I was as interested in the picture being good as he was, and that when this

fact sunk through his thick head we would get along. I could see that he was angry. I knew that he was capable of violence and I knew he could whip me . . . . Eventually, we grew to like each other." − *Don Siegel.*

Marilyn Monroe

🎥 ⌐She is as famous now as when she was alive, because of her short, tragic life and a mere dozen movies. It's impossible now to separate the two − life and career − since her temperament and insecurity, plus fights with the front office, made most of the later films into battlegrounds. It's impossible, too, to de-

▲ *"I'm Going To File My Claim" sings Marilyn Monroe to other prospective gold diggers in* **River of No Return** *(1954).*

cide where the screen Marilyn finished and the real one started − an intelligent woman who nevertheless read highbrow books because she wanted to appear educated, a woman who reveled in being admired, in being a sex object, yet who at the same time desperately wanted to be something more than that; a woman who hated being "used", but still, at the beginning, slept with people she thought could help her career; a woman of incandescent beauty before the camera, making sex both desirable and funny at the same time − much more than Mae West and Jean Harlow, neither of whom came close to possessing Marilyn's most endearing quality, her vulnerability.

She was born in Los Angeles in 1926, illegitimate, to a mentally sick

▲ *Marilyn Monroe at the peak of her reign as the cinema's sex queen in the comedy* **The Seven Year Itch** *(1955). A year later she appeared in* **Bus Stop** *which included this* ▼ *ominously portentous shot — six years later Monroe was found dead in her bed, an empty bottle of sedatives by her side.*

mother and had an unhappy childhood. Modeling took her into pictures — she got a bit part in **Dangerous Years** (1947) and a lead in a B, **Ladies of the Chorus** (1948). She

eventually received showy supporting roles in two important movies, **The Asphalt Jungle** (1950) and **All About Eve.**

Press attention won her a contract with 20th Century-Fox, who, after more minor roles, gave her the lead as a murderess opposite Richard Widmark in **Don't Bother to Knock** (1952). When Monroe fever refused to subside she was starred in another melodrama, **Niagara** (1953). That comedy was her true forte was proved by **Gentlemen Prefer Blondes** and **How to Marry a Millionaire.**

After **River of No Return** (1954) and **There's No Business Like Show Business** she began to fight for better material, and got it, with Wilder's **The Seven Year Itch** (1955) and with **Bus Stop** (1956). She produced, and Laurence Olivier directed, **The Prince and the Showgirl** (1957), and then was sensational in **Some Like It Hot** (1959), which was followed by the weakest of her late films, **Let's Make Love** (1960), the only one of this quartet made on her home lot. The other is **The Misfits** (1961), written by her then-husband with regard to her wondrous gifts.

Her inability to show up on the set of **Something's Got to Give** resulted in 20th Century-Fox firing her in 1962. Within weeks she was dead from an overdose of barbiturates.

♥ Married: Lockheed shift worker Jim Dougherty (1944-6); baseball player Joe Di Maggio (1954); dramatist Arthur Miller (1956-61). Lovers include movie moguls Joseph M. Schenck and Harry Cohn; Howard Hughes; TV star Milton Berle; vocal coach Fred Karger; agent Johnny Hyde; co-star

Yves Montand; President John F. Kennedy and his brother Robert.

Paul Newman

Paul Newman's blue eyes were his passport to movie stardom. At least, his looks were more impressive than his acting in his first film. He became a passable actor quite quickly, and, almost before we realized it, a formidable one. Although he has retained his good looks, his current top box-office appeal is almost entirely the result of a long line of very fine performances.

He was born in 1925 in Cleveland, Ohio, and, after a number of false starts, studied drama. Warners saw him on Broadway and gave him a contract, plus his début role in **The Silver Chalice** (1955), but his more notable work was done elsewhere: **Somebody Up There Likes Me** (1956), **The Long Hot Summer** (1958), **Cat on a Hot Tin Roof, The Hustler** (1961) and **Sweet Bird of Youth** (1962). He won an

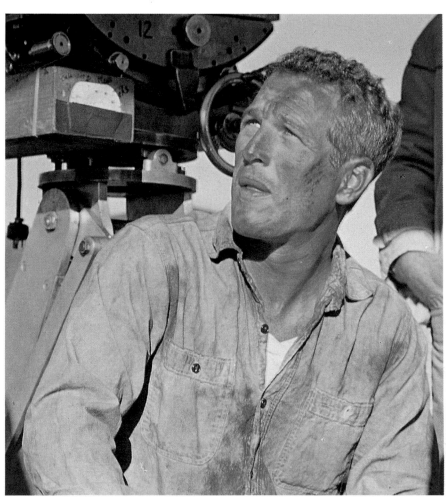

▲ *Newman in one of his most popular films,* **The Sting** *(1973).*
▶ *Many movie stars of Paul Newman's generation are now executives. Newman has produced and directed his own movies, but despite the camera and the agonised expression he was only the star on this one,* **Cool Hand Luke** *(1967).*

Oscar for **Hud** (1963), which was followed by **The Prize, Torn Curtain** (1966), **Harper, Hombre** (1967) and **Cool Hand Luke.** He proved to be an excellent director with **Rachel, Rachel** (1968) and produced (and also directed) several of his subsequent films. Notable titles include: **Butch Cassidy and the Sundance Kid** (1969), **The Mackintosh Man** (1973), **The Sting, The Towering Inferno** (1974), **Slap Shot** (1977) and **The Verdict** (1982). Just before this he told reporters that he was tired of movie-making, but that was not apparent in his last film to date, **Harry and Son** (1984), which he also directed.

♥ Married: actresses Jacqueline Witte (1947-56) and Joanne Woodward (1958).

❝ I like and respect Richard Burton tremendously, but I can't drink with him since he intimidates me simply because he's such a celebrity. Now, Paul and Joanne Newman are old friends — ten years ago my first play was his second play, and I was his little brother for a year . . . . I never think of him as being a movie star, probably because he's still the same nice guy, and to me he's still a big brother." — *George Grizzard.*

"Paul had by 1961 made himself equally distant and elevated [like Olivier and Heston, playing 'noble' roles] — a star whom it was easy to admire and with whom it was natural to sympathize; but not one who ever really seemed like the common man or the boy next door. It was to be left to such stars as Michael Caine and Dustin Hoffman to reduce to vanishing point the gap between stars and public . . . . As a person, he retained an aura of mystery and withdrawal. As a screen symbol, he was almost always an outsider or one who would end up as an outcast or martyr — an alienated modern hero."
— *Lionel Godfrey.*

Sidney Poitier

Sidney Poitier was born in Miami in 1924 to West Indian parents, and because of his citizenship served in the US army, after which he studied with the American Negro Theater. There had been some stage roles and he made a movie documentary, **From Whence Cometh My Help** (1949), before his feature début, **No Way Out** (1950), for 20th Century-Fox. Despite excellent notices there were few offers, but he made **Cry the Beloved Country** (1951) in Britain, **The Blackboard Jungle** (1955), **Edge of the City** (1957) and **Virgin Island** (1958). He had become a star on talent alone, and was now in leading roles — even if **The Defiant Ones** and **Porgy and Bess** (1959) could not be called good movies. He won an Oscar with **Lilies of the Field** (1963) and five years later was voted the top draw in the US, partly because of three very popular films, **To Sir With Love** (1967), **In The Heat of the Night** and **Guess Who's Coming to Dinner?**.

He defended the upright roles he played by saying that as long as he was the sole black star, blacks would be shown in a good light; and because of him, black actors were much in demand. He directed and starred in **Uptown Saturday Night** (1974), which was one of the few successes of his last films. He now directs and has not acted in a movie since **A Piece of the Action** (1977).

♥ Married: Juanita Hardy (1950); actress Joanna Shimkus (1976). Also lived with singer Diahann Carroll.

❝ Sidney has a greatness and professionalism and a deep, deep sensitivity . . . . He's an absolutely beautiful man, inside and out." — *Stanley Kramer.*
"He is big, black, and beautiful. His talented presence lends dignity and power, not only to the screen but wherever he is to be observed." — *Roy Newquist.*

▼ *Sidney Poitier was a fine actor from the start, but it was not until the sixties that his roles revealed his depth of talent in some very good films such as* **In The Heat of the Night** *(1967).*

Elvis Presley

Elvis, "The King", casts a vast shadow over the popular culture of the fifties and sixties. He changed the notion of popular song, which he performed in an electrifying

▲ *A happy day for Elvis Presley and his bride, Priscilla, but not for his adoring female fans, many of whose dreams were shattered.*

manner, gyrating his body as swiftly as his mouth spat out the lyrics. As an actor he was much less charismatic, so they invented a persona — a young loner and maverick, quick with his fists but basically decent and really a mother's boy in wolf's clothing. His career was manufactured, too, but that doesn't detract from his immense popularity.

He was born in Tupelo, Miss-

▲ *Elvis in action, in* **Girls, Girls, Girls** *(1962). His partner in red is Stella Stevens. This rather anodyne still is true to the spirit of his films, alas.*

▲ *Peter Sellers always admired Alec Guinness, and appeared with him in one of his (Sellers') first films,* **The Ladykillers** *(1955). Sellers looks amazed at Danny Green's treatment of Katie Johnson.*

issippi, in 1935 and while still in his teens began to make his reputation as a singer of country music. By the time he was a national figure his manager, "Colonel" Parker, was committing him to films: **Love Me Tender** (1956), **Loving You** (1957), **Jailhouse Rock** and **King Creole** (1958), before his much-publicized military service, and **G.I. Blues** (1960) afterward. He continued to make two films a year, but with the exceptions of **Wild in the Country** (1961) and **Follow That Dream** (1962), they were increasingly bland affairs, tailored for family audiences after his teenage fans grew up. The later ones failed at the box office and documentaries of his concerts showed him as only a ghost, if a fat one, of his former self. He died of a heart attack in 1977.

♥ Married: Priscilla Beaulieu (1967-72), whom he met when she was 14.

❝ I decided that this guy had the same animal magnetism of Brando. I couldn't care less about his singing." – *Hal B. Wallis.*
"He never contributed a damn thing to music . . . . He was successful — hard to account for. Oh, he sings well enough, I suppose." – *Bing Crosby.*

Peter Sellers

🎥◁ The mimicry and mercurial talents of Peter Sellers made him and the studios a mint of money: there are a dozen classics among the movies he made. Unfortunately, he lost his way in the latter part of his career, and he alienated many colleagues by his vanity and an obsessive demand for perfection that seemed to border on childishness.

He was born into a theatrical family in Southsea, Hampshire, in 1925 and became a stand-up comic and minor radio star. He made his film début in a short, **Let's Go Crazy** (1950), and his first feature the following year, **Penny Points to Paradise** (1951), but occasional films did nothing for his career till he did two good ones, **The Ladykillers** (1955) and **The Smallest Show on Earth** (1957), respectively as young punk and old fogey. A triple role in **The Mouse That Roared** (1959) further widened his reputation in the US art houses and he enlivened **Man in a Cocked Hat** and **I'm All Right Jack** as an obdurate union steward, perhaps his greatest performance. Stanley Kubrick's **Lolita** (1962) and **Dr Strangelove; or, How I Learned to Stop Worrying and Love the Bomb** (1964) made Sellers a world star, and in Blake Edwards' **The Pink Panther** he presented his most popular manifestation, the incompetent French *flic*, Inspector Clouseau.

The World of Henry Orient (1964) was his first Hollywood movie and his last good one for a long time. There were some half-successes in the late sixties, but many disasters (unshown or unfinished) in the seventies, until Blake Edwards – whose career was also going badly – offered **The Return of the Pink Panther** (1975), which put them both back on the top. The subsequent films, including some more Pink Panthers and excluding (perhaps) **Being There** (1979) were terrible. Sellers died of

a heart attack in 1980 and **The Fiendish Plot of Dr Fu Manchu** was released posthumously.

🖤 Married: Anne Hayes (1951-63); starlet Britt Ekland (1964-8); Miranda Quarry (1970-4); and Lynne Frederick (1976). Lovers include Sophia Loren, while they were making **The Millionairess** (1960), or so he implied; Liza Minnelli, to whom he was engaged for a few days; Janette Scott and Mia Farrow.

❝ He was ruthless, absolutely ruthless, as all great artists are ruthless. Behind that soft exterior he had an obsessional impulse to get his way. He was a child in that sense." – *Roy Boulting.*
"The problem with Peter was that he could never like a girl who liked him. It was the old Groucho Marx routine about not wanting to join any club that was willing to accept him as a member." – *Harvey Orkin.*
"I think [his mother] had gained such an incredible influence over him that he virtually abdicated his own right to

▲ *Sellers' remarkable talent in some British movies provoked Hollywood interest.* **The Return of the Pink Panther** *(1975), the second in the series, boosted his flagging career.*

any individual personality. He just couldn't register on his own, without Peg. Finally, he had to invade other bodies to register at all . . . . He was not a genius, Sellers, he was a freak." – *Spike Milligan.*
"He is the most difficult man I know." – *Princess Margaret.*

Simone Signoret

🎥 As a young woman she played minxes, whores and other loose ladies; now she plays grandmothers, spinster schoolteachers and stolid wives. The transformation happened quite quickly but she didn't mind because she was always less a star than an actress — and one of the very best of the French cinema.

Simone Signoret was born in 1921 in Wiesbaden, Germany, to French parents and grew up in Paris, where she became a film extra — firstly in **Le Prince Charmant** (1942). The director Yves Allégret (whom she married) gave her a brief role in **La Bôite aux Rêves** (1945) and the lead in **Les Démons de l'Aube**. Although she did a British film, **Against the Wind** (1947), and was both impressive and sexy in two by Allégret, **Dédée d'Anvers** (1948) and **Manèges** (1950), fame did not come till later that year in Ophuls' **La Ronde** and Becker's **Casque d'Or** (1952): the latter won her awards in Britain. **Thérèse Raquin** (1953), **Diabolique** (1954) and **The Crucible** (1957), with Yves Montand, were followed by **Room at the Top** (1958) for which she won an Oscar.

Changing her image, she filmed in Britain, Hollywood and France: **Term of Trial** (1962), **Ship of Fools** (1965), **The Sleeping Car Murders** with Montand, **The Deadly Affair** (1966), **Games** (1967) and **The Confession** (1970) with Montand. She has filmed only in France since then, and only **La Vie Devant Soi** (1977) has been seen much abroad, retitled **Madame Rosa**. Her recent films include **Guy de Maupassant** (1982) and **The Northern Star**. She died in 1985.

🖤 Married: director Yves Allégret (1944-9); actor and singer Yves Montand (1951).

▼ *Simone Signoret appearing in* **Diabolique** *(1954) – an apt title since the film is devilishly clever and is one of the finest horror films ever made.*

▲ *Simone Signoret is one of France's first film actresses. She graduated from portraying lovelorn women to more mature matronly roles, winning an Academy Award from* **Room at the Top** *(1958) and being nominated for another with* **Ship of Fools** *(1965).*

66 I suppose it is fair to say that I fell hopelessly in love with Simone Signoret the very first time I clapped eyes on her in a modest Ealing film called **Against the Wind** (1947) . . . . I placed her then on the very peak of her profession, and as far as I am concerned she has never budged from it and I still love her dearly." – *Dirk Bogarde.*

"Her hair grayish-white now, her voice hoarse, Simone Signoret has crossed 60 and grown rather stout, yet she's more of a movie star than ever. What the American audience – particularly older moviegoers – responds to in Signoret is not so much her talent but her moral authority as a woman. This is one aging actress who will never ask an audience to mourn her ruined beauty. She will not yield to easy pathos." – *David Denby.*

Jean Simmons

She was enchanting, spring-like, when she came to movies in adolescence, and she didn't lose these qualities as she matured into a remarkably fine actress in Hollywood; at the onset of middle-age she concentrated on TV movies, continuing to astonish us with her range and sensitivity.

Jean Simmons was born in London in 1929 and educated at a school for child actors; she made her movie début in **Give Us the Moon** (1944) and thereafter was never far away from the studios. Rank gave her a contract and plum roles in Lean's **Great Expectations** (1946), **Black Narcissus** (1947) and Olivier's **Hamlet** (1948). These brought her to stardom; also **The Blue Lagoon** (1949) and **Adam and Evelyne**, with Stewart Granger, followed. She married Granger and, since he had a Hollywood contract, Rank sold hers

▶ *Jean Simmons in one of her early Hollywood movies* **The Robe** *(1953).*

◄ *Jean Simmons' career took off in the mid 1940s, followed quickly by marriage and stardom.*

to RKO, who put her into one good movie, **Angel Face** (1952).

Following litigation, she was free to accept some of Hollywood's best and/or biggest films: **Young Bess** (1953), **The Actress, The Robe, Desirée** (1954), **Guys and Dolls** (1955), **The Big Country** (1958), **Home Before Dark** and **Elmer Gantry** (1960), directed by Richard Brooks, whom she married. She worked much less, her films including **Spartacus** (1960), **All the Way Home** (1963) and **The Happy Ending** (1969), which Brooks fashioned for her. Her last cinema film to date is **Dominique** (1978). In her TV work she was outstanding in "The Thorn Birds" (1983).

♥ Married: Stewart Granger (1950-60); Richard Brooks (1960), but the marriage was over by the mid-seventies.

"" She was one of the most undemanding, professional actresses I've ever worked with but I could imagine what it must have been like to be married to tigresses like Crawford or Davis." — *Stewart Granger.*
"A dream . . . a fantastically talented and enormously underestimated girl. In terms of talent [she] is so many head and shoulders above most of her contemporaries, one wonders why she didn't become the great star she could have been . . . . It's true, it's not that important to her. It doesn't matter to her much." — *Joseph L. Mankiewicz.*
"She is surprisingly appealing in a part [in **Guys and Dolls**] with almost no potential, and her Havana dance is a high point of the picture." — *Stephen Sondheim.*

Frank Sinatra

Frank Sinatra was made famous by the bobbysoxers who swooned when he crooned. He wasn't then, as either singer or actor, a strong candidate for a long career, but after a rough period there was a new drive in his work; he was particularly good as a stubborn, somewhat cynical bullet-headed cop. Arrogance and a refusal to do more than one take made him unpopular with some colleagues, while there has never been much love lost between him and the press — perhaps resulting in unfortunate references to his associations with mobsters.

He was born in 1915 in Hoboken, New Jersey, and found fame via a radio amateur hour and as vocalist for Harry James and Tommy Dorsey, with whose orchestra he made his film début, in **Las Vegas Nights** (1941). His success as a solo performer led RKO to sign him and he made **Higher and Higher** (1943) at that studio, but his most memorable films were at MGM, where he teamed up with Gene Kelly in **Anchors Aweigh** (1945), **Take Me Out to the Ball Game** (1949) and **On the Town**. But without Kelly he was not box-office and Hollywood lost interest, which was revived when he did a "serious" supporting role for a small salary in **From Here to Eternity** (1953). He won an Oscar and returned to stardom: **Young at Heart** (1954), **The Tender Trap** (1955), **Guys and Dolls, The Man with the Golden Arm, High**

▲ *Frank Sinatra's early movies don't exactly overwhelm us with his talent, apart from singing: but he was at his most likable in* **Anchors Aweigh** *(1945), in which he co-starred with Gene Kelly.*

Society (1956), **Pal Joey** (1957) and **A Hole in the Head** (1959).

Ocean's Eleven (1960) was the first of several increasingly resistible films with the Sinatra "rat-pack" (Dean Martin, Sammy Davis Jr). After a while playing swinging playboys and war heroes he found his niche as a cop, in **Tony Rome** (1967) and **The Detective** (1968). He retired after

◄ *Sinatra in* **The Tender Trap** *(1955). This is the sort of still which decorates his album covers of the era — records made at his peak and now not only fondly remembered by his fans (and others) but constantly reissued.*

the failure of **Dirty Dingus Magee** (1970) but later returned to singing and then films, the latest of which to date is **Cannonball Run II** (1984).

♥ Married: Nancy Barbato (1939-51); film stars Ava Gardner (1951-7) and Mia Farrow (1966-8); Barbara Marx (1976), former wife of Zeppo.

❝ He's the kind of guy that, when he dies, he's going up to heaven and give God a bad time for making him bald." – *Marlon Brando*. "So much has been written about Sinatra, of his talent, his generosity, his ruthlessness, his kindness, his gregariousness, his loneliness and his rumored links with the Mob that I can contribute nothing except to say that he is one of the few people in the world I would instinctively think of if I needed help of any sort. I thought of him once when I was in a bad spot: help was provided instantly and in full measure without a question being asked. It was not, incidentally, money." – *David Niven*.

Elizabeth Taylor

🎥 Elizabeth Taylor is the greatest film star that ever was – if greatness can be measured by press coverage alone. For a long time she was beautiful; her acting,

▲ *Elizabeth Taylor as Katharina rehearsing a scene from* **The Taming of the Shrew** *(1967) with director Franco Zeffirelli.*

however, has always had its detractors, and despite two Oscars she has given them too much ammunition. Before she met Richard Burton she did too little and after, too much.

She was born in 1932 in London, but was living in Los Angeles with her parents when offered a small role in a Universal B movie, **There's One Born Every Minute** (1942). Her association with MGM began with **Lassie Come Home** (1943) and she became a star in **National Velvet** (1944), as a girl mad about horses.

She made very few movies, but successfully made the transition to adult star – in **Little Women** (1949) and **Conspirator** (1950). She had successes with **Father of the Bride** and **A Place in the Sun** (1951), the latter directed by George Stevens, who gave her her next one with **Giant** (1956). Huge publicity over her marriages and for these films did not necessarily mean good box-office for **Raintree County** (1957), **Cat on a Hot Tin Roof** (1958), **Suddenly Last Summer** (1959),

▼ *Taylor was happiest in contemporary settings, such as* **Cat on a Hot Tin Roof** *(1958), based on Tennessee Williams' play.*

Butterfield 8 (1960), for which she won an Oscar, and Cleopatra (1963).

Because of her salary and her affair with Richard Burton, Cleopatra became the most publicized, as well as the most expensive, American film yet made; the two of them were briefly box-office, in The VIPs, The Sandpiper (1965), Who's Afraid of Virginia Woolf? (1966), for which she won another Oscar, and The Taming of the Shrew (1967). After Reflections in a Golden Eye and The Comedians she had a series of box-office disasters — including Stevens' The Only Game in Town (1970) so that her customary $1 million fee was down to $100,000 for A Little Night Music (1977), yet another flop and her last cinema film to date except for The Mirror Crack'd (1981), in England.

 Married: hotel heir Nicky Hilton (1950-1); actor Michael Wilding (1952-7); producer Mike Todd (1957, widowed 1958); singer Eddie Fisher (1959-62), ex-husband of Debbie Reynolds; Richard Burton (1964-74 and 1975, briefly); lawyer and politician John Warner (1976-82).

" The incredibly beautiful and curvaceous Liz Taylor ... disappointed me by having a rather squeaky voice, but you can't have everything, can you, and she had practically everything else in abundance." — Stewart Granger.
". . . that pristine untalentness called Elizabeth Taylor." — John Simon.

Joanne Woodward

 Joanne Woodward has had only a sporadically successful screen career, but with the exception of some films made under contract, her work has varied from admirable to outstanding. She has versatility, sensitivity and an underlying humor; and she almost manages to hide her film starriness.

She was born in Thomasville, Georgia, in 1930 and studied acting; a 20th Century-Fox executive saw her on TV and offered her a contract. She made her film début in Count Three and Pray (1955) for Tyrone Power's film company, and after one forget-

table piece won an Oscar for her portrayal of a multi-personality schizoid in The Three Faces of Eve (1957). After No Down Payment, she did The Long Hot Summer (1958), the first of several teamings with Paul Newman, including Rally Round the Flag Boys and From the Terrace (1960). The Fugitive Kind, The Stripper (1963) and A Big Hand for the Little Lady (1966) did not have the success they deserved, so husband Newman directed her in Rachel, Rachel (1968), designed to demonstrate her superior talents. It did successfully from all points of view, but a further director-player collaboration, The Effect of Gamma Rays on Man-in-the-Moon Marigolds (1972) was not a hit, though she was fine in it.

She lost interest in filming after Summer Wishes, Winter Dreams (1973), turning more to TV movies, and she was tremendous in Sybil (1976). Her last cinema film to date is Newman's Harry and Son (1984).

 Married: Paul Newman (1958).

" For a long time when anyone mentioned her name, I got a lump in my throat. She's a wonderful lady. She has so much strength and love and warmth that you instantly fall into. There isn't any actor ego where she's fighting for a scene. None of that weird stuff. With Joanne, it's 'How can we make this scene better?' She was just lost in the work, like me." — Sally Field.
"Joanne Woodward, already a proven actress of remarkable range, has never been better [than in Rachel, Rachel]. In one red-rimmed close-up, tears seem to happen to her remorselessly, like rain down a windscreen." — John Coleman.

▼ Joanne Woodward with husband Paul Newman in The Long Hot Summer (1958).

143

The Stars of Today

In the 1960s the world flocked to see Julie Andrews in **Mary Poppins, The Sound of Music** and **Thoroughly Modern Millie.** Here was a big star in the old tradition. Then, equally decisively, the world turned its back on **Star!** and **Darling Lili.** Both had opened "big", in the industry's expression, but the fans simply didn't show up and the film industry went into shock. The films weren't that good, but they weren't abysmal. No one has ventured any explanation of this sudden failure, but what seems most likely is that the public love affair with movie stars was, after sixty years, over.

The public didn't wholly reject Julie Andrews; it still turned up to see **The Sound of Music** on reissue and, when it was shown on television, audiences watched in record numbers. It seems the public remained interested in stars — in reading about them or watching them on talk shows — but no longer felt obliged to go out and see them on the big screen.

Star decline

This new attitude was for a time disguised by the fact that there were some very popular names in the box-office hits of the seventies, namely **The Godfather, The Sting, All the President's Men** and **One Flew Over the Cuckoo's Nest.** But equally, the star names — Marlon Brando, Paul Newman, Robert Redford, Dustin Hoffman, Jack Nicholson — all made movies which drew only tiny audiences. Indeed, the characteristic of today's stars is that they have all appeared in failures, and sometimes a string of them. Burt Reynolds and Clint Eastwood both seemed to

*They just can't believe he's real...
Harrison Ford as the man who made
the Fedora famous, with co-star Kate
Capshaw in* **Indiana Jones and the
Temple of Doom** *(1984).*

have a stronger following than most of the stars of the decade, but this was largely because they appeared in a certain type of reliable action adventure. By the eighties the public was beginning to tire of the sameness of their movies and these stars, too, have appeared in the occasional unsuccessful movie.

Blockbusters without stars

The evident turning point came in 1977, with the release of **Star Wars** and **Close Encounters of the Third Kind.** Richard Dreyfuss, the only big name in the second movie, immediately won an Oscar for his performance in the hugely popular **The Goodbye Girl,** but his few films since have hardly caused a stir at the box-office.

The best-known name in **Star Wars** was Alec Guinness, the elderly British character actor whose days of stardom were long over and who would hardly mean much to the young audiences flocking to see the film, while the youngsters Mark Hamill and Carrie Fisher demonstrated little talent and are still largely unknown beyond their appearance in this science fiction series. Harrison Ford, however, enjoyed another huge success four years later with **Raiders of the Lost Ark** and again with its sequel, **Indiana Jones and the Temple of Doom,** but few would claim that he was the main reason for the popularity of these adventures. It seems that films no longer need a big star to be successful — and having a star is by no means a guarantee of box-office popularity.

Today's movies often have no stars at all. As the big star names narrowed to just a few in the seventies, their financial demands rose to new and dizzy heights. Studios discovered that they might pay a star as much as $3 million, for instance, only to find that on this particular occasion the public was not interested.

▲ *Christopher Reeve in* **Superman III** *(1983), poses the question about fantasy films: which is the star, the actor or the special effects?*

Looking back at the failures of the past decade it is sad to think that much good work could have gone largely unseen and unappreciated — but, of course, it is not wasted. Many cinema failures have become TV successes, and movies that didn't seem worth the effort and expense of a night out are attractive once they are for rent at the local video store.

The new audiences
Star names have lost much of their luster, but it would be wrong to accuse audiences of becoming more fickle, although it is certainly true that they are increasingly selective in the films they will stir themselves to see. And now it may be the direction, the story interest or the special effects that people look for, rather than just the stars.

It would be too simple to say that audiences are now too sophisticated, for teenagers are still star-crazy — at least where pop and rock singers are concerned. The problem may be that the few at the very top are over-exposed on television and in the press. We have become blasé; stars are too well known, they hold no mysteries — unlike the stars of the thirties and forties who were never so intimately interviewed, and so remained somehow larger than life.

The excitement of hero worship in the past was due in part to the idol being seen only at a distance — that certain mystique essential to stardom was thus always maintained. Not so now, when screen stars are available at the flick of a TV switch — Clark Gable or Burt Reynolds, Gary Cooper and Clint Eastwood, past and present stars alike. And if there is no movie on one of the channels, there will no doubt be a showbiz personality or former screen star letting us know that they are just like the rest of us.

Today's talent
Obviously talent must be rewarded if the film industry is to survive. If so, then the delicious Valerie Perrine and Margot Kidder of **Superman** fame deserve to be more popular — and the marvelous Stockard Channing should be making more movies. And who, apart from his agent, realizes how very good Tommy Lee Jones can be?

At times, the film industry itself seems fickle in its casting. For example, talented as they are, there is little to distinguish Gary Busey from Nick Nolte — and it's open to question whether Bo Derek has any real following. Again, perhaps it was too much taken for granted that David Bowie could act, or that Gene Wilder and Dudley Moore were always funny. Moore's **10** (1979) and **Arthur** (1981) presumably had their attractions, for although neither was particularly well received by critics, the public clamored to see them. Yet Dudley Moore's other movies have had no success at the box-office, with the exception of **The Best Defense** (1984), which also featured Eddie Murphy — albeit in a supporting role. This may be why the film's revenues were only one tenth of the amount realized by Murphy's other films, which were each gigantic hits.

Eddie Murphy is unquestionably a big star, in the same class as Michael Jackson, though Jackson hasn't yet starred in a movie. But watch Jackson in the video film **The Wiz** (1978); indeed, you can't help watching him, for he steals the show every time he appears. Both Murphy and Michael Jackson have star quality — but how long will the audiences' love affair with them last? Has Murphy a box-office flop in his future? Almost certainly. There used to be an old saying in Hollywood: "You're only as good as your last picture." It was never more true than it is today.

▶ *Jessica Lange as Frances Farmer, in this classic forties pose from* **Frances** *(1983).* ▼ *Eighties heart-throb Richard Gere (left) in* **An Officer and a Gentleman** *(1982).*

Woody Allen

Woody, as director and actor, has made a fortune making jokes about his sex life (i.e. lack of), his shrink, his appearance, being a Jew, cowardly and unprepossessing.

He was born in Flatbush, New York, in 1935 and was writing jokes in his teens, from which he turned to scriptwriting and performing. He wrote **What's New Pussycat?** (1965) and played a supporting role in the film; he has written and directed all his subsequent films except **Play It Again, Sam** (1972) — which is based on his play — and **The Front** (1976). **Take the Money and Run** (1969) and **Bananas** (1971) were not too well received, but Allen began to build up a public through **Everything You Always Wanted to Know About Sex** (1972) to **Annie Hall** (1977), which brought Allen three Oscars (but not for acting). **Manhattan** (1979) was popular, but Allen was off-form with **Stardust Memories** (1980) and **A Midsummer Night's Sex Comedy** (1982). **Zelig** (1983) and **Broadway Danny Rose** (1984) were up to his best standard. His latest to date is **The Purple Rose of Cairo** (1985).

♥ Married: teacher Harlene Rosen (1956-9); and actress Louise Lasser (1966-9). Lovers include co-stars Diane Keaton and Mia Farrow.

❝ Woody is at two with nature." — *Dick Cavett.*
"He seems to strive for some kind of excellence for himself in what he does that keeps him from anything that might smell of smugness." — *Tony Roberts.*
"At the end of **Manhattan,** making a list of the things and people that make life worth living, Allen compiles a list of just such glories: Groucho

▲ *Woody Allen muses on the former in* **Love and Death** *(1975), a Russian literature spoof.*

Marx, the second movement of Mozart's 'Jupiter' Symphony, Louis Armstrong's recording of 'Potato Head Blues', Flaubert's *A Sentimental Education,* Cézanne's still lifes of apples and pears, among others. As it happens, he leaves out one

▼ *Allen and Charlotte Rampling in* **Stardust Memories** *(1980), one of his more low-key and for many, self-indulgent movies.*

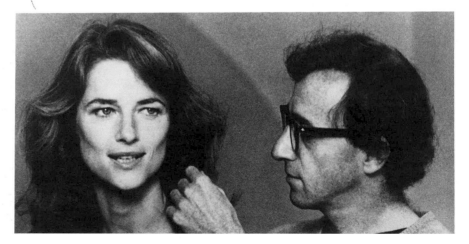

important name, somebody who belongs on anyone's short list of today's essential cultural clarifiers and consolations. That name, of course, is Woody Allen." – *Richard Schickel.* "When Woody Allen ceases to be comic, he has nowhere else to go. He seems unable to understand or describe reality, and turns instinctively to the hollow and portentous images of fantasy. He tries to intellectualize without being intelligent, to be witty without first being perceptive . . . . One tires very quickly of his second-hand insights, his borrowed culture, and his self-conscious naïvety. Woody Allen is in love with his own image — and, like some tiny Narcissus, is now drowning in his own inanition." – *Peter Ackroyd.*

Julie Andrews

Mary Poppins, Maria von Trapp: the public took fresh-faced, fresh-voiced Julie Andrews to heart, and it has loved her in countless revivals. She remains a great star despite having made a habit of appearing only in bad movies, but even they cannot hide her cheerful, no-nonsense personality and her skill as a comedienne.

She was born in 1935 in Walton-on-Thames to a showbusiness family and was on the stage in childhood. She was in two Broadway hits, "The Boy Friend" and "My Fair Lady" before being invited by Disney to film **Mary Poppins** (1964), which won her an Oscar. Two more musicals, were gigantic successes, **The Sound of Music** (1965) and **Thoroughly Modern Millie** (1967), and she was delightful in some straight roles — **The Americanization of Emily** (1964), **Hawaii** (1966) and **Torn Curtain.** She appeared in **Star!** (1968), as Gertrude Lawrence, and as a musical comedy spy in **Darling Lili** (1970), but the public didn't want to see her in these roles. The latter was directed by Blake Edwards, who,

▶ *Julie Andrews, as ravishing as ever in the movie* **S.O.B.** *(1981), written and directed by her husband Blake Edwards. It was a semi-autobiographical account of the way he felt when* **Darling Lili** *(1970) flopped. Ironically, Paramount produced both films.*

with the exception of **Little Miss Marker** (1980), has directed all her other films to date: **The Tamarind Seed** (1974), **10** (1979), **S.O.B.** (1981), **Victor/Victoria** (1982) and **The Man Who Loved Women** (1983).

♥ Married: designer Tony Walton (1959-68); director Blake Edwards (1969).

❝ The last of the really great dames." – *Paul Newman.* "The girl's got everything. She's young and she's pretty. She can dance and sing. What more do you want?" – *Beatrice Lillie.*

"How's she got to the top? It cannot be all just talent. A lot of talented people don't begin to make it the way she has made it. There is a genuineness about her; an unphoniness. She goes right through the camera, on to the film and out to the audience. Julie seems to have been born with that magic gene that comes through on the screen." – *Robert Wise.*

"It takes a star to convey the magic vibrations of another star, and the miracle of Julie's performance is that she has located the essence of Gertrude Lawrence's individual aura . . . . She once again proves that she is an actress of considerable range and stature. Her presence on this occasion is breathtaking." — *Clive Hirschhorn.*

"I mean, you in Britain have some of the best comediennes. Julie Andrews is a comedienne — oh yes she is!" — *Lucille Ball.*

Warren Beatty

📽️ Warren Beatty has not been a prolific actor (he's turned down one out of every two important Hollywood movies in his two decades at the top) but he was a useful leading man, handsome and humorous, before becoming an astute actor/producer.

He was born in Richmond, Virginia, in 1937, the younger brother of

◄ *Warren Beatty as the hairdresser who was not quite as gay as he seemed in* **Shampoo** *(1975); with him are leading ladies Julie Christie, left, and Goldie Hawn.* ▼ *Beatty and Faye Dunaway in* **Bonnie and Clyde** *(1967), a film accused of social irresponsibility, of romanticising crime and encouraging violence.*

Shirley MacLaine. The dramatist William Inge saw him in stock and recommended him for films of two of his own plays, one being **Splendor in the Grass** playing opposite Natalie Wood. After **The Roman Spring of Mrs Stone** (1961), he starred in a handful of indifferent films until his career was resurrected by the gangster movie **Bonnie and Clyde** (1967), which he also produced.

With the exception of **McCabe and Mrs Miller** (1971), the few other films in which he appeared were flops, even the excellent **The Parallax View** (1974), until his tremendous successes with **Shampoo** (1975) and **Heaven Can Wait** (1978), which he also produced, co-directed and co-wrote. He won a Best Director Oscar for **Reds** (1981).

♥ Longest liaisons seem to have been with co-stars Julie Christie and Diane Keaton; he was cited in the divorce case of another, Leslie Caron, while Joan Collins has claimed him as a lover. Before Keaton there was Michelle Phillips, who had lived with his friend Jack Nicholson, and Natalie Wood.

❝ Warren is a teddy bear, though I used to become annoyed when the teddy bear hugs turned to bottom pinches." — *Susannah York.*

"Warren, for the most part, occupies the penthouse suite at the Beverly Wilshire when he's in town. There's

a little old lady, Pasadena-type, lives below him. She is always going down to the desk and complaining: 'What do they do up there all night?' " — *James Bacon.*

▲ *Jean-Paul Belmondo in* **A Bout de Souffle/Breathless** *(1960), the film which made him a star.*

Jean-Paul Belmondo

📽️ Belmondo was *the* star of the New Wave and demonstrated great versatility in the films that followed, playing with equal conviction a cocky young hood and a gentle priest, a clumsy farmboy and a shy student. He stayed faithful to the New Wave directors until they provided him with flop after flop; he had already embarked on a series of action-adventure melodramas playing a larger-than-life hero patterned on his cheerful self. Those are all he does now, and though they are done to a formula, they are always France's box-office hits.

He was born in Neuilly-sur-Seine in 1933 and studied acting; he began appearing in films with **Sois Belle et Tais-toi** (1957) and after starring on the Paris stage was given leads in **Leda/Web of Passion** (1959) and **The Big Risk**; but it was his brilliant hoodlum in Jean-Luc Godard's **Breathless** which made him an overnight sensation. Inundated with offers, he appeared to most advantage in **Moderato Cantabile** (1960) opposite Jeanne Moreau, **Two Women** with Sophia Loren, **The Love Makers** (1961), with Claudia Cardinale, Godard's **A Woman is a Woman**, Jean-Pierre Melville's **Léon Morin, Priest**, **Doulos** —

▲ *For over twenty years Belmondo and Alain Delon have been rivals for the position of France's "biggest male star". Here they are seen co-starring in* **Borsalino**, *released in 1970.*

The Finger Man (1963) and **L'Aîné des Ferchaux,** and Phillippe de Broca's **That Man from Rio** (1964), a wonderful comic/action strip which was his biggest success to date. There were several follow-ups and, at this time, foreign offers: **Casino Royale** (1967) and **Le Cerveau/ The Brain** (1969), but he was interested in neither learning English nor becoming a star abroad.

The best of his later films with the New Wave directors are Louis Malle's **The Thief of Paris** (1967) and the last, Alain Resnais' **Stavisky** (1974), while his teaming with a rival, Alain Delon, in **Borsalino** (1970), must be acknowledged as one of his biggest hits. With such movies as **Flic ou Voyou** (1979) and **L'As des As** (1982) he left Delon far behind at the box office. His last film to date is **Joyeuses Pâques** (1984).

♥ Married: dancer Elodie Constant (1953), divorced. Accompanied film star Ursula Andress in the sixties when she filmed in Britain or the US.

❝ One of the three best actors in the world." — *Henry Fonda.* "He is the most accomplished actor of his generation . . . . He can play any given scene in 20 different ways, and all of them will be right." — *Jean-Pierre Melville.*
"[Alain] Delon moves through [**Borsalino**] like a still-warm stiff en route to a comfortable slab in the morgue, but Belmondo, mugging furiously and retaining just the right air of detachment, compensates by providing enough energy for this and at least three other movies." — *Jay Cocks.*

James Caan

🎥 In another age, the cheerful, swaggering presence of James Caan would have made him the major star he is often said to be. He has just been associated with too many poor movies: you probably wait to see them when they're on TV, only to find that he's the best thing about them.

▼ *James Caan as heir apparent to* **The Godfather** *(1972), before he was gunned down in the street.*

▲ *Caan was one of more than a dozen stars in* **A Bridge Too Far** *(1977), but he was one of the few successes.*

He was born in New York City in 1940 and studied acting. He was getting TV work when he had a small role in **Irma La Douce** (1963) and he had a featured part in **Lady in a Cage** (1964). Howard Hawks offered fine chances in **Red Line 7000** (1965) and **El Dorado** (1967), and Caan advanced to stardom in two by Coppola, **The Rain People** (1969) and **The Godfather** (1972). Other highlights are **Cinderella Liberty** (1973), **California Split** (1974), **Funny Lady** (1975), **The Gambler, Rollerball, Comes a Horseman** (1978) and **Chapter Two** (1979).

In France he made two unintelligent movies for Lelouch, **Another Man, Another Chance** (1977) and **Bolero** (1981), in return for the American profits, but the Americans sensibly declined to turn up as the French had done. His last film to date is **Kiss Me Goodbye** (1982).

♥ Married: Dorothy Jeanne Matis (1961-6).

 Caan allows his glistening teeth to wag his entire performance [in **Comes a Horseman**], and there are a few nocturnal exterior long shots in which the whole valley seems to be illuminated solely by the light of those silvery teeth." – *John Simon.*

"He's a damn good actor, and as we started rolling the more we got into it. He got a lot of laughs playing it perfectly serious. He didn't know he was playing it perfectly serious. He didn't know he was playing comedy . . . ." – *Howard Hawks.*

"In the title role of **The Gambler,** James Caan is something of a revelation, showing a subtlety and depth in his ulcerous playing that overrides the more predictable moments of conscious masculinity. There is a callousness in his manner which is at first unendearing, but as the film progresses this is shown to be part of a much greater whole." – *Derek Elley.*

Michael Caine

Michael Caine is more in demand than some stars with better looks and more charisma. There are certainly actors with a greater range. His fee is considerably less hefty than some others of his generation, in addition to which he is cooperative, with no illusions about his status. If he has an image, it's of an easy-going ordinary guy; when he doesn't depart too far from it he can

▶ *Michael Caine in a characteristic mood as secret agent Harry Palmer, a role he played three times. This is the second outing,* **Funeral in Berlin** *(1967).*

be a pleasing fellow to be around. Reliability is why he's in demand.

He was born in Bermondsey, South London, in 1933, and moved from amateur to professional actor, making his movie début in a small role in **A Hill in Korea** (1956). His break came when actor/co-producer Stanley Baker saw him in a West End play and, at the insistence of the director, Cy Endfield, put him into **Zulu** (1964), as an aristocratic officer. Thereafter Caine reverted to his usual cockney persona, in **The Ipcress File** (1965), the first of three about secret agent Harry Palmer, and **Alfie** (1966).

He first filmed in the US in **Hurry Sundown** (1967) and has since worked here, there and everywhere, most notably in **The Italian Job** (1969), **Sleuth** (1972) opposite Laurence Olivier, **The Black Windmill** (1974), John Huston's **The Man Who Would Be King** (1975), **California Suite** (1978),

▲ *Other successes in* **A Bridge Too Far** *(1977) included a determined Michael Caine (left), here being driven off by Edward Fox to tackle the Germans – the Allies look on suitably relieved.*

John Huston's **Victory** (1981), **Deathtrap** (1982), **Educating Rita** (1983) and **Beyond the Limit**. His last to date is **Water** (1985).

 Married: Patricia Haines (1955, divorced); Shakira Bakesh (1973).

" Wonderfully good company, ceaselessly funny and a brilliant actor." – *Laurence Olivier.*
"He is without doubt the nicest human being I've ever worked with. I mean, *what a pleasure!* It would be nice if I could only do Michael Caine movies from now on. I'd be very happy." – *Valerie Perrine.*
"I had a very good idea of what to expect from Michael Caine. He's the pure, elegant professional: two or three 'takes' and that's it." – *John Mackenzie.*
"The astonishing truth about Caine's

career is that one's memories of his strongest performances, even in the clinkers, endure; one's memories of the flops themselves recede. Only a special breed of actor can maintain a reputation for excellence despite a slew of such embarrassing credits as **Hurry Sundown, Beyond the Poseidon Adventure** [1979], **The Island** [1980] and, to bring his follies up to date, **The Hand**." – *William Wolf.*

Julie Christie

Julie Christie, just out of her teens, was the liberated girl of the sixties: you could confide in her as

easily as slip into bed with her. She has lent her elegance and humor to too few films, for she dislikes stardom and for a while, too, most roles and/or films offered. Living and left-wing causes mean more than tinsel.

She was born to British parents in Assam, India, in 1941, and trained as an actress in London. Some roles in theater and TV led to **Crooks Anonymous** (1962), which was seen by John Schlesinger, who featured her to stunning effect in **Billy Liar** (1963); his **Darling** (1965) brought her an Oscar. Her most memorable

▼ *Julie Christie in John Schlesinger's* **Darling** *(1965), for which she won a Best Actress Oscar.*

154

▲ *Julie Christie in* **Doctor Zhivago** *(1965), as that gentleman's true love. The music "Lara's Theme" is still much played, and though rather sickly it's pleasing to be reminded of Christie as Lara.*

movies since are **Doctor Zhivago**, Schlesinger's **Far From the Madding Crowd** (1967), **Petulia** (1968), **The Go-Between** (1971), **McCabe and Mrs Miller, Shampoo** (1975) and **Heaven Can Wait** (1978) — these last three with Warren Beatty – and **Heat and Dust** (1982). She was recently in the independent feminist production **The Gold Diggers** (1984).

♥ Has never married, but has lived with Warren Beatty and journalist Duncan Campbell.

❝ She's one of the great actresses in the history of films." – *Warren Beatty.*
"Someone recently said to me, isn't it strange to be a movie star *and* an actress. I said, that's been going on for years, at least since Julie Christie and **Darling**." – *Faye Dunaway.*

"She's the girl who's been around, who takes off when she feels like it and returns just as simply to the nest. She throws [**Billy Liar**] off balance, she adds a touch of stardust, but she's so strong and so damned bewitching that it doesn't matter. She has a quality of love." – *David Shipman.*

Sean Connery

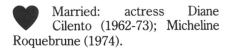 Sean Connery wasn't very good when he first played James Bond, but he became *the* only Bond and now has a screen presence of power and authority. Escaping from Bond, he was only marginally better, but apart from proving himself the heir to Clark Gable or Spencer Tracy — as a leader — he has shown a greater range than either.

He was born in 1930 in Edinburgh and did a variety of jobs before getting work in the chorus of "South Pacific" because few of the others auditioned had sufficient brawn. He went into the theater and made his film début in **No Road Back** (1957).

Television was kinder than movies, but by 1961 he was playing leading roles. He first played Bond in **Dr No** (1962) and then again four more times before relinquishing the role after **Diamonds are Forever** (1971). He was unimpressive in Hitchcock's **Marnie** (1964) but excellent in Sidney Lumet's **The Hill** (1965). His other fine performances are in **The Molly Maguires** (1970), Lumet's **The Anderson Tapes** (1971), **The Offence** (1972) and **Murder on the Orient Express** (1974), **The Man Who Would Be King** (1975), Richard Lester's **Robin and Marian** (1976) and **Cuba** (1979), **Outland** (1981) and **Five Days One Summer** (1982). He played Bond again, for a different management and with a say in the production, in **Never Say Never Again** (1983); his last film to date is **Sir Gawain and the Green Knight** (1984).

♥ Married: actress Diane Cilento (1962-73); Micheline Roquebrune (1974).

▼ *Sean Connery as the guilt-ridden cop in* **The Offence** *(1972), directed by Sidney Lumet.*

◄ *Connery as James Bond, the one and only true Bond. The film is* **Diamonds are Forever** *(1971) and we may suppose from his appearance that there's a lady somewhere near.*

"Much more attractive without his wig on." – *Barbara Carrera.*

"The best Bonds also had Sean Connery, whose absence is sorely felt here [**The Man with the Golden Gun**]. An actor of considerable resource, Connery played 007 with just the right combination of conviction and detachment. He also had a self-mocking aplomb that would be hard to duplicate. His Bond is definitive." – *Jay Cocks.*

". . . and Connery's startling performance provides the dramatic momentum. He has a powerful presence – his physical movements are those of a caged but dangerous animal; and his characterization is rich in shadings. Connery has given strong performances in the past but his performance in **The Offence** has a depth of feeling that will amaze people who still associate him with James Bond." – *Stephen Farber.*

"Sean Connery, a scoundrel in gentleman's clothes, a man who took advantage, brought an edge of sexual aggression to James Bond, but [Roger] Moore is a passive, weary, and put-upon Bond." – *David Denby.*

Robert De Niro

Robert De Niro sinks himself in his roles, and the results for audiences have been fairly stunning.

▼ *Robert De Niro in* **Raging Bull** *(1980), giving a remarkable performance as the champion boxer Jake La Motta.*

▲ *De Niro's best performances have been as misfits, outsiders or, as here in* **Taxi Driver** *(1976), as the problem-tormented.*

"Mystique, in partnership with romanticism, has always been a key component of stardom but there is a calculated mystique about De Niro that undermines romance. De Niro is too volatile and self-absorbed for that. He is the negative side of stardom but he's a great actor and a brilliant technician." — *Adrian Turner.*

"Robert De Niro is an extraordinary actor and he is going to enrich the films that are made for years to come." — *Francis Ford Coppola.*

"De Niro, who bears a striking resemblance to Jughead, may be destined to replace Dustin Hoffman as our foremost portrayer of wacky, guileless dolts." — *Peter Schjeldahl.*

He has, so far, specialized in misfits, but has given such brilliantly detailed portrayals that there is probably nothing he cannot play. He will continue to astonish us.

He was born in 1943 in New York City, where he studied acting; his first film, as an extra, was **Trois Chambres à Manhattan** (1965) and his first major role was in Brian De Palma's student effort, **The Wedding Party** (1969). Shelley Winters chose him to play one of her sons in **Bloody Mama** (1969), after which his roles became more important, until he won a Best Supporting Oscar for **The Godfather Part II** (1974). He had first acted for director Martin Scorsese in **Mean Streets** (1973) and he was the best thing about some other Scorsese films, **Taxi Driver** (1976), **New York, New York** (1977), **Raging Bull** (1980), for which he won an Oscar, and **The King of Comedy** (1983). Other movies include **The Last Tycoon** (1976), **The Deer Hunter** (1978), **True Confessions** (1981) and the last to date, **Falling in Love** (1984).

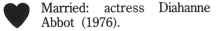 Married: actress Diahanne Abbot (1976).

◄ *For his magnificent performance in* **Raging Bull** *De Niro won an Academy Award for Best Actor.*

Faye Dunaway

She has an extremely forceful personality and an image somewhere between high chic and campy. She's not exactly endearing, but her roles have not required her to be. Faye Dunaway was born in 1941 in Tallahassee, Florida, where she studied theater; success on Broadway brought an offer from Otto Preminger for a featured role in **Hurry Sundown** (1967); and after one more film Warren Beatty chose her to play opposite him in **Bonnie and Clyde** (1967), which established her. After romancing Steve McQueen in **The Thomas Crown Affair**

▼ *Faye Dunaway, heiress to Barbara Stanwyck and Bette Davis, the* actress *of contemporary cinema.*

▲ *If Dunaway is a throwback to the era of the great screen then so was* **Chinatown** *(1974), Polanski's attempt to emulate the convoluted thrillers of the forties and fifties.*

"She's a 20th century fox, a calculating lady who repels even as she attracts." — *Bart Mills.*

"I never met anyone with such a demoniacal drive to succeed as a movie star." — *Estelle Parsons.*

(1968) and seducing Kirk Douglas in **The Arrangement** (1969), she was a hooker in the old West in **Little Big Man** (1970) and in **Doc** (1971).

Despite her Milady in **The Three Musketeers** (1973), her career had lost momentum until revived by **Chinatown** and **The Towering Inferno** (1974). She won an Oscar for her career executive in **Network** (1976). She was Joan Crawford in **Mommie Dearest** (1981), the most notable of her few recent cinema movies, the last of which to date is **Ordeal by Innocence** (1985).

♥ Married: rock star Peter Wolf (1974, divorced); photographer Terry O'Neill (1983), father of her son. Lovers include Lenny Bruce, Jack Nicholson, co-star Marcello Mastroianni, and director Jerry Schatzberg.

❝ Of all actresses, to me only Faye Dunaway has the talent and courage to be a real star." — *Joan Crawford.*

Robert Duvall

Robert Duvall has unmemorable looks: one of the reasons he was such a satisfying character actor is that you would be watching him awhile, admiring his work, without connecting him with the fellow

you'd seen in several other movies. Having progressed to leading roles he brings the same intensity, always putting the character before the star.

He was born in San Diego, California, in 1930, studied drama and in the late fifties began to appear on TV. Among the plays in which he acted was one by Horton Foote, who recommended him for the role of a redneck in **To Kill a Mockingbird** (1962), whose screenplay Foote wrote. Duvall remained in Hollywood to make **The Chase** (1966), **The Detective** (1968), **Bullitt, True Grit** (1969), **The Rain People, M★A★S★H** (1970), **The Revolutionary, THX 1138** (1971), **The Godfather** (1972), **The Great Northfield Minnesota Raid,** as Jesse James, **Joe Kidd, The Conversation** (1974), **The Godfather Part II** and **Network** (1976).

His portrayal of a military man in **Apocalypse Now** (1979) was particularly admired and he had a similar role in **The Great Santini** (1979), this time starring. He also starred in **True Confessions** (1981) and **Tender Mercies** (1983), for which he won an Oscar. He directed **Angelo, My Love.** His last film to date is **The Natural** (1984).

♥ Married: actress and producer Gail Youngs.

❝ Perhaps never before in the history of American movies have there been so many first-rate

▼ *Robert Duvall in* **Apocalypse Now** *(1979), Coppola's statement about the Vietnam War.*

▲ *Duvall with Tess Harper in* **Tender Mercies** *(1983), in which he expressed his love of music and won an Oscar.*

leading actors doing so many different kinds of roles. I'm thinking specifically of Dustin Hoffman, Al Pacino, Robert Redford, Jack Nicholson, Clint Eastwood, Roy Scheider, Jon Voight and, the most consistently surprising and rewarding of the lot, Robert Duvall . . . . Now it's time to recognize Robert Duvall as one of the most resourceful, most technically proficient, most remarkable actors in America today . . . . When I say 'one of . . .' I don't mean to weasel out of anything. At this moment, having just seen Mr Duvall in **The Great Santini,** I think he may well be the best we have, the American Olivier." – *Vincent Canby.*

"[In **The Great Santini**] Duvall has an ironclad forehead, a frightening shark's smile, paranoid eyes, and a lusterless, bullhorn voice that doesn't provide much shading or variety. He's an accomplished, powerful, uningratiating actor." – *David Denby.*

"He has been called 'the American Olivier', but although he has appeared in 32 films in the last 20 years . . . he can still walk down a street without being recognized." – *Leslie Bennetts.*

Clint Eastwood

He was "The Man With No Name" who became Dirty Harry – tough, taciturn and with a grainy sense of humor. He can be ruthless and even cruel when roused, the great icon of modern cinema. Comparisons of the past are ill-advised for Gary Cooper, unlike Eastwood, attempted all genres. Eastwood has more or less restricted himself to Westerns, cop thrillers and good-natured anything-goes "good ol' boy" adventures: some of them are very much more enjoyable than the reviews would suggest – and the prime reason is that monolithic figure in the spotlight.

He was born in 1933 in San Francisco and, although well educated, was a delivery man when a friend arranged a test at Universal. His first film was **Revenge of the Creature** (1955) and his roles had hardly got bigger when he was dropped. Eight years starring in TV's **Rawhide** brought the offer of a Spaghetti Western, **A Fistful of Dollars** (1964) – and by the time he had done two more for the same director, Sergio Leone, he was an international star.

In the US, **Hang 'Em High** (1967) got his renewed career off to a fine start and **Coogan's Bluff** (1968) started a rewarding association with director Don Siegel. Eastwood did a Western musical, **Paint Your Wagon** (1969), directed himself in the tense thriller **Play Misty for Me** (1971), and was Siegel's **Dirty Harry,** which has rated three sequels. The other notable Eastwood

◄ *Clint Eastwood made his name playing strong, silent men in Spaghetti Westerns. Here he is in* **Hang 'Em High** *(1967).*

▲ *Clint being tough in* **Every Which Way But Loose** *(1978). The trouble is, people will keep on picking on him in bars. They seldom win.*

▶ *Sally Field shortly before winning an Oscar for her performance in* **Places of the Heart** *(1984).*

movies are **The Outlaw Josey Wales** (1976), **Every Which Way But Loose** (1978), **Escape from Alcatraz** (1979), **Tightrope** (1984) and **City Heat.**

♥ Married: Margaret Johnson (1953), which lasted virtually until his relationship with Sondra Locke, his co-star in every other film since **The Outlaw Josey Wales,** began in 1979.

❝ The hardest thing in the world is to do nothing and he does it marvelously." – *Don Siegel.*
"He appears to do nothing and does everything, reducing everything and everybody . . . like Mitchum and Tracy." – *Richard Burton.*
"Clint Eastwood is no publicity manager's invention; he came after the decline of the studios, and no studio invented him or helped him edge to the top. He is very modest about his success, and grins engagingly: 'Any actor going into pictures has to have something special. That's what makes a star while a lot of damn good actors are passed by.'" – *DeWitt Bodeen.*

Sally Field

🎥 Because of her TV image, Sally Field, pretty and petite, had some difficulty in being taken seriously; but those who saw her early movie work, full of charm and humor, could not be surprised that she gave an impassioned performance in **Norma Rae** (1979), winning a much-merited Oscar.

She was born in Pasadena, California, in 1946, to an actress mother who enrolled her in a Columbia Studios workshop; while there she was offered a TV series, **Gidget,** though it was the later **Flying Nun** which made her famous. Before it, one movie: **The Way West** (1967). After it: star roles in **Stay Hungry** (1976) and **Heroes** (1977), plus three delightfully teamed with Burt Reynolds, **Smokey and the Bandit, The End** and **Hooper. Beyond the Poseidon Adventure**

(1979) was followed by the Oscar movie. Field also gave a terrific performance in a TV film, **Sybil** (1976).

Recently she has made **Smokey and the Bandit II** (1980), **Back Roads** (1981), **Kiss Me Goodbye** (1982) and **Places in the Heart** (1984).

♥ Married: Steve Craig (1968). Liaison with co-star Burt Reynolds.

❝ This girl is really more vulnerable than Jane Fonda and therefore finally more touching. Jane is probably our best all-round actress, but Sally is going to be a big star. They're both indomitable ladies." – *Martin Ritt.*
"Sally is one of the best, perhaps *the* best, actress I've ever worked with. Her rushes on [**Norma Rae**] were so good that I found myself crying over some of the more dramatic scenes. She's simply astounding." – *Martin Ritt.*

Jane Fonda

🎥◁ Other actresses complain that Jane Fonda, daughter of Henry, gets offered all the best of the few good female roles first, even as she moves into early middle-age. Moviegoers don't. She is a wonderful actress, in Hollywood's great tradition, tackling a wide spectrum of roles with vigor and sensitivity.

She was born in 1937 in New York and had acted on stage when family friend Joshua Logan offered her the lead opposite Anthony Perkins in **Tall Story** (1960). She impressed increasingly through **The Chapman Report** (1962), **Sunday in New York** (1964), **Cat Ballou** (1965) and **Barefoot in the Park** (1967). She also met and married Roger Vadim, who directed **Barbarella** (1968), the best of her films made while living with him in France.

Despite fine notices for **They Shoot Horses, Don't They?** (1969) and **Klute** (1971), plus an Oscar for the latter, Hollywood offers were few, due to her anti-Vietnam campaigning. In a changed political climate she found herself much in demand, and her political and feminist views surfaced in some of these fine films: **Julia** (1977), **Coming Home**

(1978), **Comes a Horseman, The China Syndrome** (1979), **Nine to Five** (1980) and **Rollover** (1981).

♥ Married: director Roger Vadim (1965-73); political activist Tom Hayden (1973). During the separation from Vadim she lived with co-star Donald Sutherland.

❝ In **Klute** she is profoundly and perfectly Bree: she makes all the right choices, from the mechanics of her walk and her voice inflection to the penetration of the girl's raging psyche. It is a rare performance." – *Jay Cocks.*

The two sides of Jane Fonda:
▼ *looking glamorous as* **Barbarella** *(1968), at a time when she was making mainly frivolous movies, and* ▶ *as the writer Lillian Hellman in* **Julia** *(1977), one of the better serious dramas she has made in more recent times.*

"She did this remarkable thing with her life. At 32, Jane performed a total reverse that was completely unexpected. I don't mean just her anti-war activities, but a complete reversal of her values and beliefs. People love energy, individualism and daring, and Jane's actions are almost in the area of mythology because of what she was and what she became." – *Jon Voight.*
"She's just about the best actress walkin' around today." – *Henry Fonda.*

Harrison Ford, an ikon for the eighties, even though his two films as "Indy" were set back in the thirties.
◀ *This is the second,* **Indiana Jones and the Temple of Doom** *(1984).* ▲ *Ford has also had the good fortune to be in another hugely successful box-office series,* **Star Wars** *(1977) being the first of the trilogy. In* **Witness** *(1985) he proved that his acting was equal to his good looks.*

Harrison Ford

He's a nice-looking man, dependable. He has vigor and energy. He has been in some of the biggest movies ever made, but you cannot hold him in the memory as you do Bogart or Gable. Perhaps stardom will bring a little more individuality.

Harrison Ford was born in 1942 in Chicago; he acted at college and in stock. Trying Hollywood, he was given one line in **Dead Heat on a Merry-Go-Round** (1966). Other movie roles were not much bigger though he was luckier in TV, until 1970 when he gave up showbusiness.

Director George Lucas gave him a role in **American Graffiti** (1973) and, after **The Conversation** (1974), one of the leads in **Star Wars** (1977), a role repeated in the sequels, **The Empire Strikes Back** (1980) and **Return of the Jedi** (1983). Ford became an all-purpose leading man in a handful of movies including — his biggest roles — **Hanover Street** (1979) and **The Frisco Kid.** Lucas sent for him again when producing **Raiders of the Lost Ark** (1981),

another so popular that it called for a sequel, **Indiana Jones and the Temple of Doom** (1984); between the two Ford made his best movie, **Blade Runner** (1982).

♥ Married: Mary (1963, divorced); screenwriter (**The Black Stallion, E.T.**) Melissa Mathison (1983).

" Harrison was so obviously right to play Indiana Jones that George Lucas and I approached him the next day. Harrison was a remarkable combination of Errol Flynn in **The Adventures of Don Juan** and Humphrey Bogart in **The Treasure of Sierre Madre.** He can be villainous and romantic all at once." — *Steven Spielberg.*

Richard Gere

He shares many qualities with John Travolta — both are young, city-, if not street-, wise; neither, interestingly, is macho; neither has a great aura but Gere has a febrile intensity which might make him in the end the more interesting actor.

He was born in Syracuse, New York, in 1948 and changed his ambition from music to drama. Off-Broadway roles led to the first in a movie, **Report to the Commissioner** (1975). Two small but striking roles — in **Baby Blue Marine** (1976) and **Looking for Mr Goodbar** (1977) — led to **Days of Heaven** (1978), the first of several leads including **Blood Brothers, Yanks** (1979), **American Gigolo** (1980), his biggest and you could say only success, **An Officer and a Gentleman** (1982), **Breathless** (1983), **Beyond the Limit, The Cotton Club** (1984) and **King David** (1985).

♥ Bachelor.

" Richard Gere's role is obsessive and everything in [**Beyond the Limit**], all the action, stems from him. Without him, nothing

▼ *Richard Gere doing what comes naturally. The film is* **American Gigolo** *(1980).*

really moves. I look upon him as a sort of James Dean of the eighties, maturer and older, perhaps, but still moody and with a definite aura and personality that comes across. He's very quick to pick up what you're telling him and he had a lot of good ideas himself for expanding the character." – *John Mackenzie.*

"Richard Gere has taken his shirt off in every movie he's made. He's falling out of his clothes." – *Christopher Reeve.*

"As the chief luxury item [in **American Gigolo**], Richard Gere is thoroughly self-centered, which is probably right for the character. Gere is muscular but not heavy and blockish in fantasy-queen style; the sweetness in his dark eyes and around his mouth is set off by a large, bold, streetfighter's nose. Physically, the mixture of tenderness and roughness, strength and grace, is perfect, but

▶ *Richard Gere, Over Here from Over There. The film was* **Yanks** *(1979), which showed just what the GIs got up to in the UK during World War II.*

here, as in his other movie roles, Gere never really develops a character. This actor lacks a strong sense of his own identity." – *David Denby.*

Mel Gibson

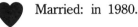 Ingratiatingly boyish, light of foot, enthusiastic, Mel Gibson may well be the most talented of all the talented Australian actors, yet he wasn't born there, but in Peekskill, New York, in 1956.

The family emigrated to Australia when he was 12, partly because his father didn't want his sons to fight in Vietnam. Gibson studied drama and made his film début in **Summer City**

(1977); he had the leading role in his second film, **Mad Max** (1979), and its international success has been followed by **Gallipoli** (1981), **Mad Max 2**, **The Year of Living Dangerously** (1982) and **The Bounty** (1984). **Mrs Soffel** and **The River** (1985) were made in the US and were followed by **Mad Max 3**.

♥ Married: in 1980.

▼ *Mel Gibson on location for* **The Bounty** *(1984), in the role of Fletcher Christian, played in earlier versions of the story by Clark Gable and Marlon Brando.*

❝❝ Mel is the new Australian. He is going to be a very good star. He is quite different from the Australian everyone knows — the kind Rod Taylor represents." – *Peter Weir.*

"Mel is the most gorgeous man I have ever seen." – *Sigourney Weaver.*

"I haven't seen a star with his sex appeal and style since Paul Newman." – *Freddie Fields.*

Goldie Hawn

She came on strong as the daffiest, dimmest and most deliciously dizzy of dumb blondes and her screen image hasn't strayed too far from that. The press assure us that she is like that in life, but

◀ *Goldie Hawn in the title role of* **Private Benjamin** *(1980), which has proved to be one of her biggest screen successes.* ▼ *And if she looks as though she has rather more on her mind than acting, it's because she also produced the film.*

she starred in **There's a Girl in My Soup** (1970). Since then, she has made **Butterflies Are Free** (1972), **The Sugarland Express** (1974), **The Girl from Petrovka, Shampoo** (1975), **The Duchess and the Dirtwater Fox** (1976), **Foul Play** (1978), **Private Benjamin** (1980), **Seems Like Old Times, Best Friends** (1982), **Swing Shift** (1984) and her last to date, **Protocol.**

♥ Married: actor/dancer Gus Trikonis (1969-76); rock star Bill Hudson (1976-81).

❝ She was launched with an idiot giggle, a remorseless inclination to squeak and if a brain hummed behind those dumbfounded eyes the secret never leaked out." – *Donald Zec.*

"Goldie is a knock-out girl. Honest as

a child's stare and full of fun and giggles." – *Roderick Mann.*

"Goldie is one of the sharpest ladies I've ever worked with. She doesn't miss a thing. She's my greatest audience. She laughs at all my stories, and in the right places, too." – *Burt Reynolds.*

"Ditsy, my eye, she's the brightest dumb blonde since Queen Boadicea sliced Roman kneecaps." – *Victor Davis.*

Dustin Hoffman

Although he found fame as the confused bourgeois youngster in an adult's world – in **The Graduate** – Dustin Hoffman has not been content to play variations on this role, but has seized ferociously any chance to widen the basic Hoffman persona. Unprepossessing in appearance and stature, he might have fallen by the wayside in an age when stars are expendable: instead (partly by choosing soundly) he has reached the stage where he is safe among the Hollywood immortals.

He was born in Los Angeles in 1937 and supported himself in odd

interviews and the fact that she's her own producer prove otherwise.

Goldie Hawn was born in Washington in 1945 and trained as an actress and dancer. She made her film début in a brief role in **The One and Only Genuine Original Family Band** (1967) and became famous as one of the regulars in TV's "Rowan and Martin's Laugh-In". After a supporting role in **Cactus Flower** (1969), for which she won an Oscar,

▲ *Dustin Hoffman in* **The Graduate** *(1967) getting to know his possible future mother-in-law.*

jobs while attempting to make a career as an actor. Odd acting jobs included one scene in **The Tiger Makes Out** (1967) and an off-Broadway play which was seen by Mike Nichols, about to direct **The Graduate.** Hoffman's other most memorable performances are in **Midnight Cowboy** (1969), **Who Is Harry Kellerman and Why Is He Saying Those Terrible Things About Me?** (1971), **Papillon** (1973), **Lenny** (1974), **All the President's Men** (1976), **Straight Time** (1978), **Kramer vs. Kramer** (1979), for which he won an Oscar, and **Tootsie** (1982).

♥ Married: dancer Anne Byrne (1969-77); Lisa Gottsegen (1978).

❝ He's energized and the greatest combination of the generous and the selfish that ever lived. He wants to be the greatest actor who ever was." — *Meryl Streep.*

"Hoffman has the reputation of being a difficult man to work with, but the result of his perfectionism has made him an exciting and surprising personality." — *Ronald Bergan.*
"There are those directors and producers within the Hollywood establishment, as well as a fair number outside of it, who wouldn't work with Hoffman to save their celluloid souls.

▼ *Hoffman has made a fine star career playing character roles: this one was in* **Midnight Cowboy** *(1968).*

The man, it seems, drives a hard bargain. 'Yes, that's true. I'm not easy to work with'." — *Carmie Amata.*
"Valentino was an extremely handsome man, but [Ronald] Colman was handsome in a different way. Physical beauty of the males in Hollywood was really a thing . . . . There were none of these drab-looking people like Dustin Hoffman — can you believe any girl looks at Dustin Hoffman and gets a thrill? I can't." — *Ruth Waterbury.*

Diane Keaton

🎥 Diane Keaton's infectious high spirits made her an agreeable partner for Woody Allen, since she managed to cheer him up; and even in her serious roles she seems unable to quite suppress her sunny disposition.

She was born in Los Angeles in 1949 and studied drama. She met Allen when they both appeared on Broadway in "Play It Again, Sam" and she repeated her role in the film version (1972); meanwhile she had made her film début in **Lovers and**

Other Strangers (1969). She was in both **The Godfather** (1972) and the sequel (1974), and also in **I Will I Will . . . for Now** (1976) and **Harry and Walter Go To New York,** but her most rewarding work was with Allen: **Sleeper** (1973), **Love and Death** (1975), **Annie Hall** (1977),

▼ *Diane Keaton made her reputation in the comedies of Woody Allen, usually playing the giddy girl. Here they are together in one of their earlier movies,* **Sleeper** *(1973), a sci-fi spoof.*

▲ *Diane Keaton, here with Michael Caine in* **Harry and Walter Go to New York** *(1976).*

for which she won the Oscar, **Interiors** (1978) and **Manhattan** (1979). As their private and professional relationship ended she made **Reds** (1981) with Warren Beatty; her other notable serious roles have been in **Looking for Mr Goodbar** (1977), **Shoot the Moon** (1981), **The Little Drummer Girl** (1984) and her latest to date, **Mrs Soffel.**

♥ Long liaisons with Woody Allen and Warren Beatty.

❝ She has no compunction about playing a lovable and gangly hick in **Annie Hall** and then very neurotic and disturbed women in **Interiors** and **Manhattan.** That's the mark of an actress and not a movie star. Keaton also has the eye of a genius, as you can see in her photos, collages, silk screens and wardrobe. She can dress in a thousand more creative ways than she did in **Annie Hall.** When I first met her, she'd combine unbelievable stuff — a hockey shirt, combat boots, some chic thing from Ralph Lauren." — *Woody Allen.*
"She's totally alive, she's totally personal, she's free, she's herself. She really cooks, she's a great actress, she teaches us a lot. I congratulated her at the Academy Awards and said 'I think you're luminous, I think your work is extraordinary'." — *Jon Voight.*

Nastassia Kinski

🎥◁ Nastassia Kinski has a habit, at times, of looking like Ingrid Bergman, which may be disconcerting but cannot be bad. She has some

▲ *Nastassia Kinski as* **Tess** *(1980), toying with forbidden fruit before being seduced and abandoned.*

other qualities in common, charm, radiance and sensitivity — and, in a changed industry, the intelligence to choose films because of the creative talent involved.

She was born in 1961 in Berlin, the daughter of actor Klaus Kinski. Brought up by her mother, she studied in various parts of the world, including New York, where the subject was drama. However, she made her film début in Germany in **Falsche Bewegung** (1975), and then did a trio of undistinguished films before meeting Roman Polanski, who made her his **Tess** (1980) — and a star.

Then followed a series of flops,

including Coppola's **One From the Heart** (1981), Schrader's **Cat People** (1982), **The Moon in the Gutter** (1983) and **Unfaithfully Yours;** but **Paris, Texas** (1984) and **Maria's Lovers** put her back in favor with the moviegoer.

♥ Lovers include Roman Polanski (1979), Milos Forman and Ibrahim Moussa, father of her child.

❝ The tantalizing teenage temptress." — *Tim Ewbank.*
"She does not sound like a brainless nymphet jerking to the strings pulled by her Svengali. She has a core of healthy, middle-European toughness and adolescent openness that is very attractive." — *Clancy Sigal.*

"She combines the innocent look of an angel with the guilty appeal of a sex kitten." — *Terry Willows.*

Jessica Lange

🎥 Not since the advent of Jane Fonda and Julie Andrews has any actress but Jessica Lange had the traditional attributes of the movie star — beauty, wit, intelligence, presence and instinctive talent. What is more, she is clearly one of the charmed that is loved by the camera.

She was born in Cloquet, Minnesota, in 1950 and studied mime in Paris and theater in New York. She was chosen for **King Kong** (1976), whose producer gave her a long-term

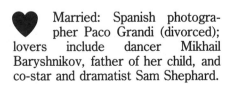 *Jessica Lange as* **Frances** *(1982). The film is based on the life of the thirties movie star Frances Farmer. Hollywood drove her to the bottle and later, to lengthy stays in mental institutions.*

contract; but after the film's critical failure there was no film work until a small role in **All That Jazz** (1979). After **How to Beat the High Cost of Living** (1980), she stunned everyone with her sexually provocative performance in **The Postman Always Rings Twice** (1981) and then as actress **Frances** (1982) Farmer. She should have won an Oscar for it, but at the same ceremony won one for a supporting performance in **Tootsie.** Her latest film is **Country** (1984).

♥ Married: Spanish photographer Paco Grandi (divorced); lovers include dancer Mikhail Baryshnikov, father of her child, and co-star and dramatist Sam Shephard.

❝ Jessica Lange, the ex-model who was the only good thing in the **King Kong** remake, uses her dreamy voice and her thin, slightly twisted upper lip, drawn back from her teeth, to suggest an inexhaustible erotic ravenousness. Lange might have had a triumph in [**The Postman Always Rings Twice**] if she had been given some better lines and a handsome, vibrant young actor to work with." – *David Denby.*

"She is like a delicate fawn, but crossed with a Buick." – *Jack Nicholson.*

"Tall, blonde and athletic, Jessica Lange is one of those natural beauties who seem regularly to be shipped out of the American mid-West along with the cows and the corn." – *Joan Goodman.*

Liza Minnelli

🎥 In some ways the daughter of Judy Garland has reached greater heights than her mother, but a prolific movie career has been denied her — which is our loss, for she is a consummate performer with many of Judy's qualities, although not perhaps so great a singer and as an actress lacking some of Judy's vulnerability.

She was born in Hollywood in 1946 and made her film début in the final sequence of Garland's movie **In the Good Old Summertime** (1949). She started performing in her teens and later with her mother after making a name for herself. As an adult her first film was **Charlie Bubbles** (1968) in Britain. After **The Sterile Cuckoo** (1969) and **Tell Me That You Love Me, Junie Moon** (1970), she had a huge success and won an Oscar with **Cabaret** (1972); but since then she was the best thing about three failures, **Lucky Lady** (1975),

▼ *Liza Minnelli singing the title song of* **New York, New York** *(1977), which has since become that city's official song.*

◀ *Liza Minnelli as Sally Bowles, the Chelsea girl in the decadent Berlin of the thirties. Since her terrific performance brought her great popularity and an Oscar it's never been quite clear why movies haven't yet offered her a comparable role.*

A Matter of Time (1976) and **New York, New York** (1977), and it is curious that there haven't been more offers. She has continued to star on Broadway and elsewhere, restricting her film performances to **Arthur** (1981) and a cameo in **The Muppets Take Manhattan** (1984).

♥ Married: Australian singer Peter Allen (1967-72); producer Jack Haley Jr (1977-8); producer Mark Gero (1979). Her name has also been linked with Desi Arnaz Jr, pop musician Rex Kramer, Peter Sellers and director Martin Scorsese.

❝ What she has is presence, and that's a gift like perfect pitch. She has something to make your eyes follow her, yet she's not pretty and far from a beauty. Her shoulders are too broad, and one's higher than the other. She suffers from curvature of the spine and looks round-shouldered. Her eyes are slightly irregular. But she has only to move, to loosen into a dance or hit a badminton shuttlecock a swinging smash, and she becomes supple as a scarf. You see then the articulate dancer's body: you see what she wants you to see." – *Marcelle Bernstein.*

"I love Liza. She is an *original*. People speak of her in terms of her mother, but she is herself, very definitely. A good, strong, unique person." – *Myrna Loy.*

"She's the greatest musical actress and performer we have." – *Cy Feuer.*

"I think she decided to go into show-business when she was an embryo, she kicked so much." – *Judy Garland.*

Eddie Murphy

◀ He's sassy, street-wise, flamboyant and even more hip than Richard Pryor (mentor and idol); he's enlivening. Eddie Murphy was born in New York in 1962 and was 15 when he turned from amateur to professional stand-up comic. His performances on TV's "Saturday Night Live" got him into **48 Hours** (1983) and, as **Trading Places** opened, an exclusive five-picture deal with Paramount worth $15 million. Since then, he's made **Best Defense** (1984), and **Beverly Hills Cop.**

▲ *Eddie Murphy, who in 1984/5 carried* **Beverly Hills Cop** *into one of the biggest hits in movie history.*

 Bachelor.

“ His effect was dazzling. There was a ding! when he walked on, almost like Marilyn Monroe.” — *John Landis.*
“Despite all his success, Eddie acts like he's 22 years old. His life is cars and girls, girls and cars. More cars. More girls.” — *Jamie Lee Curtis.*
“Eddie can hear the rustle of nylon stockings at 50 yards.” — *Walter Hill.*

Jack Nicholson

Jack Nicholson has said that he enjoys stardom, and it becomes him inasmuch as he's one of the best actors in the world — magnetic, versatile, uninhibited and, unlike some, unfearful of his image.

He was born in Neptune, New Jersey, in 1937 and studied drama in Los Angeles. Director Roger Corman saw him on stage and gave him a role in **Cry Baby Killer** (1958). With a couple of exceptions, Nicholson spent the next decade in fringe movies, sometimes involved in writing and production, often with Corman. When Rip Torn bowed out, he played the role of the hip alcoholic lawyer in **Easy Rider** (1969) and stole the notices from the stars. His at-odds bourgeois son in **Five Easy Pieces** (1970) confirmed his own stardom and he went on to **Carnal Know-**

▲ *Jack Nicholson with Faye Dunaway in* **Chinatown** *(1974), in which his private eye had the qualities we associate with him – his self-confidence and sardonic humor.*

ledge (1971), **The King of Marvin Gardens** (1972), **The Last Detail** (1973), **Chinatown** (1974), Antonioni's **The Passenger** (1975), **The Fortune** and **One Flew Over the Cuckoo's Nest,** which won him an Oscar.

He is one of the few stars not to mind taking supporting roles, as in **The Last Tycoon** (1976), **Reds** (1981) and **Terms of Endearment** (1983), which brought him a Best Supporting Oscar. Other recent films haven't worked out well, including **Goin' South** (1978), but he was superb in **The Shining** (1979), **The Border** (1980) and **The Postman Always Rings Twice** (1981).

♥ Married: Sandra Knight (1961-6). Other ladies in his life have included Mimi Machu; actresses Susan Anspach, Candice Bergen and Faye Dunaway; singer Michelle Phillips and Anjelica Huston (since 1974), daughter of director John Huston.

“ Some [actors], like Olivier, are very intellectual, others, like Brando, are organic. Jack! You see how angry he gets in a scene? Unbelievably scary! He cannot stop, he goes into a kind of fit, you dunno whether he is acting any more! He is one distinct acting school, almost opposite to Stanislavsky. You build danger by getting it physically, pounding tables, people; it comes not mentally but by inducing it in your body.” — *Roman Polanski.*
“Jack Nicholson always tells the truth — in his acting and in his life . . . . He has somewhat what Brando also has

▲ *Al Pacino in* **Dog Day Afternoon** *(1975), the bank robber with a difference – the proceeds were intended for a sex-change operation.*

the sequel (1974); but his best chances (and best films) were in Lumet's **Serpico** (1973) and **Dog Day Afternoon** (1975), respectively as unconventional cop and gay bank robber. These were followed by failures: **Bobby Deerfield** (1977), **And Justice for All** (1979), **Cruising** (1980), **Author, Author!** (1982) and **Scarface** (1983).

▲ *Nicholson, with Shirley MacLaine, in* **Terms of Endearment** *(1983), amusingly cast as an over-the-hill ex-astronaut.*

tion when he made his movie début in **Me, Natalie** (1969) and was an award-winning Broadway player when he did **The Panic in Needle Park** (1971). He became a movie star as the son who succeeds in **The Godfather** (1972) and he won a Best Supporting Oscar for the same role in

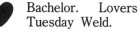 Bachelor. Lovers include Tuesday Weld.

– complete comfort with and in his body. He knows who he is and accepts himself as he accepts others. He's an enormously loving and creative man." – *Mike Nichols.*
"He's the only person I know who gives you a feeling of what movie stars were like years ago. He has great personal flair and a great sense of life." – *Richard Sylbert.*

▼ *Pacino gave a strong performance in* **Scarface** *(1983), a revamping of the 1932 gangster thriller, which was not enough to save it at the box-office.*

Al Pacino

During five years this forceful, fearless actor was nominated for four Oscars and was considered a box-office star. Something then went very wrong, perhaps because he has versatility but not variety; he hasn't acquired the necessary temperament for stardom, which is a pity.

Al Pacino was born in New York City in 1940 and studied drama; he had acquired an off-Broadway reputa-

Robert Redford

There is a dream movie star or so in every era: one the opposite sex fantasizes about, one their own sex would like — in an ideal world — to emulate. Robert Redford has been this male for a long time, partly because age has done little to decrease his handsomeness. He is a political activist, an ecologist and many other things, including being an actor before he is a star, or so he claims. Probably no one has worked harder at being a star since Joan Crawford.

He was born in Santa Monica, California, in 1937 and studied acting. He had done some Broadway work when he made his movie début in **War Hunt** (1962); he became a Broadway star in "Barefoot in the Park" (1963) and the film version (1967) was the best of his several movies; but he was regarded as promise unfulfilled till he partnered Paul Newman in **Butch Cassidy and the Sundance Kid** (1969). **Jeremiah Johnson** (1972) and **The Candidate** proved him a good chooser; **The Way We Were** (1973) and **The Sting** confirmed his box-office appeal. So, too, did **The Great Gatsby** (1974) and his **All the**

▲ **The Sting** (1973), *with Robert Earl Jones (father of James Earl Jones), who played his side-kick in this popular heist movie. If he looks uncharacteristically unkempt, the more usual Redford may be seen ▼ in* **The Great Gatsby** (1974) *with Mia Farrow. Unfortunately he lacked some of the raffishness provided by Alan Ladd in the 1949 version.*

President's Men (1976), which he also produced. Among his recent films have been **Ordinary People** (1980), for which he won an Oscar for direction (he didn't appear in it), and **The Natural** (1984).

♥ Married: Lola Van Wangemen (1958).

❝ I mean, Robert Redford is a smart man. I have the greatest respect for him. He does not say anything about anybody or anything. He goes to the mountain and he saves trees, and he makes movies, and he makes good movies, and he picks good scripts." – *Burt Reynolds.*
"Robert Redford has always been a natural, intuitive, unemphatic movie actor who draws us close with his good looks and his sweet candor and then shuts us out by never revealing much of himself. Redford has considerably less identity than, say, Burt Reynolds or Jack Nicholson." – *David Denby.*
"Redford does not want to be an actor, he wants to be a movie star." – *Arthur Laurents.*

Christopher Reeve

◁ Whether he's a box-office attraction when he's not being Superman is still open to question. He's perfect as Superman in both guises, bringing both humor and the

required physical attributes; further, he doesn't want to coast on his success in the role, and has accepted some challenging ones, though perhaps with only modest success.
Christopher Reeve was born in New York City in 1952 and was acting before studying at Cornell. A daytime soap led to a Broadway role with Katharine Hepburn and a part in **Gray Lady Down** (1978). He acted in **Superman** and the two sequels, made in 1980 and 1983. His other films include **Somewhere in Time** (1980), Lumet's **Deathtrap** (1982), in which he played a gay man, **Monsignor** (1983) and **The Bostonians** (1984).

♥ Unmarried. British model Gae Exton is the mother of his two children.

❝ What seemed such a nice, simple, artless performance in **Superman** was the finest kind of acting. Reeve's timing – and humor – had to be just about perfect to make the character come off." – *Sidney Lumet.*

▶ *"Who said that man could fly?" asked the slogan for the three splendid Superman movies. Here Christopher Reeve in* **Superman II** *(1980) shows that it's really quite easy.*

"Chris is good-looking in the prewar mold when movie stars looked like movie stars and not like the local wine shop manager." – *William Marshall.*

Burt Reynolds

◁ Good ol' Burt projects a strong macho image, but he lets in a bit of camp from time to time. He doesn't take himself seriously – or doesn't appear to – and that makes him one of the most attractive stars since Gable.
He was born in Palm Beach, Florida, in 1935 and chose a career in acting rather than football. He did a lot of TV work before making his movie début in **Angel Baby** (1960). His movie career didn't get off the ground till TV had made him a national figure; **100 Rifles** (1969) and **Sam Whiskey** helped, but **Deliverance** (1972) and a *Cosmopolitan* centerfold did more. He became a box-office star in such films as **Shamus** (1972), **White Lightning** (1973), **The Longest**

Burt Reynolds has fashioned his successful career around the easy-going guy image, sometimes not quite within the law, as in **White Lightning** *(1973)* ▲, *a bootlegging caper with the sequel,* **Gator** *(1976). In* **Hooper** *(1978)* ▶, *Reynolds plays a movie stuntman.*

Yard (1974), **Gator** (1976), **Smokey and the Bandit** (1977), **Cannonball Run** (1980), **Sharkey's Machine** (1981) and **The Best Little Whorehouse in Texas** (1982). There were also some failures, and after several in a row he co-starred with his only rival among the big male stars, Clint Eastwood, in **City Heat** (1984), his last movie to date.

 Married: actress Judy Carne (1963-5). Much publicized liaisons with singer Dinah Shore and actress Sally Field.

❝ It's the man's tremendous wit that just keeps coming across. Listen, there *is* no acting *style*. Most people just play themselves. Spencer Tracy used to say to me after a scene, 'Did I ham that one up?' If I

said yes, he'd say 'OK, let's do it again.' There's that same honesty in Burt Reynolds. He's a throwback to the old school." – *Myrna Loy.*

"He turned out to be a thinking man's actor, working his tail off to make it look simple. Just like the old guys. Sure, he plays himself, but there's a technique to that. He's got it. And he's got that comic timing that really sparkles in drama – the deadpan reaction." – *Alan Pakula.*

"Playing a passive, put-upon man, Reynolds performs comic miracles [in **Starting Over**] with his deadpan mug and semaphore-like eyebrows." – *David Denby.*

"What I look for mostly in a man is humor, honesty and a mustache. Burt has all three." – *Sally Field.*

Arnold Schwarzenegger

Pumping Iron (1977), a documentary about bodybuilding, turned into a tribute to the muscle king, who was clearly no blushing violet. That same self-

◄ *Arnold Schwarzenegger, the bodybuilder who went back into the Dark Ages, in the two Conan films, to sort out anyone who dared step out of line before coming up-to-date in* **The Terminator** *(1984).* ▼ *Here he's seen with Ann-Margret in* **The Villain (Cactus Jack)** *(1978).*

confidence has turned him into an actor (of sorts), though whether his body will be an enduring feature of movies remains to be seen.

He was born in Austria in 1947 and settled in the US after winning various world titles in his chosen field; his high profile landed him a part in Rafelson's **Stay Hungry** (1976) and he also acted in **The Villain** (1979). His role as **Conan the Barbarian** (1981) seemed like a one-off, but there was a sequel, **Conan the Destroyer** (1984). He moved from the Dark Ages to the future with **The Terminator.**

♥ Engaged to Maria Shriver niece of John Kennedy. They met in 1978 at a tennis match, and have been together ever since.

❝ I have always been rather worried about Arnold. Having been elected Mr Universe on no less than four occasions, Mr Schwarzenegger can out-ripple a lot of bodybuilders, but all that pumping iron seems to have given him an ethereal gaze and the toneless voice of an automaton. And it makes me wonder: is he really one of us?" – *Iain Johnstone.*

"Arnold has done a fantastic job – and real progress in this art of acting: but as he has an accent I've been obliged to work him twice as hard." – *Richard Fleischer.*

"Of course, if Arnold hadn't existed we would have had to build him." – *John Milius.*

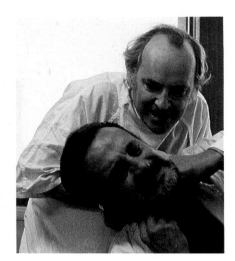

▲ *That fine actor George C. Scott had a host of problems in* **The Hospital** *(1971), not the least the attentions of a homicidal maniac, played by Barnard Hughes.*

George C. Scott

George C. Scott doesn't fit into the usual movie star categories. Only briefly was he box-office, on account of his talent and dynamism. He is best suited to character playing, but is too "big" and energetic an actor to take supporting roles, which may be why he prefers to star on Broadway or in TV movies. Their gain is our loss, for he possesses the essential qualities for mastery of his profession – daring and attention to detail.

He was born in 1926 in Wise, Virginia, and became a teacher before turning to acting. He was established before accepting supporting roles in **The Hanging Tree** (1958), **Anatomy of a Murder** (1959) and **The Hustler** (1961). He had leading roles in **The List of Adrian Messenger** (1963), **Dr Strangelove; or, How I Learned to Stop Worrying and Love the Bomb, Petulia** (1968) and **Patton** (1969), for which he was awarded an Oscar. His refusal to accept it and some subsequent failures lowered his stock in Hollywood, but there are some Scott performances to be savored – in **The Hospital** (1971), **The New Centurians** (1972), **Movie Movie** (1978), **The Formula** (1980) and **Taps** (1981) – his last to date, although his TV Fagin in **Oliver Twist** (1983) and Scrooge in **A Christmas Carol** (1984) have been released in some markets.

▲ *Scott as General* **Patton** *(1969), a role which won him an Oscar.*

♥ Married: Carolyn Hughes (1950, divorced); Patricia Reed (divorced); Colleen Dewhurst (1960-5, 1967-72); and Trish Van Devere (1972), all actresses. His name was linked with that of Ava Gardner (c. 1966).

❝ One of the best actors alive. But my opinion of him as an actor is much higher than my opinion of him as a man." — *John Huston.*
"He's difficult to deal with, but always for a purpose. I wish I had a picture with Scott starting tomorrow." — *Frank McCarthy.*
"Intelligent, constructive, decent, professional. If there was a difference of opinion between us, we worked it out in five or ten minutes." — *Richard Lester.*
"It was amazing just to stand by him and see him at work [on **Taps**] — a real experience to see such discipline and concentration." — *Timothy Hutton.*

George Segal

🎥◁ George Segal is good at panic. He's an amiable enough urban guy, but events constantly conspire against him, forcing voice and face into unholy contortions. He is an adept, likable light comedian, without any great "star" aura.

He was born in New York City in 1934 and university educated. He became an actor and was seen in the revue **The Premise** by a Columbia producer, who gave him a role in **The**

▼ *George Segal and Glenda Jackson in* **A Touch of Class** *(1973), which made sport of adulterous relationships.*

Young Doctors (1961). He was soon in leading roles in **Invitation to a Gunfighter** (1963) and **King Rat** (1965), but after **Who's Afraid of Virginia Woolf?** (1966) it was clear that his forte was comedy in such films as: **No Way to Treat a Lady** (1968), **Bye Bye Braverman, Loving** (1970), **The Owl and the Pussycat, Where's Poppa?** and **A Touch of Class** (1973). The response since then has been sporadic, but Segal's work can be enjoyed in **California Split** (1974), **The Duchess and the Dirtwater Fox** (1976), **Fun With Dick and Jane** and later in **Carbon Copy** (1981). His last film to date is **The Cold Room** (1984).

♥ Married: Marion Sobel (1956-82); musician Linda Rogoff (1983).

❝ He is sophisticated, as stylish as Cary Grant, and has an over-riding ability to make you feel he is just a little-boy-lost." – *Tim Satchell.*

"A man of zesty humor, filled with laughter and a sense of the absurd." – *Joan Robinson.*

"The only screen star laying claim to the mantle of Cary Grant, that of the true ladies' man. Not a rotter or a rake, you understand. The modern knight in shining armor is courteous, slightly bemused, well dressed and wholesome looking. He is puppyish rather than passionate and probably in the care of a psychiatrist, or at least wondering whether he should be." – *Anthea Disney.*

Tom Selleck

There is so much TV, and so many TV personalities, but there are fewer TV stars – and Tom Selleck is one of the very few really big ones. One of the reasons he has succeeded beyond all the other macho action heroes is his ease, his sense of enjoyment and that rather high,

squeaky voice which, allied to his Castro-clone mustache, suggests that he's not as virile as all that. Therein lies his charm.

He was born in Detroit in 1945 and became a leading male model; he also studied at 20th Century-Fox talent school and made his movie début for that company in a brief role in **Myra Breckinridge** (1970). Three other movie parts were similarly brief, but in ·1980 he became a star in TV, because of "Magnum". He turned down **Raiders of the Lost Ark** (and **Victor/Victoria**), but the movies he has starred in have been inferior — if cheerful — imitations of that: **High Road to China** (1982), **Lassiter** (1983) and **Runaway** (1985).

◀ *Tom Selleck in* **Lassiter** *(1983), one of his large screen adventures exploiting the cheery and courageous character which has made his TV show,"Magnum" so enjoyable.*

Married: Jacqulyn Ray (1974), separated.

❝ He is gorgeous, and he has some real power now, but he doesn't use that, or his charm, to exploit women. He genuinely seems to *like* women. For an actor, that's rare." − *Bess Armstrong.*

Sissy Spacek

🎥 In an era of ordinary guys on the screen we must expect some ordinary girls − and mousy, freckled, dreamy, sensitive Sissy Spacek would have to qualify. But who needs to be spectacular when you have her ability to fill out a role?

She was born in Quitman, Texas, in 1949, the cousin of actor Rip Torn, who encouraged her to study acting. She had had some TV parts when recruited for **Prime Cut** (1972). It was a good role but not much of a film, and it took **Badlands** (1973) for

Denied conventional beauty, Sissy Spacek would have been confined to playing the heroine's best friend or sister in an earlier Hollywood, but her talent ensured that she could not be overlooked that easily and led to performances in **Carrie** *(1976)* ▼, *for example, and more notably in* **Coal Miner's Daughter** *(1980)* ▲ *for which she won a Best Actress Oscar.*

people to notice her. **Welcome to L.A.** (1976), the awful **Carrie** (1976), **Three Women** (1977) and **Heart Beat** (1979) were followed by **Coal Miner's Daughter** (1980), for which her portrayal of Country and Western singer Loretta Lynn brought her an Oscar. Her husband, a former art director, directed her in **Raggedy Man** (1981), which was not a success, although **Missing** (1982) was.

❤ Married: Jack Fisk (1974).

❝ Sissy's a phantom. She has this mysterious way of slipping into a part, letting it take over her. She's got a wider range than any young actress I know." − *Brian De Palma.*
"She's remarkable, one of the top actresses I've worked with. Her resources are like a deep well." − *Robert Altman.*

Sylvester Stallone

🎥 Sylvester Stallone has confounded the cynics who sneered on hearing that **Rocky II** was in production: there were more to come and now **First Blood** (1982) is getting a sequel as well. True, certain other films of this rather ox-like actor haven't done well, but the public likes his strength and self-sufficiency.

He was born in New York City in 1946, not to comfortable circumstances, and for a while acting seemed a difficult career. A sexploitation movie, **Party at Kitty and**

▲ *Sylvester Stallone and Talia Shire in* **Rocky** *(1976), the first in a seemingly endless series.*

Studs, was never released. A small bit in **Bananas** (1971) was followed by a large role in **The Lords of Flatbush** (1974), but as he zoomed down the cast list again, he determined that he and only he would star in a script he was writing. **Rocky** (1976) was a huge hit and an Oscar winner, so after two flops, **F.I.S.T.** (1978) and **Paradise Alley,** which he directed, Stallone did **Rocky II** (1979). Since then, he's made **Nighthawks, Victory** (1981), **Rocky III** (1982), **Rhinestone** (1984) with Dolly Parton, and **Rocky IV.**

 Married: Sasha Czach.

❝ **Rocky II** is the most solemn example of self-deification by a movie star since Barbra Streisand's **A Star Is Born.**" – *Frank Rich.*
"Sounds like a Mafia pallbearer, they said. Looks like a bouncer. Has the vocabulary of Mike Hammer, the class of a smack in the mouth. Down-

right ugly, others said. Today, the same people are standing in line to shake his hand." – *Colin Dangaard.*
"Sly is a kisser – the best. I had to go home and lie to my husband and tell him that it's really hard to kiss people in the movies, that it was really embarrassing and uncomfortable. Sly is a great kisser." – *Dolly Parton.*

Meryl Streep

🎥◁ It's an odd quality to find in a leading player, but there's a smugness about Meryl Streep that sits intriguingly with her other dominant quality – brittleness. The smugness has gone from her recent performances (though not, to judge from interviews, her personality), which are technically perfect – indeed, technically magnificent. She has elegance, grace, mystery, class and a faultless way with difficult accents.

She was born in Basking Ridge, New Jersey, in 1951 and was educated at Vassar and Yale, where she acted. She had a supporting role in her first film, **Julia** (1977). After **The**

Deer Hunter (1978), she had unsympathetic roles in **Manhattan, Kramer vs. Kramer** (1979), which won her a Best Supporting Oscar, and **The Seduction of Joe Tynan.** She was English in **The French Lieutenant's Woman** (1981), Polish in **Sophie's Choice** (1982), which won her the Oscar, and an Oklahoma girl in **Silkwood** (1983).

❤ Had a long affair with actor John Cazale, which ended with his death in 1978. Married: sculptor Don Gummer (1978).

❝ . . . has already surpassed Faye Dunaway as the archetypal blonde *Shiksa,* yet she is still so fresh for us that every smile or dip of the head seems like revelation. It's nice to see her [in **The Seduction of Joe Tynan**] as a tough, wily, aggressive woman; indeed the flashes of avidity breaking through her southern-lady's gaiety and charm in this role make one long for her to cast off niceness altogether." – *David Denby.*
"Meryl Streep is a big star today, but she herself has no glamor. You take one look at her, and almost any sales girl in the expensive perfume department of Bergdorf Goodman's is better looking than she is. But at least she looks real." – *Sheilah Graham.*

For several years Meryl Streep has been the actress most in demand in movies, always giving impeccable performances in such films as
▶ **Kramer vs. Kramer** *(1979) and*
▼ **The French Lieutenant's Woman** *(1981).*

Barbra Streisand divides critics and moviegoers as no leading star since the Silent era. You either love her or leave her: there appears to be no middle ground. Few, however, would deny her her way with a comic song, as in **Funny Girl** *(1968)* ▲ *which won her an Oscar, but her thespian talents were somewhat less happily employed in* ◄ **The Way We Were** *(1973).*

Barbra Streisand

Few people can "sell" a song better than Barbra Streisand and no one can deliver self-deflating Jewish lines with greater effect. Beyond that there isn't much unanimity. She certainly has her fervent admirers, but her detractors find her strident, mechanical and lacking in vulnerability.

She was born in Brooklyn in 1942 and became a singer, originally as an amateur. A supporting role on Broadway led to "Funny Girl", playing Fanny Brice, and when they filmed it (1968) she won an Oscar. After two more musicals, **Hello Dolly!** (1969) and **On a Clear Day You Can See Forever** (1970), she mainly played comedy: **The Owl and the Pussycat, What's Up Doc?** (1972), **The Way We Were** (1973) and **The Main Event** (1979). **Funny Lady** (1975) and an unnecessary remake, **A Star Is Born** (1976), were musicals, as was **Yentl** (1983), which Streisand co-wrote, produced and directed.

♥ Married: actor Elliott Gould (1963-71). Lovers include politician Pierre Trudeau; Jon Peters, former hairdresser who became her co-producer on **A Star Is Born;** and co-stars Omar Sharif and Ryan O'Neal.

❝ Barbra is also one of the most impressive business people I've ever met. I find her an irresistible child, a beautiful person. I think we're close, but not very close. She insulates herself because she has to protect herself, and it's difficult for me to trust anyone who has to protect themselves from me." — *Elliott Gould.*

"The difficulty is that even when Miss Streisand labors to appear sensitive and vulnerable, she cannot conquer our impression that, were she to collide with a Mack truck, it is the truck that would drop dead." — *John Simon.*

"Barbra was real nice to work with. Fun. She and I said we'd like to someday do something like *Macbeth.* We were younger then . . . . Now I understand she wants to do classics, including Shakespeare, for television. I'm not lining up to do television, but if it's okay with Barbra . . . . We haven't seriously discussed anything, let alone the classics. But I would be willing to work with her again — on a more equitable level." — *Jack Nicholson.*

John Travolta

Strutting his stuff on the disco floor he is magnetic: off it, he isn't. Dreamy-eyed, not sexually aggressive, he represented, in his first two starring films, all the nine-to-five working adolescents in the audience — and they had had no one else of their own age group to worship in a long time.

He was born in Englewood, New Jersey, in 1954, studied dancing, became a Broadway "gypsy" and had

▼ *John Travolta, the latest in a long line of teenage favorites, in* **Grease** *(1978), with Olivia Newton-John.*

one line in **The Devil's Rain** (1975). Fame in TV's "Welcome Back, Kotter" brought a supporting role in **Carrie** (1976) and stardom in **Saturday Night Fever** (1977) and **Grease** (1978), with Olivia Newton-John. The huge popularity of these movies was followed by a flop, **Moment to Moment** with Lily Tomlin. Business was okay on **Urban Cowboy** (1980) and **Blow-Out** (1981); **Staying Alive** (1983), a sequel to **Saturday Night Fever,** did not equal the success of the original, nor did a reunion with Newton-John in **Two of a Kind.**

♥ Relationship with TV co-star Diana Hyland was much publicized after her death.

❝ The closest we've had to me lately is John Travolta. Whether he'll want to work hard enough on his dancing I don't know. Travolta moves well, but the facts of dancing life mean that you have to work very hard to keep up the level you're already at." — *Gene Kelly.*

Liv Ullmann

In the films of Ingmar Bergman, Liv Ullmann has crested the enormous demands made on her to express — eventually — all the facets of womanhood. If she has been less impressive in her English-language films it may be due to the quality of the films themselves.

She was born in Tokyo in 1938 to Norwegian parents and studied acting in London. After acting on the stage in Norway she began her film career with **Fjolls til Fjells** (1957). Among the co-stars in her next four films was

had little more success with **Pope Joan** (1972), **Forty Carats** (1973) and **Zandy's Bride** (1974), but she continued to play in Bergman's magnificent, tortured dramas: **Scenes from a Marriage** (1973), **Face to Face** (1976), **The Serpent's Egg** (1977) and **Autumn Sonata** (1978).

♥ Married: psychiatrist Jappe Stang (1960-5). Bergman is the father of her daughter.

66 I saw Liv on television being interviewed by Dick Cavett. I felt her power at once, more than in any of her films. Her face had a ravishing sensuality. Those blue eyes were veiled. She was amiable, a bit coquettish, saying kittenish little words, but there was a panther underneath. She could have swallowed Cavett in one gulp." – *Samson Raphaelson.*

"I'd seen Miss Ullmann in Ingmar Bergman's films, so when Mike Frankovich phoned and told me he had a picture with her as leading lady I said, 'I'll do it.' 'Hey, wait a minute,' Mike said, 'you don't have the leading part. Hadn't you better read the script?' I said, 'No, it doesn't matter. I'll do it.' I just wanted to work with her." – *Gene Kelly.*

Jon Voight

🎥 There just aren't many actors around as good as Jon Voight, who has made far too few films. He's one of only a few contemporaries with an upright, clean-cut WASP look, but his actual range would seem to be the widest of any, from his oafish hustler in **Midnight Cowboy** (1969) to the tender-hearted teacher in **Conrack** (1974).

He was born in 1938 in Yonkers, New York, and studied acting after college; after playing on Broadway in "The Sound of Music" he was seldom out of work. He made his movie début in a supporting role in **Hour of the Gun** (1967) and went on to star in two films hardly ever shown – even after the huge success of **Midnight Cowboy**. The Revolutionary (1970) was an undeserved failure, but of Voight's subsequent movies only a few have been outright hits: **Deliverance** (1972), **The Odessa File** (1974), **Coming Home** (1978),

Bibi Andersson, one of Bergman's favorite interpreters, and Bergman wrote and directed **Persona** (1966) for the two of them. Ullmann became famous in a series of Bergman's films: **The Hour of the Wolf** (1968), **Shame, The Passion of Anna** (1969) and **Cries and Whispers** (1972). With Bergman's customary male star, Max Von Sydow, she starred in Jan Troell's **The Emi-**

▲ *Despite her brilliant work with director Ingmar Bergman, the acting talents of Liv Ullman have frequently been wasted in some of her less than memorable English language films.*

grants (1971) and **The New Land** (1973). She had already made her English-language début in the little-seen **The Night Visitor** (1971) and

for which he won an Oscar, and **The Champ** (1979). His last to date is **Table for Five** (1983).

♥ Married: actress Lauri Peters (1960-7); Marcelline Bertrand (1971-6). At the time of **Midnight Cowboy,** his name was romantically linked with Jennifer Salt, whose father wrote the screenplay.

❝ Voight brings a sincerity and a winning naïveté to the shambling, untidy young thinker [in **The Revolutionary**] who's not above going home for a bit of bourgeois comfort or doing a little social-climbing-cum-seduction; his charm is his uncertainty, his seriousness, his essential youngness." — *Judith Crist.* "To filmgoers who recall Valentino's Latin swank, Gable's derisive charm, or Bogart's fake-hard arrogance, Jon Voight must seem a remarkably ordinary Hollywood creation . . . . His face, at first sight anyway, has the agreeable neutrality of a male model . . . . [But] in Joe Buck, the inexpert Texan hustler [of **Midnight Cowboy**], he may even have created a classic figure of the cinema, ranking with the durable Captain Bligh, Rhett Butler, and Streetcar's Stanley Kowalski." — *Peter Evans.*

▼ *Prefering to work in character roles, John Voight first gave notice of his abilities in the role of Joe Buck in* **Midnight Cowboy** *(1969).*

▶ *Proving that getting back to nature can have its drawbacks, John Voight enjoys 'down home' hospitality in* **Deliverance** *(1972).*

The Index

The main entry of each star is shown in **bold** type.

Grateful acknowledgement is made to the many writers and interviewers who are quoted in this book and to their publishers. The newspapers and magazines concerned are The Times, The Daily Telegraph, The Daily Mail, Daily Mirror, Daily Express, The Guardian, Evening News, The Standard, The Observer, The Sunday Times, The Sunday Telegraph, Sunday Express, The New York Times, News Chronicle, New York Daily News, New York Herald-Tribune, The Spectator, The New Statesman, New York Magazine, The Nation, Life, Time, Newsweek, Films in Review, Films and Filming, American Film, Film Comment, Film Fan Monthly, Radio Times, Focus on Film, The Movie, Screen Facts, Ciné-Revue, Picturegoer, Photoplay, Theatre Arts Magazine, Variety, Sight and Sound.

Grateful acknowledgement is also made to:

Agate, James: *Around Cinemas*. London: Home and Van Thal, 1946.

Agee, James: *Agee on Film*. New York: McDowell, Obolensky, 1958; Grosset and Dunlap, 1969.

Arce, Hector: *Gary Cooper, An Intimate Biography*. New York: William Morrow & Co, 1979.

Astaire, Fred: *Steps in Time*. New York: Harper and Bros, 1959.

Bacall, Lauren: *By Myself*. London: Jonathan Cape, 1979.

Bacon, James: *Hollywood is a Four Letter Town*. New York: Henry Regnery Co, 1976.

Billquist, Fritiof: *Garbo*. New York: G. P. Putnam's Sons, 1960.

Bogarde, Dirk: *An Orderly Man*. London: Chatto & Windus, 1983.

Cagney, James: *Cagney by Cagney*. New York: Doubleday & Co, 1976.

Cahn, William: *Harold Lloyd's Funny Side of Life*. New York: Duell, Sloan and Pearce, 1964.

Capra, Frank: *The Name Above the Title*. London: W. H. Allen, 1972.

Carey, Gary: *All the Stars in Heaven*. London: Robson Books, 1982.

Castanza, Philip: *The Films of Jeanette Macdonald and Nelson Eddy*. Secaucus: Citadel Press, 1978.

Castle, Charles: *Joan Crawford, The Raging Star*. London: New English Library, 1977.

Chaplin, Charles: *My Autobiography*. London: The Bodley Head, 1964. New York: Simon and Schuster, 1964.

Chevalier, Maurice: *With Love*. Boston: Little Brown & Co, 1960.

Chierichetti, David: *Hollywood Director: Mitchell Leisen*. New York: Curtis Books, 1973.

Cooke, Alistair (Ed): *Garbo and the Night Watchman*. London: Jonathan Cape, 1937.

Cooke, Alistair: *Douglas Fairbanks*. New York: Museum of Modern Art, 1940.

Crawford, Joan with Kesner Ardmore, Jane: *Portrait of Joan*. New York: Doubleday, 1962.

Crosby, Bing: *Call me Lucky*. New York: Simon and Schuster, 1953. London: Muller, 1953.

Davidson, Bill: *The Real and the Unreal*. New York: Harper and Bros, 1961.

Davis, Bette: *The Lonely Life*. New York: G. P. Putnam's Sons, 1962.

De Mille, Cecil B.: *Autobiography*. New York: Prentice-Hall, 1959.

Dickens, Norman: *Jack Nicholson, The Search for a Superstar*. New York: New American Library, 1975.

Downing, David: *Marlon Brando*. London: W. H. Allen, 1984.

Evans, Peter: *Peter Sellers, The Mask Behind the Mask*. London: New English Library, (revised edition 1980).

Geist, Kenneth L.: *Pictures Will Talk, The Life and Films of Joseph L. Mankiewicz*. New York: Scribner's, 1978.

Gish, Lillian with Pinchot, Ann: *The Movies: Mr Griffith and Me*. Englewood Cliffs, NJ: Prentice-Hall, 1969. London: W. H. Allen, 1969.

Godfrey, Lionel: *Paul Newman Superstar*. London: Robson Books, 1981.

Goldman, Albert: *Elvis*. New York: McGraw Hill, 1981.

Goodman, Ezra: *The Fifty Year Decline and Fall of Hollywood*. New York: Simon & Schuster, 1961.

Graham, Sheilah: *My Hollywood*. New York: St Martin's Press, 1985.

Granger, Stewart: *Sparks Fly Upwards*. London: Granada Publishing, 1981.

Greene, Graham: *The Pleasure-Dome*. London: Secker and Warburg, 1972.

Hampton, Benjamin, B.: *A History of the Movies*. New York: Covici, Friede, 1931.

Hanna, David: *Hollywood Confidential*. New York: Norden Publications, 1976.

Higham, Charles and Greenberg, Joel: *The Celluloid Muse: Hollywood Directors Speak*. London: Angus and Robertson, 1969.

Hirschhorn, Clive: *The Films of James Mason*. London: LSP Books, 1975; *Gene Kelly*. London: W. H. Allen, (revised edition 1984); *The Hollywood Musical*. New York: Crown, 1981.

Hopper, Hedda and Brough, James: *The Whole Truth and Nothing But*. New York: Doubleday, 1963.

Hotchner, A. E.: *Doris Day, Her Own Story*. New York: William Morrow, 1975.

Hunter, Allan: *Walter Matthau*. London: W. H. Allen, 1984.

Jacobs, Jack and Braum, Myron: *The Films of Norma Shearer*. Cranbury, New Jersey: A. S. Barnes, 1960.

Jordan, René: *Barbra Streisand*. London: W. H. Allen, 1976.

Kanin, Garson: *Great Hollywood Teams*. New York: Doubleday & Co Inc, 1981.

Karney, Robin (Ed): *The Movie Stars Story*. London: Octopus Books, 1984.

Keaton, Buster with Samuels, Charles: *My Wonderful World of Slapstick*. New York: Doubleday, 1960.

Kobal, John: *Gotta Sing Gotta Dance*. London: Hamlyn Publishing, (revised edition 1983).

Lake, Veronica and Bain, Donald: *Veronica*. London: W. H. Allen, 1969.

Lamour, Dorothy: *My Side of the Road*. New York: Doubleday & Co, 1980.

Lejeune, C. A.: *Chestnuts in Her Lap*. London: Phoenix House, 1949 (second edition).

Loos, Anita: *A Girl Like I*. New York: The Viking Press, 1966.

Marion, Frances: *Off With Their Heads*. New York: Macmillan, 1972.

Marx, Groucho with Anobile, Richard J.: *The Marx Brothers Scrapbook*. New York: Darien House, 1973.

Maugham, W. Somerset: *A Writer's Notebook*. London: Heinemann, 1950. New York: Doubleday, 1949.

McBride, Joseph: *Hawks on Hawks*. Los Angeles and Berkely: University of California Press, 1982.

Meryman, Richard: *Mank, The Wit, World, and Life of Herman Mankiewicz*. New York: William Morrow & Co, 1978.

Moshier, W. Franklyn: *The Alice Faye Movie Book*. Harrisburg, Pa: 1974.

Newquist, Roy: *Showcase*. New York: William Morrow & Co, 1966; *A Special Kind of Magic*. New York: Rand McNally, 1967.

Niven, David: *The Moon's a Balloon*. London: Hamish Hamilton, 1971.

Olivier, Laurence: *Confessions of an Actor*. London: Weidenfeld and Nicolson, 1982.

Parish, James Robert: *The RKO Gals*. London: Ian Allan Ltd, 1974.

Peary, Danny (Ed): *Close-Ups, The Movie Star Book*. New York: Workman Publishing Co Inc, 1978.

Pickford, Mary: *Sunshine and Shadow*. New York: Doubleday, 1955. London: Heinemann, 1956.

Quirk, Lawrence J.: *The Films of Gloria Swanson*. Secaucus: Citadel Press, 1984.

Ringgold, Gene and Bodeen, De Witt: *The Films of Maurice Chevalier*. Secaucus: Citadel Press, 1973.

Ross, Lillian and Ross, Helen: *The Player*. New York: Simon and Schuster, 1962.

Schickel, Richard: *The Stars*. New York: Dial Press, 1962.

Shepherd, Don and Slatzer: *Bing Crosby, The Hollow Man*. London: W. H. Allen, 1982.

Shipman, David: *The Great Movie Stars* (two volumes). New York: Hill & Wang, (revised editions 1981); *The Story of Cinema*. New York: St Martin's Press, 1984; *Brando*. New York: Doubleday & Co Inc, 1974.

Simon, John: *Reverse Angle*. New York: Clarkson Potter Inc, 1982.

Stallings, Penny: *Flesh and Fantasy*. London: Macdonald and Jane's, 1978.

Swanson, Gloria: *Swanson on Swanson*. New York: Random House, 1980.

Truffaut, François: *Hitchcock*. New York: Simon and Schuster, 1969.

Tynan, Kenneth: *Curtains*. London: Longmans, 1963. New York: Atheneum, 1961; *Tynan Right and Left*. London: Longmans, 1967. New York: Atheneum, 1967.

Von Sternberg, Joseph: *Fun in a Chinese Laundry*. New York: Macmillan Co, 1965.

Wallis, Hal with Higham, Charles: *Starmaker*. New York: Macmillan 1980.

Windeler, Robert: *Burt Lancaster*. London: W. H. Allen, 1984.

Winnington, Richard: *Drawn and Quartered*. London: Saturn Press, 1948.

Wlaschin, Ken: *The World's Great Movie Stars and Their Films*. London: Peerage Books, (revised edition 1984).

Zec, Donald: *Marvin*. London: New English Library, 1979.

Zierold, Norman J.: *The Child Stars*. New York: Coward McCann, 1965.

PICTURE CREDITS

Ronald Grant Archive 124 **Tom Graves** 14 left **The Kobal Collection** half title, 2-7, 8 bottom, 9-13, 14 right, 15-17, 19, 20 top, 21-32, 34-40, 42 top, 43-53, 54 right, 55, 56, 57 top, 58-60, 61 bottom, 62-71, 72 bottom, 73 right, 74-78, 79 bottom, 81-85, 86 top, 87-92, 94-98, 99 bottom, 101, 102 bottom, 103-112, 113 top, 114-119, 120 left, 121-123, 125-126, 127 top, 129-136, 137 left, 138 bottom, 139, 140, 141 bottom, 142-151, 153, 154 top, 155, 156, 157 top, 158, 159 bottom, 160-162, 163 bottom, 164 left, 165-170, 171 right, 172 top left, 172 top right, 173, 175 bottom, 177-179, 181-187, 189 **National Film Archive** 13 bottom, 33, 42 right, 61 top, 79 top, 102 top, 137 right, 141 top, 154 bottom **Photoplay Magazine** 41, 93, 99 top **Rex Features** 113 bottom, 128, 138 top, 157 bottom left, 157 bottom right, 159 top, 171 left, 176, 180, 188 **David Shipman** 8 top, 18, 20 bottom, 54 left, 57 bottom, 72 top, 73 left, 80, 86 bottom, 100, 120 right, 152, 174 **Frank Spooner Pictures** endpapers, 127 bottom, 163 top, 164 right, 175 top **Syndication International** 172 bottom

Front Cover: **Kobal Collection**
Back Cover: **Frank Spooner Pictures**

Many of the illustrations come from stills issued to publicize films or distributed by the following companies: ABC Pictures/Allied Artists, Anglo Amalgamated, Avco/Brut/Gordon Films, British Lion/London Films, British National, Columbia, Elmer Enterprises, Filmsonor, First National, Fox Picture, Gala Film Distributers Limited, IFD/Romulus-Horizon, Lucasfilm, Marianne/Dino de Laurentiis, MGM, Metro-Goldwyn Mayer, Noveiles Editions, Paramount, Rank/Two Cities, RKO, TCF, Twentieth Century Fox, Union Film Incorporated, United Artists, Universal, Vitaphone Pictures, Wallis-Hazen, Walter Wanger Production, Warner Brothers, Warner Seven Arts.

Multimedia Publications (UK) Limited have endeavored to observe the legal requirements with regard to the suppliers of photographic material.